13793203

HEALTH PLANNING AND
SOCIAL CHANGE

HEALTH PLANNING AND SOCIAL CHANGE

Leonard J. Duhl, M.D.

Professor of Public Health and City Planning
University of California, Berkeley

Edited by **Joanna Tamer**

 **HUMAN SCIENCES PRESS, INC.**
72 FIFTH AVENUE
NEW YORK, N.Y. 10011-8004

Printed in the United States of America
987654321

Library of Congress Cataloging-in-Publication Data

Duhl, Leonard J.
  Health planning and social change.

  Bibliography: p.
  Includes index.
  1. Health planning. 2. Health planning—Social aspects.
  3. Social change. I. Tamer, Joanna. II. Title.
RA394.D84   1986   362.1'042   86-10405
ISBN 0-89885-301-X

This book is dedicated to some of the many people who have inspired and supported much of the thinking that has gone into this body of work:

Ed Greenwood—friend and mentor from the Menninger Clinic who set me on the path to looking at health and mental health in a broad way,

Robert Aldrich—friend and joint toiler in the worlds of health and cities,

Howard Rome—guide, friend, and model physician,

John R. Seeley—best friend, researcher and general supporter through the ups and downs of life,

William Soskin—friend and guide to alternate realities,

Richard Smith—health entrepreneur, friend and brother, and

Especially to Lisa, my wife, for having read these articles in original form, using them in her own work, and encouraging me to put them together.

There are indeed many others, part of networks of friends, colleagues and family, who over the many years have been truly part of the creative process. One friend once asked, "Don't you ever do anything alone?" The answer is obvious, one doesn't live in isolation—and the context of support nourishes any flame that is within.

CONTENTS

Changes in health are in large part a reflection of a person's reality. This chapter recognizes that people must deal with understanding themselves and others in order to be involved in the change process.

Health planning moves beyond the narrow linear model and demands an understanding of ecological systems and the social environment. New models reflecting social changes are required.

Alternative models of non-Western medicine offer an ecological framework to deal with medicine and health in a non-Cartesian way.

The health planner must create opportunities for optimizing health. The Peckham Health Center serves as a model for other innovative programs.

Planning has focused classically on hard measurable data. To create true planning and change requires recognition of idiosyncratic nonrational inputs to decision making and change.

The city is the environment in which diverse populations are offered health services. Problems of the poor demand understanding of social factors impinging upon health and disease. Those in the population who are at present underserved require high priority in our resource allocation.

The attempt to be both healthy and holy is, in reality, an attempt to deal with becoming whole in one's relationship to oneself and the environment.

     FUTURE   101

     Mental health must be integrated into holistic
     health care. Connecting individuals in the
     family, into a community, and into the human
     service network is as important to healing as is
     individual therapy.

9.   THE PROMOTION AND MAINTENANCE OF
     HEALTH: MYTH AND REALITY   111

     Developmental models of growth are guides
     to human health programs. The impact of any
     environmental change on the health of indi-
     viduals, families, and institutions are ex-
     plored.

10. THE SOCIAL CONTEXT OF HEALTH   140

     A broad understanding of the sociocultural,
     economic, and environmental impact on
     health may be more important than extending
     personal care services in modifying illness.

11. HUMAN SOCIAL FUTURES   151

     Broad societal changes lead to crisis and
     stress. Our environmental context and the
     way we perceive reality determines how we
     cope with our world. Human relationships
     and processes of governance may determine
     whether we can recreate ourselves in today's
     changing society.

PART II. SOME PAST PLANS: THE GOLDEN ERA
           REVISITED

12. NEWARK—COMMUNITY OR CHAOS: A CASE
     STUDY OF THE MEDICAL SCHOOL
     CONTROVERSY   167

     Conflicting goals of diverse groups in the city
     modify and change the plans for a medical

school in an urban ghetto. The process of working through the proposal and the events that resulted from it started new processes of governance in a then-decaying city.

PREFACE

For many years I have been concerned with both personal and social change.

I have had the unusual experience of being both a psychiatrist-physician, dealing directly with clients and attempting to heal them, and I have been active in promoting public health social policy in areas of health and medical care and also in the broader social context in which health takes place. In this latter role I have worked with legislatures and communities in areas where the concern was with housing, urban renewal, and community development. Frequently my traditional concern with health has receded into the background as I have focused on issues that most people consider nonhealth issues.

In looking at my own development, which is reflected in these essays that have been published, in earlier versions, over a period of some 15 years, there is a cycle of development that started with the need for personal intervention, reached out to the larger issues of social change, politics, and now attempts to integrate and synthesize all of this into a broader socioecological model of health. My current preoccupation, as exemplified in one of the final essays, is with "the healthy city"—my way of showing how all issues of our life space impinge upon our personal health and illness.

These essays are part of my historical progression. They speak, therefore, to issues of personal development, health planning, and ways to conceptualize health issues. I have tried to show the breadth of the map of thinking required to look at personal and social health issues. Rather than give specific answers, I ask for the active participation of the reader in looking at each problem and considering ways to respond other than only with those ideas that are in good currency at present. Some of the issues are old; some more current. What they have in common is another way of understanding that is systemic, transdisciplinary, and crosses over the accepted turfs of medicine and our society.

As I have worked through a variety of issues, several points tend to repeat themselves:

- The importance of social and personal change in finding solutions to health problems.
- The need for new and alternative paradigms for any change.
- The social context of health.
- The need for alternative future scenarios.
- The difference in planning for medical care and for health.
- The need to explore ways to change our existing institutions.
- The need for participation and network development as part of change.
- The creation of new values and ways of planning and creating policy.
- The need to optimize individual growth and development in differing cultures.
- The value of finding new ways to learn.
- The problems of survival in a "hostile" world.
- How to integrate the pieces.

The attempt to look at "the healthy city" is the attempt to pull all these issues together. We find that, indeed, from each person's or organization's perspective, *They* are "right"! Each domain is a private world of values, beliefs, and actions which are continuously self-reinforcing. The problems arise as these separate worlds collide. It becomes important to bring them all together on a "common gameboard" where all the players create a mutually accepted set of rules and where differing views are negotiated and resolved. For most of us the city is such a place, for it is here that all the conflicting worlds of business and service, personal and professional interact. The outcome of this action is the health of individual citizens, for often the results of business development have more impact on illness and health than medical care by itself.

To read these essays is to attempt to take the varied steps toward changing each of our ways of being. If it is successful we may find some clues to the dilemmas we face in medicine, health, and in the broader social arena.

Leonard J. Duhl

ACKNOWLEDGMENTS

It is my particular privilege and pleasure to acknowledge the sharing of ideas, information, and assistance of the co-authors of the original versions of the chapters of this book.

Stephen R. Blum, Ph.D., for *Chapter 2*, "Health Planning: Critique and Alternatives," which appeared as a chapter in B. Checkoway (Ed.), *Citizens and Health Care: Policy Problems and Prospects for Change*. New York: Pergamon Press, 1981.

Stephan Levinson, *Chapter 6*, "The Delivery of Health Care Services," which was published as a chapter in Gary Tobin (Ed.), *The Changing Structure of the City*, an Urban Affairs Annual Review by Sage Publications, Beverly Hills, CA, 1979.

Roger Coleman, M.D., for his assistance with *Chapter 9*, "The Promotion and Maintenance of Health: Myth and Reality," which was a speech delivered at a conference on "Health Promotion through Designed Environment" in Ottawa, Canada, in October 1976 and published in the *Pro-*

ceedings of the conference by the Ministry of National Health and Welfare, Ottawa.

Nancy Jo Steetle, who was senior staff specialist, Urban Management Assistance Administration, U.S. Department of Housing and Urban Development, Washington, D.C., for *Chapter 12*. This case study appeared as an article in *The Journal of Applied Behavioral Science*, Vol. 5, No. 4, 1969, with a response from Robert R. Cadmus, M.D., one of the principals in the events that resulted in this work.

Harold M. Vistosky, M.D. and Jonathan W. Brown, for *Chapter 13*, assisted in the study of the Job Corps and the writing of this proposal for its redesign. The proposal was published in *The Journal of Applied Behavioral Science*, 7(5), 1971.

Jonathan Feinberg, M.D. and Captane P. Thomson, M.D., who assisted with the research and writing of the report that became *Chapter 14*.

Janice Volkman, then of the Department of City and Regional Planning, University of California, Berkeley, for *Chapter 17*, which was published as a theme article in *Urban and Social Change Review*, 3(2), Spring 1970.

I wish also to thank the publishers who gave permission for the articles and chapters that were originally published elsewhere to appear as a part of this book in the forms presented here. In addition to those mentioned above, thanks to the publishers and journals for the publications cited:

Chapter 1: "Our Selves and Social Change." *Main Currents in Modern Thought*, 30(5), May-June 1974.

Chapter 3: "The Dimensions of Health: Traditional Healing and Modern Medicine," in *Transactions of the National Academy of Science and Technology*, 1, 1979. National Academy of Science and Technology, Manila, Philippines.

Chapter 4: "The Health Planner: Dreaming for Health and Wellness." *American Journal of Health Planning*, 1(2), 1976. American Health Planning Association, Alexandria, VA.

Chapter 7: "Health, Whole, Holy, Healing." *Gesar,* (Spring) 1976. Dharma Publishing, Berkeley, CA.

Chapter 8: "Mental Health: A Look into the Future." *Psychiatric Annals, 8*(5), 1978.

Chapter 10: "The Social Context of Health," In A. C. Hastings, J. Fadiman, and J. S. Gordon (Eds.), *Health for the Whole Person,* 1980. Westview Press, Boulder, CO.

Chapter 11: "Human Social Futures," presented at the symposium, *The Prospects of Man,* York University, Toronto, June 3-4, 1975. Published as proceedings of the symposium by Collier-MacMillan Canada, Inc., Don-Mills, Ontario, Canada.

Chapter 15: "The University and the Urban Crisis." *Community Psychology,* April 1971. American Psychological Association, Washington, D.C.

Chapter 16: "Interdisciplinary Teaching in Health." *Interdisciplinary Science Review, 2*(4), 1979. Heyden and Son, Philadelphia, PA.

Finally, it is difficult, nay, impossible, to mention all of those colleagues and friends who have given me their time, patience, support, and inspiration over the many years that the work for this book was being accomplished. However, I am especially grateful to

Joanna Tamer, who edited the material and put the pieces together early in the preparation of this book and who acted as sponsoring editor;

Peter Fisher, who performed the heroic task, at times in the heat of summer and the gloom of midnight, of getting these articles into the word processor; and

Margaret Rudi Hall, copy editor of all the essays, who set the style for this work and acted as managing editor in the final stages of its preparation. Most of all she kept me, as a dyslexic, readable, and, it is hoped, understandable.

Part I

PRINCIPLES FOR FUTURE PLANNING

Chapter 1

OUR SELVES AND SOCIAL CHANGE

I am concerned here with several interconnected and related problems, primarily the use of the self and some of the ethical questions that arise from being an agent of social intervention. In addition to these problems, I will present several important factors which help to explain various historical currents behind some of the evolving social change agents with which we are confronted. I regret that I am not trained as a sociologist, a philosopher, or a historian. Each of these ways of seeing could further clarify what I have to say. As it is, my attempt here is to sketch, suggest, and raise questions in the minds of those interested in social change.

In part because I am trained as a psychiatrist, it is with the person as a change agent that I am primarily concerned. As I have reviewed case material of individuals involved in effecting change, I have come to see that I am a product of a dynamic constellation of unique pasts that impinged upon my developing life, which, in turn, molded and were molded by me. In addition, I am a product of a particular time and location in world history, and this I can never ignore.

Just as I am unique, so each of you is also unique. From the many lives, of past and present intervenors in society (some of whose interventions have been deliberate and some inadvertent) comes the history of our collective "now." How we all interact with the institutions which shape us, and which we shape, makes our futures. The sum of our current view of history—that is, the constant rewriting of the past—determines in large measure what we do in the present, just as the images of the future constantly contribute to rewriting the present.

From each of our histories come symbols and myths, many of which are quite individual and private. Other symbols and myths belong to groups, and still others are part of our collective consciousness. We Americans have long acted as if we were a homogeneous common symbol-accepting culture. We have learned through the strife and tension of the last few years how naive we were and how we have suppressed some myths and symbols and have been dominated by others. The dust has not yet settled, and we have not yet become aware of the many groupings of which we are a part (Currie, 1971). Do we identify fully with any one set of symbols or institutions, or are we really multirelated—a little bit of us here, a little there, in a patchwork of multiple and unique identities? By asking the question I do not doubt our current identity. Rather, I question whether we really have given up our individuality so easily to any group, institution, or ideology.

By searching, one may find that multi-identities are real, though frightening (Laing, 1965). We do not know what we are or where we belong, and that is part of why we are all so mixed up. It is simpler to be an "X" or a "Y." At least there may be fewer hard questions, choices, and uncertainties. Moreover, multi-identities are often put aside for strategic purposes, to achieve an end, to form coalitions and to make communication easier.

When the multi-identitied, those whom Robert Lifton (1970) calls "protean man," face those who appear more definite in their identities with their associated symbols, myths, and language, problems arise. These problems are formidable, for although we are all, in some sense, reasonable people, and speak English, we mean different things, and shake different historical trees, and the "communication" between us often becomes unintelligible noise. We search hard for translators in order that we may understand others by immersing ourselves in their private worlds, and we use many means to hear and be heard. Often, these fail. Our impatience, our fear of the unknown, our timidity in attempting to learn anew how to deal with other human beings, cause us to fall back upon the most primitive tools of persuasion. We often use anger, hostility, and aggression to win whatever stakes appear valuable to us. The painful paradox is that our attempt at "communication" does not resolve conflict; it may even heighten it.

Often, when we begin such a process we not only do not know "the other"; we do not know our own self. How often does our silent language, the nonverbal speech of our unconscious, communicate more than we are aware of? When I say, "He is a wonderful man," but at the same time pull on my nose, my message may be, "I don't really like him." Small muscle movements, facial expressions, body motions, and slips of the tongue often say clearly what the voice may mumble. To know one's self in all its complexity is a wide-ranging task.

If we see the self as an agent of change, we can understand that the various groups that are actively involved in the process of change are clusters of persons who share identities of one kind or another—youth, sex, minority, professional, or institutional identities, to name only a few.

For example, some members of a so-called New York intellectual neoconservative group (who are actually geographically dispersed around the country) are currently characterized by an (unexpressed) concern for their own security and the sense that they are the inheritors of those who have struggled for reform in the past. Were they not the harsh, analytic critics of the establishment a short time ago? Having achieved influence and prominence as critics of the establishment, they reject the suggestion that others may think of them *as* the establishment. Thus, as Daniel Bell has said, "ideology" was dead because he was unwilling to admit that a new form of ideology, an "ideology of value," was emerging.

On the other hand, the radical New Left (which has emerged from a variety of backgrounds ranging from the American socialism of Norman Thomas to the *Catholic Worker* radicalism of Peter Marin and Dorothy Day) is questioning the values as well as the institutions which are the basic underpinnings of our society. They are trying to rewrite history, to find new ways to question our assumptions of what must be taken for granted. They have tried many methods of achieving change—organization, protest, rhetoric, research, guerrilla theater, and even violence—each depending on a different view of how change can best be effected. Sadly, these "value radicals," for all their skill in reappraising the problem, do not recognize the human psychological processes that are so deeply involved in social change, and especially in the resistance to change (Morris, 1958; Fried, 1963). Yet they are the vanguard of the future, for all radicalism is a portent of things to come.

A third force in change, about which I have written elsewhere, is constituted by those "process liberals" who try to move change ahead without giving up all of the existing needs for security (Duhl, 1967). This group, which is trying to face the ambiguities and unknown values that are emerging, is willing to question the interpretations and histories of the past. Its members both belong and do not belong to the established order. Seeing many sides of the current dilemma while fully championing none, they are plagued by the "purgatory of nonbelonging." They are trying to re-form the problem by connecting, linking, and reconnecting different parts of the social organism without making the process too rough or provoking the repression of reaction and a fear-laden return to the past. Among these catalysts of change are the healers, therapists, and educators. Like all other agents of change, they are molded by the interplay between who they are and the roles they play. Their security comes from a *new belonging*, from an identity with others like themselves. Like members of the "invisible colleges" of the eighteenth century in Great Britain (and of the scientific community today), their informal networks give them information utilization. They thus become an elite which has a power based not on money or position but on ideas, questions, and information, coupled with other human characteristics and resources (Duhl & Volkman, 1970).

I have suggested that Americans like change disguised as conservatism: nonchanging structures which incorporate changing meanings—the "in" society which co-opts radical ideas but appears unchanged. Although this is a psychologically valid process, the current strains on our society and the burgeoning aspirations of divergent groups combine to press impatiently for a totally new world. At such times, he who questions what has been widely accepted, and thus rewrites history, is a challenge. He makes us all feel insecure, for often his questions, because they imply new values, are not clear to us. He uses intuition and feeling; he senses and wonders. His fantasies and dreams embody images and expressions that alter the ways we arrange simple, often accepted facts. We feel threatened by these new perspectives, and we react by calling him impractical and unrealistic. We try to abort him.

I have stressed *security* in this discussion because man's psychological need to belong is most critical. Human beings all recognize both a physical and a psychological territory or turf as their own. Whether radical or conservative, white or black, each of us protects this turf from foreign incursions, lives within it, and tries to expand its boundaries. Each of us wants *our* myths, values, or view of the world to stand unquestioned, especially when these values have been newly found. If we don't fight for our world view, we retreat into apathy and helplessness. Yet we feel equally free to attack, condemn, criticize, or even laugh at the ways in which others protect their myths and values. We are thus "divided selves."

How can we change, expand, or find new directions while we insist on maintaining our "invulnerable" condition? In protecting our world view, we narrow our vision. We close ourselves off from what we do not want to see or hear. If we are "radical," we wonder how anyone dares to read Falwell or Buckley, or even the *Reader's Digest.* If we are "conservative," we stress the dangers to society of "radical tracts," or even the "liberal press." Closed to what is outside the circle of our belief, we sense devils all around us. To those of us who have "seen the light," everything else is simply false.

When this condition exists, the most radical person is a conservative or, at least, radically self-serving. He becomes unaware of the fact that others do not see the world as he does: they do not share his past or his images of the future. He is the true believer who says, "Learn *my* way or take the consequences." We try all sorts of brain-washing (often immensely sophisticated) in order to convert others to our point of view. The result is often tyranny, even though the social forms adopted by the fulfilled self-blinded can be dictatorships of the conservative right or the radical left. A necessary concomitant of tyrannical forms of government is intolerance of others, especially if these others are "reformers" who do not accept the prevailing view. In such a world, we tend to fragment into groups and are unable to make coalitions for change or even to maintain stable states in a changing world. In our fear and frustration, we try to make the world whole again by stealing diversity and individual idiosyncrasy from its members. We become thieves.

Under such circumstances, we see self-defense as all important. Vulnerability is what is most feared. Yet, paradoxically, the only solution to our dilemma may be a security wherein we can be both vulnerable and open (Seeley, 1969). It is true that open negotiations, democratically arrived at, are the most difficult to achieve. They represent an idealized goal. In the present conditions of instantaneous free communication, our open society finds itself forced to turn to quiet negotiation, and thus to reliance upon an informed, decision making elite. In such a situation, trust and security become important strategic as well as personal concepts.

In brief, the history of most change includes a vanguard which promotes and achieves change according to its own views and a movement of mass support which follows along once the structures of change have been created. Thus the core issue of social change may well be the process of arriving at the *rules* for change, rather than focusing, as is more usual, upon *goals*.

It has been my theme that those who are involved in deliberate change must come to understand themselves and others, as well as the processes that are invoked.

With terms such as these, who has a right to intervene deliberately in social change? In nondeliberate change we are, of course, all involved, even if we choose not to be, for every human act is part of the fabric of the whole ecology of change. But as to deliberate change, I believe we each have a right to intervene according to our interest and ability, if only because we *are* an inseparable part of society and deeply responsive to, and responsible for, its condition. In the process of intervention, however, certain important factors should always be taken into account. I shall attempt to describe some of them.

There are limits to my knowledge, for I am human. Recognizing this, I respect your right to question my judgments or interpretations and, in turn, I will evaluate your criticisms for myself. But you must do the same for others as you do for me.

Conscious intervention should carry with it the assumption of responsibility. I see too many people trying to change an existing situation without knowing much about it. We tend to feel that what we know or believe to be true *must* apply to others as well as to ourselves without recognizing that such extrapolations from our own experience are both arrogant and invalid.

Somewhere underlying the problem of change, trust must exist between people—trust, and a sense of "no blame." In a democratic society, it is inevitable that responsibility be delegated and that we permit others in whom we trust to act in our name. In this sense, honest mistakes should be "blameless." Yet trust must be earned. No profession involved in social change gets its authority by decree. Physicians have had to earn their right; when there is doubt they must prove, not to the elite but to the layperson, that they can be trusted. The doctor gets this right from individuals who, as clients, can define his goals. How can the agents of change, dealing with groups or even in the public interest, get legitimacy from the client? There is no such profession as that of change agent. This means that there are no accepted wise men, despite various academic, intellectual, or political claims. We are still in the equivalent stage of the prescientific era of medicine as far as social change is concerned.

Science can only offer part of the answer. Some of the new utopians or technocrats have a variety of exciting tools to offer, but too often they ignore human values. Politicians fail us for similar reasons: they sacrifice or ignore the deepest human needs for the sake of immediate effects. So, while each of us tries to effect social change, each of us also partly fails—or succeeds in ways he did not anticipate or even wish for. Although I have tried to indicate that so far no group has earned the right to call itself a professional change agent, it becomes critically important to discuss the unique aspects of a profession that might earn for itself the right to "invade" the status quo and create change.

Although there is no such group, there is a common assumption that political bodies that allocate resources have been given (or have taken) the right to legislate change. Claiming any one of many sorts of expertise, some of these bodies attempt to assume as much right as possible to control decisions and, by implication, to gain increased autonomy over their own work and a degree of control over that of others.

More than any other professional, the physician, backed by his ability to use science to meet practical everyday needs of the public, has gained such a right over the past hundred years. As long as he exhibits this ability, his autonomy is not questioned. As he fails, however (as he does in many aspects of current complex medical systems), others enter the decision making process. In addition, if dissatisfaction is serious, the lay public may even attempt to deprofessionalize the medical (and other) systems.

The scientist and the academician, unlike the clinician, need not have lay acceptance or pragmatic "clinical" success (Friedson, 1970a). They are subject only to peer review and by accrediting political powers, which have the right to give or take away funding, thus often to grant permission to work. There is a distinct difference between acceptance by the lay public and by the "powers that be." In the growing concern with social change, confusion has resulted from the lack of differentiation between these various required roles. The "change agent" has little public sanction and his status, vis-à-vis the scientist-academician, is also low. Similarly, if the scientist-academician's work cannot be directly utilized or connected with pragmatic here-and-now questions (as in the case of medicine), he loses credibility with the public.

What has been missing is, on the one hand, an informed public, and on the other, a lack of "in-betweeners," people who can make visible and viable connections between knowledge and action. We still operate societally with primitive notions of change. There is no coherent skill group that could form up into a profession of social change.

What lies ahead, then, is a process of experience gathering, evaluation, and, finally, the growth of credibility. This involves building up the basic sciences (of which we may have more than we realize) and adding to them what we know of the clinical sciences of intervention. Here, too, as yet we have only fragments—a bit of diagnosis, a little therapeutic management, a few clinical teams—and no visible ethics or articulated values for those involved. I suggest, therefore, that there is a need for *social clinicians*—a professional field to which diagnosticians (planners), pathologists (critics), and a variety of other "social engineering" entrepreneurs can contribute only a part. Public administrators can certainly offer some ideas and methods, as can the political scientists. Industrial engineering embraces future planning within the business community, and the social impact of this engineering is increasingly recognized as an important part of such planning. Yet the gaps in our knowledge are broad. We have not yet put together, or even selected, all the pieces of our interventionist puzzle.

Our right to intervene can only grow out of a professionally rigorous, carefully supervised body of knowledge. But professional expertise, however important, is not enough, for without broadly based public support this expertise is in danger of becoming elitist. Therefore it must be enriched with other kinds of knowledge, experience, and aspiration. The participation of consumers and of other groups and professions affected by the struggle for social change is also a requisite. During such a long-term process, which can be hazardous, even perilous, for all of us, every person is an equal, even if some are "more equal" than others.

Who is to determine this course of development? I suggest only one of a number of possibilities: mounting an effort to produce several diverse models, which can be tested in "clinical schools" and coupled with voluntary community laboratories that begin explorations toward a solution. I will point out, however, that those involved in change within the broad social issues of medicine may well arrive first at answers to our riddle since many of the steps toward professionalization (especially in mental health) have already been taken.

What, then, lies ahead for those of us who have chosen the area of social change as our life work? We can foresee progress in many directions, but we shall have to live with ambiguity. We will have to try to know ourselves well enough to decide where we can work best: as teacher, activist, radical, or stabilizer, with individuals, groups, or the institutions that mold our values. No one can choose the roles we should play for us, for each of us must reflect our own personal history, values, and ways of using time. The problem is difficult, for we often allow ourselves to become captives of our own development and, therefore, of the institutions we choose to make responsible for our sense of security.

Nevertheless we cannot despair, nor close ourselves to unknown opportunities. On the contrary, we must open ourselves to the limits of our understanding. This means disciplined, yet open-minded studies of social issues. We must test our limits against all legitimate concerns, because only by means of such tests can we discover who we are and what we can do. We must also learn to respect others who do not see the world as we do, realizing that they hear in our words a foreign language, uttering threats to their security. To be a clinician of change is a responsibility not to be borne lightly, for *those whom we change could easily be ourselves.*

The attempt to bring many different views together within an open structure—much less to convince a wide public that the effort is valuable and necessary—will be difficult, and will take time. I see us now as only partially beginning such a process. However, we should remember that making a beginning does not mean that we ourselves will have to follow through to the end. Those of us who are by nature and talent designed for confrontation are not usually able to organize new institutions nor are we capable of running them. Each of us is unique, and therefore has a different role to play; but one of the most difficult tasks is to turn over responsibility for the next step to others. Having achieved our goal, we must not assume that we can go on with equal success to other goals. In all revolutions this assumption has been shown to be false—proven by death or, even in the best of times, removal from office. If we know ourselves, the strength of our purpose can be verified by our awareness of when and how to bow out. As Warren Bennis has taught us, our society is more and more a "temporary one" (Bennis & Slater, 1969; Toffler, 1970). Certainly this quality of impermanence is intrinsic to social change, and a criterion for the individuals participating in it.

Applying these points of reference to myself, I see myself as a starter—not a radical but a clinician, a questioner, a rephraser, a linker and connector. I am not a theoretician, nor a planner, nor an administrator. I am not a hedgehog who burrows deep, but a fox who circles and is unsure of his ultimate goal (Berlin, 1957). I am neither a belonger, nor non-place oriented (M. M. Webber, 1964), a person who questions not only the world, but himself. In addition, being identified with the oppressed and with those whose situations I attempted to change, I feel within me their torment and resistance as if it were my true self. But for an accident of history, rather than American, white, Jew, psychiatrist, physician, professor at Berkeley, or all else that I am, I could be any one of you—or of those for whom we hope the world will change.

If we look within ourselves, we will find there open for exploration an unknown domain as great as any in the outside world. Our intrapersonal tools are still primitive; none furnishes us with the means or the answer, yet inside ourselves we begin to perceive a basic core that makes us *not unlike* all other humans (Satprem, 1970). Despite all of our differences, it is within ourselves that we may find clues to that which makes us diverse and individually unique, yet homogeneously *human*. It is possible that within each of us we may find answers which can override our collective social failures, our often divisive personalities and specific differences. Out of such a fundamental recognition of our humanness, it may be possible to create a society which permits difference and yet encourages each and all of us to grow, to have aspirations, and to live peacefully together.

Chapter 2

HEALTH PLANNING

Critique and Alternatives

Although there is evidence that rational health planning is declining in usefulness, this paper is not an investigation as to whether planning is "dead," nor an overview of the process by which it has been replaced by other activities such as regulation or deregulation. Neither is the focus of this chapter on the day-to-day activities of the health planner. Rather, alternatives to planning as it has ordinarily been understood are presented here with the goal of moving it from the impoverished context of contemporary policy-making to new conceptions and visions of planning in the field of health. Change in health can only be achieved when planners have real insight into just what social change is and how it takes place. Under what conditions is planning even possible at all? Understanding these issues is especially crucial today because of the accelerated pace of change throughout the world.

THE PERILS OF RELYING ON THE PRESENT

Current planning in its pragmatic day-to-day practice is perhaps the easiest kind of planning to understand and describe because it involves clear, limited goals that are to be achieved in a short period of time. But as the concern with the long-term future increases, our sense of ambiguity increases, and our "quest for certainty" grows stronger (Dewey, 1960). Knowing less, we seek the comfort of believing that we can control the future by making it as much like the present—or past—as possible. This "conservative impulse" may be seen as an effort to protect ourselves from the sense of loss we associate with change (Marris, 1958, 1975). As the planning process moves from areas that are specific, immediate, and known to the distant, ambiguous future, it is essential that we learn to understand and depend on the continuing process of "inquiring systems" to define and redefine what is involved (Churchman, 1971, 1979a, 1979b). Indeed, the very conception of planning itself, its actors, objectives, systems, and processes will change as time spans lengthen.

It has been virtually an article of planning faith that if we look at a problem with clarity and precision we can, at least in principle, understand and comprehend all aspects of it. The health planner works with a complex set of systems connected to health and medical care, trying to define a mass of critical variables, then to project an understanding of their dynamic interaction in order to get a clear picture of what can or should lie ahead. The goal is to identify opportunities to intervene in these intertwining processes in order to deliberately shape the future.

However, although simple, short-term problems may be addressed with such seemingly precise short-term approaches, precise methodology becomes inappropriate and difficult to apply when the problems being addressed are multifactorial in nature and when planning is to extend to the uncertain future. It seems, in fact, that the arena where we have the ability to predict and control phenomena has contracted markedly.

As professional power has become more concentrated and more systematic, unintended side effects have increased both in medical care and in health planning and policy (McKeown, 1976; Haggerty, 1972; Winkelstein, 1972). Clinical iatrogenesis has bred what Illich (1976) calls a social and cultural "expropriation" of power and control from individuals and this has led to a pervasive sense that both health practitioners and health and social planners cause more harm than good (Gaylin, 1978). These crises of health and medical care in America today are clearly of long standing (Committee on the Costs of Medical Care, 1932). Possible solutions will profoundly affect many major sectors of the society (H. Blum, 1976a, 1981; Duhl, 1980a).

Health planning in the last years has begun to move beyond specific medical issues related to care, treatment, and rehabilitation. The reality of health care is that it is more—far more— than only the provision of medical care services (Navarro, 1976; Relman, 1980). A hospital in a central city, for example, not only performs its medical functions, but it also participates in the employment picture, in social unrest, and in all the human services and sociopolitical issues that make up the central city and the community around it (Duhl, 1968). If health and medical care facilities and their parent corporations are not to cause more problems for its neighborhood and community than it solves, planners and administrators must understand these institutions in their full context.

Because health care (which is primarily medical or disease care) accounts for almost 10 percent of the Gross National Product of the United States, its concerns must be related to those of the larger society. To some extent, therefore, health planning has become societal planning. The health planner is not free to exercise "professional dominance" in making decisions about health care (Friedson, 1970b). Planners must take into account not only their "own" field but also an array of centrally-related issues in the community: those legal, financial, social, and political considerations that in the past may have held little significance to the disease care planner concerned with preexisting "standards."

A vision of the interconnectedness of systems and of the ecological nature of all activities—biological, social, economic, political, conceptual, and even spiritual—is central to an understanding of change (Brody, 1973; H. Blum, 1976a). The determinants of health have enlarged to the totality of the planet earth, but at the same time planetwide change has become so extensive and significant that we have often lost control of specific actions in the field of health. We seem to be at a point where we can no longer have an impact in the formal, standard, and ultimately simplistic manner that many of us once understood could effect health change. It is no longer clear, for example, as it once

seemed to be, just what type of a national health insurance policy would answer our current needs. Certain versions of such a
scheme may be counterproductive for providing a "just" program for medical care, and, importantly, for health promotion
and well-being.

To understand this we need to examine the differences between the medical model of change, which has served most
health planners until now, and a new health model of change
that planners should adopt in order to plan for the complex future. Medical care focuses on a defined and limited set of difficulties, symptoms, or illnesses that require prevention, treatment, rehabilitation, maintenance, or some combination of
these. Health, on the other hand, encompasses the normal processes of growth, development, and decline. It is made up of
interdependent biological, psychological, social, and spiritual
foci in human development. During stress or crisis these foci
normally allow for coping and adaptation, but when this adaptation process cannot take place, *dis-ease* results. Dis-ease can bring
either social, physical, psychological, or spiritual "illness" or
often a confluence of two or more kinds of "illness." While clinical medical treatment often deals with specific disorders me-
chanically and in relative isolation, an interdependent notion of
healing seeks to return the whole individual to an optimal state
of well-being and growth. Healing reintegrates and reconnects.

We now know that although there are normal, generally determined processes of development, the path to health varies by
culture and society. Even the very definition of health is socially
constructed (Berger & Luckman, 1967; Strauss & Glaser, 1967;
Estes, 1979). Rational planners in the past have not always taken
this diversity of cultural or ethnic pathways and norms into account. They have tended to assume that all healthy development
was essentially the same and that goals and norms were similar
whether one was black, Caucasian, Asian, or American Indian.

To further complicate the planning process, planners need
to recognize that people living in heterogeneous societies have a
more difficult time achieving health than those living in homogeneous societies: the skills they require are more specialized
and they often live in multiple, conflicting worlds. As people
who have been "invisible" to the majority culture become more
visible, stress increases for individuals, for institutions, and in

policy itself (Ellison, 1953). However, when the attempt to achieve healthy development breaks down under stress and crisis, the dis-ease that occurs often takes a particular form. Typically, disease and the form it takes depend upon the predominant culture. As a result, minorities in heterogeneous societies are often alienated from their own more traditional cultural definitions of disease and health.

In a relatively predictable and homogeneous social situation the stresses are relatively clear, and the health planner may well have ways to determine what those stress situations are and how to plan to cope with them effectively. In heterogeneous societies, however, as stresses become increasingly complex and unpredictable, planners may find that the institutions designed to cope with stress are under stress themselves and are thus incapable of dealing either with their own difficulties or with those of the people whom they were supposed to serve (Holmes & Masuda, 1970; Slote, 1969; Berkman & Syme, 1979; Marris, 1958, 1975).

Finally, health and planning for health must be spelled out in the full context of our contemporary health environment. Our "natural" environment, if there ever was such a thing, has been supplanted by a man-made environment that seems at least as uncontrollable, so that much of our dis-ease is both man-made and difficult to cure. Dis-ease becomes illness in a variety of forms depending on a multitude of factors. Does the present high incidence of drug abuse, alcoholism, mental illness, and suicide reflect an epidemic of individual illnesses, even failings, or is it a product of particular social, man-made conditions? If, as we believe, these diseases are neither completely individual nor completely social in origin and course, so, on the other hand, is health also a synthesis of the individual's internal environment with the entire external environment—physical, social and spiritual, man-made and "natural" (Lalonde, 1974; Califano, 1979; Dubos, 1959, 1968)?

WHITHER PLANNING?

Planning represents a set of strategies to organize and implement hope, to produce change for the better, or at least to attempt to prevent change for the worse. The idea that planning is feasible at all has several premises: that social change is both possible and desirable; that the future can be affected positively by deliberate intervention; and that the social activity of policy design will function to clarify present confusion and will lead to a deliberate outcome. This outcome will be a set of plans or programs designed to be implemented as the intended interventions of the policy designer. The emphasis on *control* of policy design leads to the notion that the planning process is characterized by deliberateness.

This calculated belief in deliberate intervention, however, can and does go awry. When it goes awry in a systemic way, authors like Ivan Illich (1976) point out that iatrogenicity no longer confines itself to biomedicine but begins to characterize most social systems in most industrialized countries. Narrowly defined, iatrogenicity means that an illness is unintentionally caused by the physician or the health care system or both. As a society becomes "developed," it is frequently more dominated by a rational medical model of illness and a parallel model of planning. Such a society tends to view most problems and issues with a singleness of approach, one that is often particularistic, paternalistic, and tending toward professionalization with its specialization and consequent narrowness of vision and alternatives. Such an approach is epitomized, according to social critics such as Illich, by the limited vision of contemporary biomedicine. It can also be seen in approaches to health care that describe health as a business or industry to be understood and undertaken using the language of corporate market analysis rather than of equity (Vladeck, 1980; Relman, 1980).

Health planners and policymakers need to address this notion of iatrogenic policy and, for that matter, the idea of iatrogenic illness. To do so will require a different paradigm from that reigning model of social change that now dominates both scientific and social scientific inquiry. This "dominant paradigm," as Kuhn (1970) calls it, relies upon inquiry that uses particularistic and discrete methodologies rather than upon the "macro" approach that we advocate and which is now often termed "(w)holistic" (Pelletier, 1977, 1979; Duhl, 1980a).

Current conventional efforts at planning, policy-making,

and social change all share inherited assumptions that seem increasingly plausible and dysfunctional. Planning is now not where we want it to be nor where it *ought* to be, and we use the word "ought" deliberately in order to emphasize that planners must be explicit about values. Planning, policy-making, and social change are all, and always, we believe, both political and value-laden. The present striving after a rational planning approach seeks to remove these taints and constraints from planning theory. We argue that the reverse may well be necessary: both values and politics need to be understood and incorporated as primary and endemic aspects of planning, policy-making, and social change (Veatch & Bronson, 1976).

The wish to "cleanse" ethical and political considerations from planning and policy-making is at best naive and at worst an untenable reductionism that leads one systematically to exclude key factors from consideration in conceptualizing both health and planning. While such exclusions have what may seem to be "obvious advantages," not the least of which is the illusion of parsimony, they ultimately result in a pristine and misleading clarity. This desire for a false sense of clarity is rooted in what William Barrett (1979) called "the illusion of technique." It is the belief that problems of virtually any complexity can and should be reduced to discrete entities, thereby becoming malleable and open to solution. As a method for dealing with the systemwide problems that face us today, this approach is more and more questionable. Planners need not to break "macro" problems down into "micro" size, but rather to gain a critical understanding of the dynamics of the relation between micro-person and macro-policy. This relational process must avoid the pitfalls of reductionism, victim blaming, and false clarity (H. Blum, 1980; Ryan, 1976).

The multiple discrete, iterative, and often quantitative techniques that at present make up much of the planning process in health are of only limited usefulness when it comes to understanding a social and politicized world that appears to be ever more ambiguous, intricate, and independent. Our world is more complex than present models can portray. We do not, however, deny the power and appropriateness of quantitative tools—such a denial would be that of twentieth-century Luddites. We are concerned that the use of such tools has come to *replace* a more complete, more human approach that looks at problems from many perspectives simultaneously.

Quantitative tools are necessary but not sufficient to plan for the ambiguous future; they are tools to be used as aids *for* interpretation, for consensus and discensus, and for our scenarios and visions of a future. To the extent that these tools *replace* interpretation, to that extent we may find ourselves in a statistically robust and socially arid wasteland, where method subsumes content and problem alike. We would be symbolically powerful, and actually impotent to understand, or plan for, change (Edelman, 1971; Alford, 1975).

WHITHER HEALTH? SOME PRESUPPOSITIONS

Before proceeding with our argument, it would be useful to summarize our underlying convictions, assumptions, and values about health and planning, and to offer evidence for these where possible.

There is a significant difference between medical care and health care; they are far from synonymous. Present evidence indicates that the treatment activities that make up medical care account for only about one-quarter to one-third of the determinants of health status (McKeown, 1976; H. Blum, 1981). The other two-thirds to three-quarters, in short, the critical determinants of health, are apparently unrelated to medical care. Biological and genetic factors in the individual determine health status to a significant extent, but the major determinants of health are the ways individuals live their lives and the kinds of physical and mental environments in which they live and work (Califano, 1979). The medical model of health, however, dominates health planning and health care. It has led to what one physician-critic calls "the medical industrial complex" (Relman, 1980). Indeed, the rhetoric and the resources for prevention, wellness, and environmental planning are dwarfed by the enormous influence, power, and resources wielded by the "care and cure" branch of the contemporary biomedical enterprise.

Policy-making and planning are quite possibly not best accomplished via discrete, linear, and primarily quantitative tasks. This method of intervention, although effective in solving small problems that can be isolated, decreases in utility as problem complexity increases. Planners should adopt a "systems approach" instead (Churchman, 1979a). Such a perspective demands and gives attention to the continuous, dynamic interrelationships between an array of circumstances, issues, and values, many of which cannot be reduced to "variables." The major reason that many health policy and planning issues remain intractable is that the "dominant paradigm" no longer works: it is stalled by its inability to map the interrelationships between politics and values on the one hand, while espousing, on the other hand, a way of doing planning that attempts to deny the influences of these very factors.

Following this, we argue that the activities of professionals may often be surprisingly inappropriate, even iatrogenic, especially when these professionals are operating "normally," that is, with a combination of professional autonomy and professional dominance. In addition, the actions of professionals may well be unresponsive to the wishes or the needs of clients and consumers (Wiseman, 1970). Where once there may have been trust between experts and the public, more and more people would agree with George Bernard Shaw's characterization in *The Doctor's Dilemma* that "All professions are conspiracies against the laity."

In our society, where the delivery of health care, like that of other social services, is highly differentiated, planning cannot be undertaken without developing a philosophy of intervention. We need a theory to explain how—and why—we should bring about social change, and who should be in charge of doing so. It is no accident that the distrust of professionals coincides with the rise of a consumer movement, however limited this movement may be, and with a growing public interest in self-care and self-help. Evidence for these latter concerns can be seen in almost any bookstore, and yet training about traditions of self-help and self-care is virtually absent from the education received by any health professional.

The distrust of professionals has spilled over from those who deliver direct services, such as lawyers, social workers, and health care providers, to planners and administrators as well (Barber, 1980). As a tragic by-product of the emphasis on professionalism in our society we have produced a class of professional experts who see with great sharpness and penetration but in a very limited fashion (Larson, 1977). Our professional class may become increasingly ineffective, even counter-productive, as the magnitude of our pressing worldwide problems—population growth, the leadership crisis, and institutional fragmentation and disarray—becomes greater.

ALTERNATIVE WAYS OF SEEING, PLANNING, AND BEING HEALTHY

We have described planning as either reactive or as being paralyzed by particularity. We have shown that concern with health has been overshadowed by the attention given to medical care in the contemporary biomedical enterprise. We see all this taking place in an atmosphere of institutional torpor, where societal guides, in the form of plans, goals, and programs appear to be firmly grounded in a prior view of the world. But what alternatives—what ways of seeing and doing differently—are available?

Jonas Salk, in an attempt to expand his thinking beyond his training and research as a bacteriologist and virologist, applies the biologist's law of the S-shaped curve to our planetwide dilemma. Salk (1973) sees the growth of bacteria and viruses on agar plates as a metaphor for the world's situation. Salk believes that environmental nutrients are no longer capable of sustaining the increasing growth of the population, but also that most institutions are no longer capable of sustaining their ability to deal effectively with problems. When the middle of the S-curve shifts from experiential growth toward a plateau, or no growth, a transition into a new epoch is required, one that Salk calls Epoch B, where the metalanguage, or the way one conceptualizes issues, needs to become markedly different. It would be nihilistic to end our discussion with a diagnosis that the present crisis is so severe that we are fundamentally incapable of dealing with it: we do not believe this to be true. But we are all, to one degree or another, inept, because we are products of a way of thinking that emerged in the previous epoch, in what Salk would call Epoch A. We need to begin to see ourselves and our problems as taking place in the midst of the profoundly unsettling transition from Epoch A to Epoch B.

What is this transition or shift all about? In *The Structure of Scientific Revolutions*, Thomas Kuhn (1970) suggested that at the point where issues cannot be understood and assimilated in terms of accepted "truths," then a change in paradigm takes place, in conceptual framework. If and when the paradigm in good currency is fundamentally challenged we get—or are forced to face—varieties of evidence for "alternative realities" (Castenada, 1968; Zukov, 1979; Forward, 1980).

We suggested earlier that a basic problem of traditional planning and policy was the need to control a hostile environment and that this need has caused the concept of control to become central to our Western approach to knowledge (Webber & Rittel, 1973). We invade, divide, and analyze in order to *know*. Such knowing requires a "left brain" that rationally understands (Ornstein, 1971). Accompanying this form of knowing has been a belief that we *can* know everything and that we *must* act out of knowledge and with a specific type of information called "data." Thus the metalanguage of the epoch, Epoch A, that we are leaving, is essentially a language of controlling the data.

It has been the inhabitants of the Northern hemisphere, and especially of the West, who have been preoccupied with control and with the paradigm, metalanguage, and conceptual systems that have gone with it in Epoch A. In early human development, the tribal peoples of the Northern hemisphere indeed found it necessary to exercise control because the environment was hostile and the Ice Age left the North a harsh and dangerous place. Those in the Southern hemisphere found themselves in a very different situation. In the Southern hemisphere, which was relatively untouched by the calamities of the glacier, groups of people did not need to develop the precise analytic techniques of the control that were used in the North and West. In the South, they could communicate without the use of a highly concrete language, while their sense of time, space, and precision met their needs, although it could not have met the needs of the North. In recent centuries the colonizing ("developed") nations of the North have superimposed their culture both on the East and the South, so that they have become more and more "like us." The tragedy of developing nations and of many development planners is the denial of original heterogeneity.

Colonizing Northerners have seen the people of the Southern hemisphere as unintelligent because they did not use the analytic skills or techniques of the North and West. The absence of concern with calibration and precision appeared to leave them in a "fuzzy" state where they dealt with nebulous and ghostlike images unacceptable to a social system dominated by analytic, left-brain, conceptual models. The view of the world that was not centered in control created a different model, a model that may also have existed in the North before the Ice Age calamities. We now often refer to behavior that arose from a noncontrol model as "primitive." Yet in this noncontrol model individuals are an integral part of the total ecology, they appear to understand the interrelationship of forces to which they have given names, and they understand that as they interact these forces impinge on their actions and on their very being.

This "primitive," noncontrol model is merely one of many that may facilitate an understanding of the heterogeneous development necessary to achieve a perspective for global social change and habit. We can also look to the work of some Western scientists for Epoch B models. If we are indeed moving into a society in which the totality of the earth should be understood as a single organism, then it may be useful to use the human organism as a model for the larger organism of the earth. This does not mean, as in older organic theories, as a system of organs dominated by the head, but rather as an organism that is complexly interconnected in ways that we are only beginning to understand (Pribram, 1977).

Some neuroscientists have begun to find clues about communication devices between cells and about how cells and organs interact with each other. Biologists now teach that bodily organs, both in predetermined biological function and in response to stimuli, are relatively autonomous and self-governing and yet at the same time interdependent and cooperative. Earlier models of the body that presented the brain as ruler and controller of the system paralleled earlier social and political models of hierarchy and patriarchy where king, pope, or chairman of the board controlled the organization. Recent research suggests, however, that even if it is the mind that "rules," this mind is not confined to the brain but is instead distributed throughout the organism. Some even argue that individual bodily organs have their own memories, injunctions, indeed, almost their own consciousness. Organs are not puppets dancing for a ruling brain; they are active in making decisions. We have but minimal information of these matters, although as compared to 50 years ago our knowledge is tremendous (Handler, 1970; Ferguson, 1980).

Emergent alternative models, then, envision no single center, but recognize that the pieces of our individual and social organism are independent yet joined, separate yet part of the whole. These alternatives suggest that we are moving toward a new understanding of ourselves, and of the processes and goals of planning as well. For example, with such an alternative view, the process of governance will be markedly changed because it will require processes that are neither hierarchical nor totally collegial (Thayer, 1980).

Planners and protesters have spent a good deal of time fighting social and political models of hierarchy, only to come up with alternative models that are primarily collegial. They have defined equity as numerical equality of input and of outcome. If, however, a population cannot be described best as a collection of equal integers but rather as an interdependent organism of markedly different subgroups, then equity should be redefined as a planned developmental process by which each group maximizes its opportunity to develop in a full and total manner. In order to recognize and plan for social heterogeneity we need to develop a wide variety of health and planning processes, including planning to favor those presently least advantaged in order to grant them justice (Rawls, 1971). The "melting pot" should no longer be an appropriate designation nor a desired social policy.

We are beginning to understand that a family, for example, need not be seen only, or even optimally, as a paternalistic hierarchical organization, nor yet as one of complete equals. The family can be seen instead as a situation in which individuality is valued and yet those who participate in it are held together by a set of processes that comprise living in the family (Satir, 1975). This is a very different notion of governance, a new departure from the ethos where paternalism and control were primary.

As we begin to face the problems of moving to a new epoch, many have rediscovered—through certain forms of community action, through travel, drugs, music, art, and through contacts with non-Western teaching and teachers that certain aspects of our rational system can be expanded and modified by what traditionally has been called the nonrational. Our definition of knowing can and must change to include more than that which we understand analytically so that it incorporates "primitive" or right-brain thinking. The education and training of people for left-brain and right-brain thinking are quire different and this can and does make communication between cultures difficult. It is encouraging to note, however, that the basic genetic and biological template upon which the learning takes place is probably similar and that it is only social learning that directs people in one or the other direction. We may yet devise a sense of "organized empathy" that will diminish such a deep division in ways of seeing and being. If, as we move out of Epoch A to the new ways of being and understanding that will become Epoch B, we cannot bring this mutual empathy about, we shall surely be both imperiled and impoverished.

ARE WE THERE YET?

Does all this bear on planning for the future? As we move from Epoch A to Epoch B we are faced with a need for alternative models, because the first temptation, as we confront the existential and social deprivation of this transition, is to emphasize increasingly sophisticated controls over both environment and people. In this crisis, however, we may have an alternative choice: to accept a completely different set of metavalues. The metavalues of planning based upon collaboration and of health seen as wellness rather than disease control could lead us to learn to live more wisely.

There well may be laws for these new alternatives, laws that at this moment are undiscovered. Epoch B may well also redefine the notion of a law so that it becomes less a "confirmation of the data" and more a shared understanding. The very ideas of "law" and "proof" may expand and change in Epoch B. Planning in this new setting may become a proactive undertaking to understand alternatives even when we have little knowledge about the full context and contours of the future.

Let us then speculate as to the meaning of health in the emerging world, that David Bohm sees as a holographic universe (R. Webber, 1978). We are aware that all of the universe is connected; within the hologram, health may mean the ability to choose the appropriate reality (or the appropriate dream) depending upon the issue that needs to be faced. Such an interconnected universe implies that the so-called "side effects" of one issue, problem, or solution can more properly be seen as a whole set of health issues. Such a central issue is the "grieving for a lost home" that many feel at present and the seeking a "new home" that can offer us the well-being of wellness that is the true definition of health (Fried, 1963; S. Blum, 1973).

Health professionals need to recognize that health may be the utilization by individuals, as part of a communal society, of all their senses, even those beyond the ones we normally recognize. It is this direction that health is taking: a direction away from the purely technical and manipulative and towards the integration of the technical with the synthetic, the rational with the spiritual, the analytic with the intuitive (Moore, 1980).

This essay has been designed to show planners concerned with health some of the multiple frustrations that they are facing, frustrations that may arise from the pace of contemporary change, which is beyond the control of any individual. In order to be effective, planners must become affective and cognizant of the variables of change that are taking place within individuals, institutions, systems, and in fields as diverse as psychology and physics. Only then can they design policy that will permit alternative ways of discovery and of being. The belief that there is a single path of development for individuals, that institutions and interventions are similar for all, no longer works. We must move toward a pluralistic system that meets the variety of needs and the levels of development and culture of this planet's people. To do less is to be condemned to the limiting vision of the impoverished present. The challenge is ours.

Can we exist with this heterogeneity? Can we keep together as part of a whole or must we separate and change and move toward being members of tribes who do battle with each other and ultimately destroy our home, the earth? As dramatic as this question is, just so are the needs for reseeing ways to foster planning for wellness and for equitable social change.

Chapter 3

THE DIMENSIONS OF HEALTH

Traditional Healing and Modern Medicine

A major task facing us today is that of finding new ways to conceptualize the relationship between health, illness, and what is commonly known as "health care." This is a particularly dangerous task because, even on the surface, it is so complex. Then, in our humble efforts to describe these difficulties we find that the vocabulary of modern medicine and science contains few words appropriate to this task. As a result, we must draw upon other fields, other conceptualizations, and other points of view.

The symptoms are familiar. Wherever one turns, expenditures for medical services are growing in staggering amounts, due to rising individual expectations as well as increases in costs related to the exponential growth of technological investments. In addition, around the world, patterns of health manpower utilization are changing dramatically. The organized medical system is being expanded on the one hand by physicians' assistants, MEDEX (medical extenders) personnel, and a host of ancillary manpower, and on the other by the slow reincorporation of indigenous, more traditional, non-Western practices of medicine.

Problems resulting from the blurring of distinctions between so-called "health issues" and other kinds of social issues such as crime, education, and even poverty are beginning to have medical overtones. We may be finding an increase in the number of phenomena that are placed in the hands of the medical professional with the expectation that he or she should be responsible for coping with them.

In the so-called developed nations, as infectious diseases and some of the other basic medical conditions are being conquered, a new collection of illnesses or medical conditions, such as aging and environmental hazards, are gaining attention.

We find the realm of medicine extending even further as we begin to understand the implications of the changes in all our societies and to see how those changes are influencing the patterns of illness that are produced. We are thus forced by the very nature of the etiology of disease to focus more and more attention on the general structure of society and how it impinges upon the human organism.

For many years we have used the words medicine or medical care interchangeably with health and health care. People have talked of "health insurance" as if the individual's ability to deal with illness medically would, in fact, improve the general health and well-being of a society. Indeed, when one deals with major infectious diseases such as smallpox or malaria, it is true that the general well-being of a society can go through vast changes due to the very processes of improving the care or prevention of medical conditions.

However, as cultural aspirations rise with affluence, and illnesses that are conquerable begin to disappear, we are faced with the question of what we mean by healthy living and well-being. The general quality of life becomes the issue, and we begin to raise such questions as what we need to do to meet the basic needs of people.

It is only recently that such august bodies as the World Bank and the United Nations have defined people's basic needs as food, clothing, clean water, and shelter; and rediscovered that these needs, accompanied by a minimum of medical care, may in fact have an important effect both on illness rates and the quality of life in any society.

And as one looks more deeply at the question of needs, one

may find, much to one's surprise, that needs may be even more subtle, and that such things as touch, belonging, being part of social networks, of family, community, and even nation are critically important to people's well-being. One soon discovers that such questions as self-esteem are central to health in much the same way that one requires food and clothing and shelter.

It is here that we begin to raise questions about the *meaning* of well-being, because we find that for most of us, issues which are foreign to the world of medicine, nutrition, and housing, such as religion, ritual, and cultural belief systems, take on prime importance in our concern with illness and its care and the maintenance or achievement of healthy living.

We are faced with a tremendous dilemma because people at different stages of personal and social development, coming from different cultures, orientations, and ways of conceiving the world's reality, end up with different definitions of health. Illness becomes the inability of the body to meet the expectations or limitations of a society or, if we are to extend this further, when the body gets out of balance with the external environment, that is, when the internal and external environments are not synthesized, we may develop ill health.

Furthermore, when one's life cycle or experience is incongruous with one's self-image, as, say, during times of revolution, war, catastrophe, other severe stress, or even during psychotherapy, one falls out of balance with oneself. Often mental or physical illness or dis-ease is a temporary or chronic attempt to regain homeostasis. The same stress may be experienced by others as a time of change and growth.

We have just opened what may appear to be a strange door because as we talk of individual differences as well as cultural, social, and developmental ones, we are beginning to suggest that societies are full of different realities about our world. We have always experienced our societies in which the dominant and majority cultural force has indeed determined the criteria by which we define reality. That force has indeed determined the cosmology of the society within which questions of dis-ease, health, and illness are defined. The questions have become decidedly political, in that society after society does battle within it as various groups jockey for power to determine right and wrong, good and bad, health and illness. This is not to say that there are not illnesses that cross over cultures and belief systems, yet on the whole they may have become determined by social forces.

It is here that we would like to focus on the question of how we define the realities of medicine and of the health care professions. The Western model, a scientific model of Cartesian proportions, has determined how the body works and, in fact, determines the questions of how we are to render our medical and other services. Science, as we have known it up to now, has focused on its biochemical systems, its infectious and allergy responses, and a whole host of other phenomena that we associate with Western scientific medicine.

Clearly, the Western model is different from basic traditional concepts of Native Americans, or for that matter the model of the Tao, which the Chinese have espoused for many generations. The Tao model is based on energy systems, and social and individual equilibrium. It employs treatment procedures such as acupuncture, which are foreign to Western medicine. We raise this point to illustrate that if one were to design a medical and health system based purely on the models of energy, one might create, even in the world of modern science, models that are akin to what we have called primitive belief systems. The American Indian, the Hawaiian, and other so-called primitive cultures around the world have talked about the connection of all beings to one another. They have posited the belief that one is one with the earth and all its beings, rather than disconnected as a human from everything else. As such, these models of health allow the energy to flow and the individual becomes one with the universe by a variety of means—physical, psychological, religious, and spiritual. Thus, what we have called primitive ritual has become part of the system of ongoing life, and indeed part of what is called treatment or medicine within that cosmology.

We have raised the question of energy models because it is a foreign reality to those of us trained in Western medicine; yet this view is an accepted part of daily life in many cultures. In this connection I refer to some interesting questions about waves and energy. To do this requires that I take license and talk about a field that I know nothing about—water and land—and that I try to refer some of those issues to some of the issues of energy systems.

One of the most interesting properties of water is not its chemical composition, or the fact that it is so prevalent a part of our environment, but rather its style, for water never seems to flow in straight lines. It is subject to the rhythms of the moon; it flows even in the deepest ocean, in its own streams; its temperatures vary a few feet apart. There are eddies and currents and whirls and waves so that it is in continuous motion.

If we look from the air at pictures of the earth, especially that part of the earth where man has not had an impact, we see that the ground is made up of the same kinds of curves and hills and sharp peaks, and what we see are the endless flows and processes across the land. In viewing the earth from the air, it is interesting to see how human beings have dealt with the curves, the flow, and the rhythms of the earth and water. What we see may be described, charitably, as a sign of human need to control the environment. We have done so in order to improve our way of life. Thus our quality of life was improved by interfering with the normal patterns of energy flow—interference necessary in order to protect ourselves from the climate, from the environment, and from predators. Further, we began to find techniques both to husband our resources and to protect ourselves against the potential harmful effects of famine.

To resort to Native American imagery, one can easily imagine the view that as the civilizing or colonization process has advanced from one phase to another, a switch in cosmology changed the free flow of the human being with its total environment to a cosmology which emphasized human control of the environment. Since we are never separate from the environment (it influences our feelings and attitudes while we make our mark on it), it is no surprise that as the environment itself was conquered, the human perception of the enemy broadened from the environment to include other humans who perceived the universe as one of the scarce resources.

In the process of husbanding and protecting the resources from others, society developed techniques and beliefs which were concomitant with that behavior. Thus, the behavior that resulted from this agricultural determinism led to a belief system which not only determined the behavior of individuals but also became the controlling force in the behavior of science, and its practice of medicine and health. In a competitive, growing world it was important to have a health system, or medical system that dealt primarily with the control of death and with techniques to cope with the competitive arrangements of others.

In a nomadic pre-agricultural society in which people were "one with the environment," there was neither ownership nor land nor competition. What *was* present was a cosmology and a belief system which led to the concept of health having to do with a *balance* of energies. Health, then, was defined as those human behaviors and beliefs which would coexist with the natural flow of the rivers and the streams and the hills and the valleys, and consistent with the ebb and flow of the seasons, the currents, and the weather. As soon as that society emerged which needed to conquer its environment, it not only straightened out the natural energies by creating land that was cut up in straight lines, but water had to flow in straight lines in irrigation ditches, canals, and pipes. People had not only to control each other through timed schedules, law and order, and structural education, but they had to learn to control their own emotions and physical processes. That view of controlling society led to its fragmentation and ultimately to the theoretical models which were the models of science, its medicine, and its concept of health and well-being.

At present a series of changes seem to be occurring in our society. On one hand it is as if the values of the so-called primitive societies are infiltrating those with which the West is preoccupied. In the West, concepts of "nonrationality" are beginning to enter into rational thinking. What may be surprising, however, is that suddenly we are beginning to become aware that there is rational, scientific proof of some of the processes that heretofore have been considered unscientific.

In addition to scientific proof, there are changes in moral and ethical perceptions, just as there were when the natural world began to be controlled. We now seem to be in the midst of a shift of major proportions as we face the inability to deal with current problems. As our society becomes more and more crowded and the problems of one fragmented field after another—medicine, education, city planning—begin to overlap into another fragmented field, what emerges is a need for and thus the creation of a concept of systems. "Systems theory" thus developed as a way of managing organized complexity. The paradox, however, is that organized complexity does not behave in a purely rational manner; thus the concept became one of living systems—systems which continually learn and are therefore in a state of perpetual flux. We call these "inquiring systems."

Despite this trend, the crises continued to build so that each fragment overlapping each other fragment led to further and further complexity. Consequently, instead of talking about pieces of the earthly universe, it is becoming easier to conceive of the earth as a total organism. Such a perception is being proposed in modern physics and in neurophysiology and the holographic universe and the holographic mind. We cannot separate the Native Americans from the rest of the United States, China, Japan, or the rest of the world, nor can we separate the concepts of health from politics, governance, economics, or even the price of oil. We are talking about a total living organism.

We could face the issue with the concept of One World, or of "Spaceship Earth" as described by Buckminster Fuller. We then come up with the notion that we have an earth that is a whole, that the resources are limited, and that we must find ways, not of competition, but of collaboration, and that we must slowly return to being one again with that environment which is the earth and which is the context of our lives.

We would like to turn now to the concept previously mentioned, of the hologram, because the physicists, in their analyses of the various quanta, have become more and more preoccupied with studying and finding the particles which make up the atoms or matter of the universe. If the physicists discover more and more particles, some even suggest that if they search endlessly, they will find as many particles as they set out to find. Some physicists are beginning to propose that the issue may very well be how particles are organized and that the organization of the particles is based upon the space between the particles, which they call "consciousness." For those of us in the field of psychology, consciousness has a similar meaning, in the sense that consciousness is the way we organize reality. The physicists hypothesize that the way reality is organized determines how the particles get together. They further suggest that if a shift of consciousness is produced by shifting the energy pattern, what we call physical reality will change. Thus, reality is a reflection of our consciousness about the universe in which we exist (Capra, 1975).

But let us take it one step further and go way out in concepts and then return. The physicists have even suggested, following some of the concepts of Einstein, that if one were to leave our present perception and move endlessly in space and in time, we would also at the same time be back at the present. There are some physicists, like David Bohm, who suggest therefore that the universe is indeed a hologram. A hologram is basically the concept that any piece contains within it all of the whole (Bohm, 1978).

Geneticists, in their concepts of cloning, have suggested that in each cell there resides the whole organism. Thus through the cloning of any cell, not just the sex cell, the whole can be derived.

Karl Pribram, a neurophysiologist at Stanford University, postulates that the mind is made up of cells which both perform their pragmatic function and have within them the total memory of the universe. Thus each cell is a hologram of all knowledge. To take this still further, not only would the brain have this memory, but all cells would as well. But the proposition that Pribram raises for us is that through our formal and social education we have learned one particular decoding of the hologram and by common agreement we see the same thing. If we were to learn a different decoding, we would see something different, and *that* reality would exist. Thus, *all* realities exist.

If we go back to the concept of the physicist that all space and time would endlessly come back to the same point, if we could abolish space and time, then all knowledge would be available to us within the present point. Techniques such as meditation, or techniques by which one is in tune with the energy of the universe through a variety of religious practices, lead to being in tune not only with energy but with the all-knowing, which in nonmedical languages has been called "God." There are experiential techniques practiced by Buddhists and Tibetan lamas which remove space and time and thus make available to one's self knowledge from all sources. We then arrive at the possibility of behaviors which have heretofore been mysterious.

Let us consider as a possibility for scientific study (indeed as a possible reality) such activities as healing, as practiced by traditional healers, reincarnation experiences which we have denied scientifically, and other phenomena which we have heretofore classified as mysticism. We may find that the mystic learns to decode the hologram in a different manner than the rest of us and therefore he may have available to him knowledge that others do not have. Healers may have available to them not just scientific knowledge but the ability to tune in to energy which may be able to heal. If one were to abolish space and time, and were to lose one's fear, one could possibly utilize the energy or be in tune with the energy of the universe in order to become healthy. This is the concept that we have called primitive religion, but it is also the concept of people who have healed themselves or who have been healed by healers, all of which is foreign to the medical practice of Western scientific medicine.

We have noted the familiar point that this is a time of great stress and crisis and nonsolution, the point which Jonas Salk (1973) calls the transition from Epoch A to Epoch B. He metaphorically uses the sigmoid curve of the growth of bacteria on an agar plate as it shifts from one slope to another. He suggests that as part of the upward curve there develops a metabiological and philosophical system of behavior which is different than when the curve begins its second shift. The shift from Epoch A to Epoch B means a shift in the metabiological system of belief system. Our present dilemma is how to adjust our thinking, our institutions and organizations, and our values to this new system.

Thomas Kuhn (1970) suggests that major scientific advance occurs with paradigm shifts, and that these occur at times of crisis—crises which force people to look for alternative ways of perceiving reality. In the process of crisis one cannot fall back on old cosmologies because they are no longer useful; accordingly, we search for new ones.

We are poised in that moment of transition from Epoch A to Epoch B. We have evolved a step in social evolution—that is, social development or social learning. It is not that the hologram develops new knowledge, but rather, since all knowledge may be present, it is that our societal learning has developed to the point where we may now better decode the hologram. In fact, what may be occurring now is that we are forcing ourselves to devise new decoding techniques to unscramble the hologram, and thus to remember what is already known but has not been decoded. Thus the only secrets that exist are secrets that result from our inability to understand, see, conceive, or develop a decoding technique to reach an alternative conceptual model.

We are faced, then, with a dilemma of governance, politics, and of the conflict between peoples' different models. Many people are fighting to meet their basic needs and to meet their level of self-esteem. They want to feel capable to ask for things for themselves. There are those who were the wandering, aimless hippies of the sixties, then mainly interested in being high or "mellow," living commune-style, who now confront their own individualism, their own desires. But these one-time "hang-loose" individuals are generally very controlling in their new identity — of themselves and of others. There are still others who have reached a point where those needs are met, and they then move on to new questions. It is these people who, because their basic needs and self-esteem have been fulfilled, *can* move on to these alternative models.

The paradox, is that those who have the most and those who have the least may be at that point in time where their search for models may be in synchrony. The models of people who have what we call primitive views of the universe and of those who are frustrated with the so-called advanced views are coming up with parallel and compatible views of what the universe may be. It is only those in the middle, who have moved on and have started the upward spiral, who feel they must follow in all the traditional steps (so that ontogeny repeats phylogeny in this group), and in so doing, need to repeat the steps of their predecessors. Thus the neocolonialists who have gotten rid of the colonial masters have become more colonial than the previous masters. These people are holding onto the model that has been successful for their forebears despite the fact that now the organism known as the earth no longer is capable of being dealt with by these old models. Since the earth is one earth, we are at the moment where we can ill afford to have cosmologies which do not meet the needs of all.

It is clear that the problems of our society—our total earth, the lands of the Native American, the United States as a whole, Iran, Israel, Egypt, or any place—cannot be dealt with in separation or in fragments. It is clear that the problems of medicine cannot be dealt with separately from the problems of education and health. Indeed, as Martin Buber has said, the problems may very well be the notion of the changing concepts of what a human being is on this earth.

As was earlier suggested, in looking at the problem of medicine and health, health may indeed be the synthesis of the internal and external environments. Health may be, as René Dubos says, the ability to use all of one's senses. If this is so, health then becomes the ability to move from one reality to another, as the problem requires. It is also the ability to experience all of one's feelings and perceptions invited by the situation. For the schizophrenic, his reality is real; his problem and his illness are that he cannot move from that reality to another. For us, to move from Epoch A to Epoch B, our problem is that as long as our emotional and perceptual life is stunted and rigidified in a controlling and controlled style, we will be unable to move from our own narrow survival mechanisms to living on a holographic level where options are open.

We are bound by our own emotional and perceptual styles. For those who are caught in a fight for emotional ego and personal survival, freedom to use all of one's senses feels dangerous. Not only does this style produce asthma, ulcers, migraines, but by necessity a rigid notion of reality. When people are comfortable or skilled with a broad range of experiential capabilities, internally and with others, they no longer need to exert control over reality but are free to move from one option to another.

This experiential limitation, or limiting of emotional and perceptual skills, besets ordinary individuals, families, and communities as well. When people are de-skilled emotionally, they are not able to feel or express the broad range of affects available in their person. Perceptually, having confined their view of the world to that which is culturally acceptable, they must remain blind to each other and themselves as unique and paradoxical personalities.

It is a challenge to us in medicine, especially, to be able not only to understand all the realities of our patients and clients, but to understand the different realities and cosmologies that make up our world, and to participate, as we go through the transition from Epoch A to Epoch B, in the creation of a new reality and cosmology. Health in our new epoch involves not only the quality of life, but the way we live and what we consider important. That will determine the needs of our society. To meet those needs we address health and the problems and crises that lead to illness.

These ideas take us on a trip of the mind, a trip that extends far beyond the mind and body, beyond the brain or mind into the mind that makes up our holographic universe. I have raised these questions here primarily because I believe that these problems are the problems of our whole earth, and that the problems faced by everyone on this earth are deeply interrelated.

Chapter 4

THE HEALTH PLANNER

Dreaming for Health and Wellness

Almost every planner is, at heart, a dreamer with a conscience, deeply concerned, motivated, and sometimes driven in the search for a better world. Faced by the immensities of the task, the urgency of the constant crises, the planner responds in the manner that is most human to what is most critical. The pressures of nationwide regulations often create conflict. The counterpressures of state, local, community, and special group interests and other issues lead to crisis planning (H. Blum, 1974). Given the obstacles, even the little that has been accomplished is amazing. Despite those obstacles, each of us, in the back of our mind, has a dream: a healthy world and a better place for our children and, we hope, for ourselves.

We, as planners, may be able to take some steps toward this dream, even within the present prevailing atmosphere of crisis and apparent helplessness. But can we create opportunities for health where those who wish to can focus more steadily on their own and society's well-being? I believe there is evidence that this can be done. I would first raise questions, then offer recommendations for the consideration of planners. I would ask:

- What is the relationship between health and medical care?
- What role do planners play as part of the process of change?
- What are the potentials for health inherent in PL 93-641 (the National Health Planning and Resource Development Act)?

HEALTH AND ILLNESS

Health is not a special commodity. It is not something that can be bought and delivered, or will happen as a result of the work of doctors. Health is related to *life*—how we are created, grow, live, and die. It is how we are and how we feel, as well as how we relate to those around us who are important to us and those with whom we have less contact but who affect our lives. It is related to the environment within which we live, in all its forms, including all the living organisms that make up our world.

It is almost as if the living organism most relevant to us is the earth, and each of us is part of that alive being. As with many living organisms the whole can be healthy while a piece is sick or dying, and yet we know the sick piece cannot but affect the whole. The converse is not true, for if the whole is sick and dying all the parts die also.

The ancients knew this well; the shaman dealt both with the ill person and with the community. As the shaman removed the ill part, the whole community was engaged in coming together, joining its energies in a variety of activities which regenerated the whole at the same time as dealing with the part.

To expect the best of medical care nowadays (and in many ways it is superb) to deal with health is to ask the physician to deal with the whole community as well as with the patient. This is too much to ask of our medical care system when the systems of the whole are not working.

Health comes from the totality of existence and not just the internal experience. The health planner, concerned with orchestrating these issues, is faced with these dilemmas. Either deal with *all* the world or, more rationally, choose to deal with the presenting crisis. Health planning as such has become planning for care, but with an implied responsibility for all of *health*.

Our job is to reassign responsibility for health back to the broader community. To do this means understanding the relationship of medical care to health. The finest medical care system in the world will not guarantee health. It is but a step.

It is my belief that *health* is in all of us, from the moment of conception. The DNA molecules and the genetic templates they lay down do not limit our growth and health, but offer broad ranges of possibilities. However, from the moment of conception, that potentiality of aliveness becomes more and more limited (Williamson & Pearse, 1947, 1965; Pearse & Williamson, 1938; Pearse & Crocker, 1947).

The environment—the uterus, the mother, the family, the community, and the world—little by little impinges upon the growing being, slowly decreasing the possibilities for aliveness.

What are these assaults? They come about through adverse nutritional, emotional, physical, and social environments. They come iatrogenically—the very things we often do to prevent, treat, or educate leave a mark or limitation on us. Oxygen administered to a premature child to save its life may leave a burden of blindness. A parent's own need may lead to an assault on a child's psyche. Food "poisoned" by processing to "preserve" freshness may have unknown impacts on a growing child. The assaults of environment, however, are most often due not to medical iatrogenesis, but rather to the very quality of life that we assume.

Often we educate our children to reproduce ourselves, to guarantee the present, which by so doing educates *out* (brainwashes) the aliveness of potential creativity (King, 1976). Health is an optimization of aliveness within ourselves in relation to the environment. It is synthesizing that relationship into a way of life.

Health has rarely been studied from this vantage point—so often it has meant the absence of disease. If health is growth, it is both the absence of disease *and* the increase of one's potential.

On rediscovering the seminal work of Williamson and Pearse (1938) which was done at the Peckham Health Center in London in the 1930s and 1940s, I realized that they had found a way to meet some of the dilemmas regarding the meaning of health. After careful examination of families in a community settlement house, they discovered that the population could be divided into three groups: the Living, the Surviving, and the Dying. Without using these words, numerous epidemiological studies suggest the same findings.

The *Dying*, or ill, make up about 20 to 30 percent of the population. They know that they are ill and they focus all their energies on coping with the illness. To stop the disease process requires a homeostatic state. Interestingly, the ill often will move out of the illness category through active participation in dealing with their situations. At Peckham, many moved to aliveness just by participating in the activities of the center.

Most of those studied—60 to 70 percent—were termed *Survivors*. These persons had "something wrong," but did not consider themselves ill. They wanted to get rid of their problems and return to their way of living. Their homeostasis was a "don't-rock-the-boat" syndrome. They wanted the world to be as it is—comfortable and safe. Both illness and aliveness is frightening, because they are unknown. The Survivors rationalize their lives, often creating a structure both social and physical which keeps things as they are. As the majority group in any society (for the very definition of a society, an institution, and most often a person, is to keep everything as is) they adhere to systems, institutions, governance, and even folklore and myths that preserve and sustain the present. Each society schools its children to the present. The alive, creative children are a threat to classroom for they demand shifts in curriculum and exploration of areas not part of the standard regulations.

The *Alive* make up less than 10 percent. They are full of the vitality and excitement of life. They are so busy being alive that they do not worry about health. If sick, they bounce back. They have a resilience and ability to "self-actualize." As Maslow (1968) has put it, they have met their basic needs, so they move on. Homeostasis means a momentary plateau, and they then go on to dysbalance and a new homeostasis. They search the new frontiers, test themselves, create new ideas and ways of being.

Obviously these categories are not so neat. All of us know ill people as well as people who are alive and vital, creative and happy. This suggests that health and illness may be separate but related issues. A healthy schizophrenic exists. But this suggests even further that illness may be *the* avenue to health: where survival is the status quo, non-health prevails.

People who are ill or have symptoms—the Dying or the Survivors—are treated just as our children are educated. The institutions we have created lock people into their current status. A good patient behaves like a patient. A patient who fights toward aliveness is a nuisance, like a creative child. Regulations are broken and the systems fought. *One Flew Over the Cuckoo's Nest* is more than a study of a mental hospital. It is the story of the control of the environment of any "alive" behavior (Kesey, 1962).

Since none of us ever gives up his or her current behavior voluntarily, illness must be received as a signal, both of something gone wrong with our internal processes and with the environment. Thus we must learn how to deal both with the presenting issues and with the manner of encouraging aliveness. How can aliveness occur through a medical system which focuses not on growth and aliveness, but only on illness? How can we plan for services that deal both with *crises* and with illness?

The work of Hans Selye (1974) on stress is to me the most significant of orientations in the medical field today. He suggests that when the body can no longer utilize its resources, to cope with assaults and stress, it breaks down at its weakest points. It would follow that too much stress guarantees illness.

What, then, brings people the ability to cope with themselves and the environment? First and foremost is *the ability to command events that affect our lives* (Seeley, 1976; Foote & Cottrell, 1956). Whether this be through meeting basic needs of security, love, or nutrition, or through skills learned by education (both school and societal learning), or through the ability of the community to respond to what is really signaled by illness or pain, the result will be a direction taken toward health.

Growth and learning must then be *whole* and not fragmented. It has been all too easy to "focus down" on issues or pieces that we can manage or understand. In doing so we have separated ourselves into parts. Schools teach cognition, families and peers teach feelings. Sports programs deal with the physical; churches have less and less dealt with spiritual issues; sexual development has been left to peers and the Pill. How rarely are these all tied together into a whole. If to permit growth out of synchrony breeds noncompetence to command events that affect our lives, it produces thereby another illness. Problems and crises are whole issues. Responses must be whole, not partial. To separate education from emotional or social learning is to disconnect. To take medicine away from growth, to give medicines as a substitute for the laying on of hands and of caring, to ignore hope and faith, to become passive and to hand over the power of our healing to machines and to high technology is to disconnect humans from the sources of wholeness. Wholeness or health (they have the same root as the words "holy" and "healing") is *the* connection to the whole organism: its outer limits, our earth, our inner limits, our own being.

Since the Renaissance and through the Industrial and Scientific Revolutions we have, as a Western world, moved more and more towards specializing our rational minds, while the Eastern world has dealt with what we Westerners call the nonrational. The recent research pointing toward the right and left brain and their various functions show how, of necessity, during the frontier stage of the Western world, we have emphasized the left brain. Somehow both East and West for different reasons have fragmented. The challenge now is the joining of the two functions—the right and left brain, the rational and the nonrational. It is the searching for all our whole function, the use of the body and the mind with the awareness that the mind is not the brain but our whole being and, indeed, the earth or the universe. With it goes memories, history to which we owe respect. For it is in our personal, social, cultural, and environmental histories that we find answers to wholeness. Further search conducted on the rational, or on any fragmented plane alone, will not give the answer.

I have suggested that crisis can lead to change. Overwhelming crisis means danger, pain, and death. But crisis faced, crisis redefined, and met with by a different means offers health and life.

People and societies are in crisis. Crisis offers the possibility of death. The nuclear arms race hints at doom. The assaults on each of us portend illness and death. Because the crisis looms so large, it affects us all. Through our period of the limitless frontier (in the U.S., up to the twentieth century—what Jonas Salk [1973] calls Epoch A), with abandon we could waste, compete, and concern ourselves with surviving. But now we have gone to the limits of growth (Epoch B). We are faced with survival requiring not the survival techniques of the past, but the *Aliveness* techniques. That which threatened survival must become the core of our survival. Unless we let "survival" institutions face their own death, and let them truly die, change cannot take place. Institutional change for aliveness requires crisis, and crisis is danger and opportunity.

THE PROCESS OF PLANNING AND THE PLANNER

"Look at our problems, view our resources, and tell us how to proceed." A heavy task, for despite the fact that we have been hired to do the job, we wonder if "they" really want it done. The planner, once a dreamer (Geddes, 1949) or a prophet (the *Bible*) who sees the world in all its essences, has increasingly become a product of the times. Rationalism and science—the beautiful product and process of our left brain—has turned the planner into a logical, rational, scientific quantifier of what is. Numbers replace intuition. Middle-ear infection becomes suppurative otitis media instead of a crying child with a distraught mother and a helpless father. People become cases, diseases, institutions, and people become disconnected from their homes, from nature, and the environment. We still separate child and parent, family and community.

What is change, and where does planning fit it? The planner, rather than being the collector and deliverer of *truth*, can become the facilitator or educator of a society's holistic learning, helping people to face the issues of health. (The Office of Economic Opportunity's *maximum feasible participation of the poor* may have led to poor programs, but it also encouraged people to be healthier and to be better able to take control of their lives [Illich, 1976]).

The fact that we are in crisis in the health field has led to more concern with decentralizing responsibility and with teaching people to know their own bodies (Boston Women's Health Collective, 1973; Samuels & Bennett, 1973). The free clinics and women's health collectives are moves toward health. Around illness we can see a movement toward health, as when a heart attack leads to a new life-style, when old people become alive through nonmedical techniques, and when children learn their holistic potential through education (Harvey, 1974).

SOME THOUGHTS FOR ACTION

As planners we are faced with a series of questions. Is health our domain? Are we willing to "rock the boat" and become advocates for health, "disturbers of the peace?" Can we become the advocates for the dying-ill and survivors, so that they do not get locked into illness but have opportunities to grow? Can we use what we find to see illness as a flag—a warning about both illness and health issues? Can we support a moratorium on the flow of money into the high technology illness system and professionalization? Could we work to increase the levels of personalization and self-power over our bodies in illness and health? Can we encourage new ways of dealing with the environment? Can we ask that at least 10 percent of the funding in health not be for the established medical care system, but for experimenting with health (H. Blum, 1976b)?

Can we follow the Canadians and recognize that sports and recreation are part of health (Lalonde, 1974; Leonard, 1975)? Can we truly encourage nutrition programs that increase the potential of fetal and growing children? Can we say *stop* to more drugs, technology, and high capital expenditures, and more for the software? Can we live with ambiguity, change, and design systems that are not locked in the status quo?

These are all big orders, but there is a chance. We can do what the society wants us to do: respond to the moment-by-moment pains. Or, we can channel Title XVI resource development funds (PL 93-641) to wellness initiatives.

What would we be asking for? I propose two things.

1. *A Health Impact Statement* should be prepared on all proposed programs that impinge upon our human environment (Duhl, 1976c). The essence of this recommendation is based on the Environmental Impact Statements now required. Although there is much about the current EIPs to criticize, they do serve several purposes. Specifications for Health Impact Statements should include these points.

    a. They may be prepared by any program proposer, inside or outside the health field, and the statements should be completed within 90 days.

    b. The opposition should be supported in order to prepare a counter-report.

    c. The discussion and acceptance should be by *the community of concern.* This requires prior presentation and communication.

    d. The critical issues would be to force discussion of the *health* implication, or, if there is none, a statement of why it should be given a priority should be presented. Various definitions should be encouraged, as should alternative solutions.

    e. The process would be one of *social learning* (Illich, 1976), whereby new ways of looking at the issue would be encouraged. Right- and left-brain concepts would be part of the dialogue.

2. As a way for a community to learn about the options for health, local programs dealing with health in new ways should be supported even if they do not appear to be the vehicles that are classical in the health field. Examples and possibilities are:

    a. *Magic Mountain School.* A program for normal ten- to fourteen-year-olds, who learn in a holistic, synchronous way using right- and left-brain skills through fantasy, body and movement work, cognition, dreams, poetry, and intuition. They learn about their bodies as well as governance of their own school by facing issues congruent with ten- and fourteen-year-olds (e.g., what is a woman, what is aliveness, what is governance?) in the context of the sciences, mathematics, writing, and reading (Luce, 1979).

b. *SAGE.* A program where old people can "turn on" by yoga, tai chi, massage, group discussion, and self-awareness so that they may become "alive" (Harvey, 1974).

c. *Project Community:* A project to aid adolescents in learning how to "turn on" (become alive) without using drugs. This is done through use of peer groups, multigenerational groups, guided fantasy sessions, workshops, and other activities. This experimental program in self-understanding for adolescents is now in its seventh year and, at present, is being developed into a 4-year program. The program is entirely experiential. It is an elective course given for credit in the high schools in Berkeley, Napa, and Walnut Creek, California. It does not utilize textbooks, lectures, or examinations.

d. *Hospices for the dying.* Places not connected with illness and focused on self-healing power, reconnecting to family, community, and the aliveness of all. At St. Christopher's Hospice, London, in 1967, Dr. Cicely Saunders opened a "way station" for the dying which is a cross between a hospital and the patient's own home. The health care is a team effort involving medical, nursing, social, psychiatric, and religious workers and family members. A similar plan is being proposed in New Haven, Connecticut, by Reverend Edward P. Dobihal, Jr., President and Chairman of New Haven Hospice (Kron, 1976).

e. *Re-Creation Centers.* Places for people who are in transition and who, in their crises, can explore a response to their pain in a holistic way and grow both through inner work and active participation (Duhl, 1976b).

f. *Utilization of alternative techniques for health creation.* Mixing and creating Eastern and Western skills; medical and nonmedical; cognitive-rational, and intuitive.

g. *Building health into the media.* What messages can the "soap operas" give that are better than what the professionals can provide?

h. *Local health fairs, education for meditation, physical educa-*

tion, among many others, offer techniques which focus on health.

The work of the Fanon Center of Charles Drew Medical Center in Los Angeles suggests that the issues are the same for minority blacks (King, 1976). For most blacks, the first years are full of life and aliveness with all the potential that the human organism offers. It is the society and its education as well as the educational system that "brainwashes" the child into a sense of helplessness and failure within the dominant society. Rather than building upon the unique potential of the child, we create "compensatory education" programs to make up a deficit that may be unreal until we create it. To do otherwise means breaking with big school systems, individualizing, and turning toward growth whereby people learn to control their own destinies.

To take the other path for the so-called disadvantaged poor is to build a ladder to nowhere. To assist the so-called have-nots to follow our rational, competitive paths may appear to be equity, but true equity is the process of assisting people to help themselves. The job of health is always a personal one, and not one for missionaries or salespeople.

How can we as planners work? I have mentioned what we can do in our roles as planners and how to use the new legislation. More important may be our need to find a path of health for ourselves so that we can, in fact, *bear witness by our behavior*. How can we assist others towards health without having experienced it? By going through the process, we learn, and by learning rather than participating, we can truly know the issues.

Planners then can become not only teachers but leaders in the process toward health.

Chapter 5

RATIONAL AND NONRATIONAL
PLANNING[1]

The tremendous pressures which our society seems to be under have led to many proposals as to how to deal with the issues involved. One such development has been the concern with planning. The environmental area, almost more than any other, points up the problems we encounter.

Planning has been with us through a long period of time. Not until recently, however, has it been so labelled. Intelligence and data have always been used. Prior to the eras of science—and more recently of economic rationality—much of the information, which was determined by the organizing concept of those worlds, was shaped primarily by the environment. It was assisted by myth, intuition, impressions, and a sense of relationships of the information then perceived as relevant. The world, as formerly understood, was what we would call nonrational. Predictive dreams of leaders and shamans, untold natural events, messages from the environment, intuitions, illnesses, and the changing relationships of the stars, seasons, and the sun and

---

[1]Testimony of Leonard J. Duhl, M.D. before the U.S. House of Representatives Subcommittee of Fish and Wildlife, June 29, 1976.

moon were often held more relevant than what we would call hard data.

As science, knowledge, and rational perception "improved"—and as we gained a "better" understanding of the issues—there has been a shift in our organizing concepts. Dreams and feelings, intuition and myth—as well as the environment—have become much less important, and thus the data utilized reflected "hard data." Hard data are analytic. These have become more clearly related to measurable facts, and it is these facts put together which form the core issues in most planning.

Planning, with hard, measurable data, has increasingly been used. Where it was once used only for a single institution, it is now a process in the relationships of institutions and the creation of priorities, options, and choices within systems of systems. Since the issues have been primarily measurable ones, we have searched endlessly for ways to quantify what we have done.

The more unsure we are, the more we work at evaluating and planning. The more we plan, the more we use quantifiable, "hard" data. We are then left with another problem.

Since life and its environment become more complex, we have somehow divided life into what is measurable and what is not. Often we call one rational and the other nonrational. Our rhetoric reflects this orientation, denying the existence of the nonrational. Though every participant in any activity *knows* in his or her heart that real decisions are not made by using hard data, we still act "as if" this were true. Nor are some of the issues in the environment that quantifiable. Green trees and open space are often things you "yell" about but cannot measure. Such things as love, along with joy and happiness, are just nonrational.

We deny and put under wraps, keep secret and hold private, the nonrational. When rational behavior and rhetoric *fail* us, the nonrational erupts; human behavior is a darker realm than anything we acknowledge publicly. Dig into private lives or public activity, and we find on one hand *Peyton Place*, or *Watergate*—and we suddenly find exploding in our society the awful facts about how life is "really lived." The turmoil of protest movements and the difficulty of dealing with poverty upsets many, for we are shaken and horrified by unpredictable events. On the other hand, we see the private pleasures of people—also kept to special times and places—as if, nonrational as they are, they cannot be considered or planned for as part of a whole life.

If both the negative and positive events are viewed as a way to look at our organizing concepts, the volcanic eruptions of the last 15 or 20 years were worth having, as are the private joys, the re-creation times, and the holy days. They remind us that *real life* is made up of both the dreams and intuitions, as well as the data and measurable rationality.

The negative feelings about planning that we hear all around us reflect our current inability to plan both ways. "No federal planning; no federal control" becomes a message not against planning but against one-sided planning. Honest and good leaders plan, but within a wholistic concept.

Leaders often report that too much data impede them. They require just enough, put within a context that they understand to be good, and then, from the depth of their being, a decision emerges.

The preliterate planners worked within organizing concepts that all the tribe accepted. Indeed, most of their perceptions of the world (the environment and themselves) existed as a totally interrelated whole. Their cultural concept of the cosmos was directly related to the decision at hand. For us, the organizing concepts are not fully accepted, especially the total interrelatedness of our world. The eruptions of the sixties, for example, with the awareness that we all are victims (albeit different kinds of victims), put us each in a different place, given where we are and with what different perceptions and organizing concepts of our cosmos and our world.

The problems of planning then are multiple, namely (1) to establish a national planning policy that recognizes the essential planetary nature of our total environment, (2) to recognize that both the rational and nonrational, the hard data and the feeling intuitions are part of life, and (3) to recognize what end and what goals toward the first steps in planning are undertaken. By what *organizing concept* do we lay out our world? And if, indeed, there are different ones for different persons and groups, how do we create an organizing concept which has room for a pluralistic society with work and pleasure, money, power, joy, and open space all differently defined that must also hold together as a whole? Our actions belie our apparent concern with wholes, for we now act in fragmented, disjointed ways.

Planning then requires a national dialogue—a stage upon which the basic questions are asked, and the tensions reduced. The dialogue must then be about governance, and not necessarily about government. For governance is the processes by which people "play by the rules of the game" in a group, culture, tribe, or family. These rules are often unstated, and are both conscious and unconscious "ways of being." It is when these rules break down that governments must provide governing.

Governance in our time is the creation of this informal "game board" on which we can play out the game of life. It is not that there is conflict between views as much as an inability to cope with differences that exist wherever people are, as to where they want to go, and how they perceive their world. There is no chance of our all developing in the same way, nor is there hope that we each make use of all the opportunities offered and become "the same." Only in an authoritarian situation can that happen. As a society we opt for an authoritative, pluralistic, and multivalued existence.

What, then, is the need for or possibility of planning on a national scale? On one level it must occur as part of our national political dialogue, but only if its leadership is perceived as leading an educational effort—one of societal, institutional, and personal learning. Leadership becomes an exercise in searching for organizing concepts and values within which we can live the lives we desire. The issue then, again, is what kind of life, what priorities, what are our nonnegotiable expectations? The focus on the environment must include nonphysical issues that are noneconomic and nonmeasurable.

One way to proceed is based on a proposal that I recently made to the Canadian government: the creation of a "health impact statement" to supplement the "environmental" one; and the proposed (U.S. Senate) family impact statement. For in my approach, *health* (not illness removal) is related to the quality of life and the environment. They cannot be separated. It is not my purpose now to speak out on such statements, but only to suggest that a National Planning Institute be responsible for creating that dialogue.

I favor national planning, but reject planning that does not reflect the wholeness of life, the rational and nonrational; the dialogue to clarify international, national, and local values; and the creation of governance that permits a pluralistic society to exist within our nation.

Chapter 6

THE DELIVERY OF HEALTH CARE
SERVICES

The effects of urban life, both beneficial and detrimental, on people and on classes of people are well documented elsewhere in this volume. The purpose of this chapter is to examine those effects as they pertain to the delivery of health and medical services. The crucial factors here are networking and networks.

Networks are a response to life involving the development of social microsystems to serve the emotional and personal needs of individuals and groups. These networks can be formal and obvious, such as family units (nuclear and extended), or more implicit, such as friends, merchants, a mass transit system, or simply a feeling of belonging, a connectedness to a perceived order of life. Indeed, we maintain that these networks, and the ability both to form and "play" them, are essential components of health for any individual—and especially so in cities, where the size and differences among the population tend to decrease the chances for feeling like a vital and contributing part of the social order. When networks break down, a negative response occurs, just as surely as when a bacillus spreads. The fact that the effects of "de-networking" are less predictable and more insidious than those of a new bacillus has kept us from recognizing and confronting the problem other than diffusely and episodically, if at all.

Throughout history, the city has been a breeding ground for devastating and depopulating epidemics of disease, as well as of outbreaks of social unrest and disorder. No more fertile spot could be imagined for the spread of such problems than where vast numbers of people gather in relatively small areas, removed from the sources of food and raw materials and dependent on more tangible payoffs.

Networks of all kinds are established to hold urban societies together in an attempt to preclude anarchy, debilitating solitude and loneliness, and anomie. Urbanites have evolved styles of living that are intrinsically dependent upon cooperation, sharing of common services, stratification of dwelling areas, and other factors, in ways that reflect socioeconomic differences, such as ethnic pride and prejudice or social standing and caste. This clustering within the larger unit of the city as a whole has been the dominant feature of Western urban life for more than 5 centuries. It also is reflected in the clustering of medical services.

Most advances in medical services have been made in cities, partly because of the gathering of large numbers of people and the epidemics that have threatened these large populations. Systems of emergency services, the older charity medicine concept, public health reforms, distribution systems for immunizations, and sanitary codes are identifiable as urban developments. Similarly, a tiered system of medical services, ranging from house calls to heart surgery could only have developed where there were enough people to need such a range of services and enough facilities and resources to offer them (Stevens, 1971).

The organization of health services in urban areas has come to be a complex and often controversial arena for discussion and action. Health systems planning, as a distinct endeavor, has gained much attention (and growing numbers of practitioners) in recent years. But there is something about the process that is still much like the reshuffling of the same deck of cards, and little attention seems to be given to searching out a new paradigm for the planning of health services, particularly in urban areas. The concept of networks and networking might provide a starting point for such a rethinking.

Health and well-being are now made possible or impossible in the context of a world that already knows much about how to deal effectively and efficiently with most of the biological threats to health, with some of the psychological threats, and with few of the social threats. But it is just these latter two categories that are at present most influential in causing ill health and disease and are at the same time perhaps most amenable to amelioration by social action, including the strengthening of networks and networking skills. Although networking is now better appreciated, there are some precise sociological and economic reasons that make relevant nurturing networks difficult, especially in urban settings. These include the flight of the middle class from the central city and the rise of the nuclear family.

At precisely the time that delivery of medical care was reaching a highly sophisticated level of stratification into primary, secondary, and tertiary care (Alford, 1972), American cities began to experience the depopulation of much of their middle-class (mostly white) residents in a pervasive move to new suburban housing.[1] Most of these suburbs and exurbs were built near small towns that had no facilities, medical or otherwise, to serve the new residents. Thus, the new housing developments had to be planned to provide these services, schools, and support systems first for themselves and eventually for the original community as well.

Included in the waves of urban exiles were physicians, pharmacists, technicians, planners, administrators, and even much of the clerical support staffs of hospitals and medical facilities. For a while these people simply commuted to the city to practice their crafts; eventually many of them abandoned the cities entirely to staff the new services where they lived.

This flight of the middle class had some easily observable ef-

---

[1]Primary care includes the delivery of services at first point of contact: family doctor or community clinic. Secondary care includes specialists, routine surgery, ambulatory care in a hospital setting, and laboratory and X-ray tests. Tertiary care includes care by "superspecialists" and such care as open-heart surgery, renal dialysis, and long-term psychiatric care.

fects, such as leaving the cities populated by the poor and the very rich, the old, and minorities who already lived there, as well as creating a vacuum that was quickly filled by new migrations of blacks from the rural South and by waves of immigration from Puerto Rico, Cuba, Central and South America, and Mexico (Orleans & Ellis, 1971). These new residents, with few exceptions, did not bring with them the medical professionals that had come in with earlier urban settlers. Nor, because of prejudice, poor education, and poverty, were significant numbers of these people upwardly mobile into colleges and professional schools to replace the losses, due to suburbanization of professionals. They came and settled and suffered poor medical care (James, 1972; Kitagawa & Hauser, 1973).

The new suburbanites, the new urbanites, and those who stayed in the cities had at least one thing in common: because of the movement of family units into or out of the cities, they all shifted from extended family units into nuclear family units. As young families dispersed from their parents and grandparents into the suburbs, as families came from other countries or from the South to the cities and left *their* parents and grandparents behind, the entire grouping pattern of families was altered abruptly. Each nuclear family had only itself in a newly made world of strangers and unfamiliar customs. Every large American city has seen this happen and felt its effects. People lost their networks of support and were unskilled in creating new ones. Social systems evolved to handle the problems of crowding, decay, and poverty. Most of these systems tended to put stress on the nuclear family and some systems, such as welfare, actually worked to destroy even that unit (Stevens, 1971). For example, as a family on welfare begins to earn money, they are ineligible for the housing they may have been getting. Thus, they can't increase income; it's a lose-lose situation.

Viewed in these terms, it is not difficult to see why medical care became another part of the urban crisis (Alford, 1972). The urban rich still had little problem in obtaining services, while the urban poor faced a breakdown in one sector upon which they had depended: charity medicine. This two-class system, which used the income generated by upper- and middle-class patients to pay for services and sufficient personnel to handle the poor, who could pay little or nothing for their care, rapidly broke down in the 1950s and 1960s (Anderson, 1968).

The issue of health care can also be examined by applying an economic model. In urban hospitals, for instance, which have the most desperate problems of all, demand for services dropped off among the middle class who had fled the cities. Demand remained relatively the same among the rich and increased geometrically among the poor—both those who were left in the cities and those who moved into the city. It is not difficult to see that a decreasing capital base coupled with increasing demand for shrinking services would cause a sharp rise in prices.

Coupled with ever more expensive technological innovations, rising wages for health workers, and increases in the numbers of health workers earning those higher wages, we have a blueprint for economic and social disaster. When this analysis of the situation is used, it is far easier to understand the sudden successes of Medicare and Medicaid legislation in 1965, after 3 decades of abortive and unfruitful attempts, than when one uses the commonly accepted wisdom that our social awareness was heightened. The overall record shows that such an altruistic analysis seems to be inappropriate.

The current medical crisis is causing a tremendous conflict among the medical establishment, insurance companies, government, and consumers. The budget restraints require a look at possible reductions in allocations for the delivery of medical care and force us to reassess our priorities. We cannot "buy" everything in the store. Discussions take place daily within the insurance industry regarding emphasis on preventive medical or health care. Similarly, the Canadian government, while putting a ceiling on medical care expenditures and trying to rearrange priorities, also encourages environmental and recreational developments as ways of dealing with health (Lalonde, 1974).

HEALTH SERVICES AND THE POOR

It is clear from our history that decreases in illness rates are frequently related to rising standards of living and *changing nu-*

trition patterns and much less directly related to the development of medical facilities and treatment procedures.

This being true, the current crisis creates a large cadre of people trying to deal with the medical system and with issues of health. Those of us concerned about the poor can use this crisis as an opportunity to participate in the reallocation of resources by making new political alliances with those who see a need to reduce medical care expenditures.

In order to do so, it is important that we look at all health and medical care activities and start to develop a balanced health care system. Whatever happens in the larger system will directly affect the health and medical care of the poor.

At this point it might be useful to examine what is now being done to alleviate our medical urban crisis. A suitable focus for this examination would be efforts to improve health services for the poor, who comprise one of the largest population cohorts in most large American cities.

Health services for the poor is an area that has been addressed only peripherally in plans for national health insurance and nationally directed planning efforts. Because of this lack of focus it has been tacitly assumed that economically depressed communities have the same needs as any others (Somers, 1971). This is not the case.

If we have learned any lessons from our idealism of the 1960s, especially from the Office of Economic Opportunity programs, it is that the health status of economically depressed communities shows significant improvement only when the people from those communities are allowed full participation in the planning and implementation of what is done to and for them (Geiger, 1972). This seems forgotten now as we plan to expand the technologically sophisticated medical care system into urban ghettos without carefully examining whether it is an appropriate move. More and more neighborhood clinics are being closed as the funding disappears. More importantly, planners have not asked the residents themselves whether they think it is a good idea. When consultation is sought, it is almost always in the framework of how much high technology to introduce and where to put it. This is the principal failure of the community representation on the boards of health systems agencies: they have successfully sought input, but are limited by not knowing which questions to ask. High technology is assumed to be needed everywhere, simply because it is available.

The issues before us have as much to do with allowing people to regain control of their own lives and destinies as they have to do with installing million-dollar X-ray scanners and building larger medical complexes in blighted neighborhoods. When people have a real sense of controlling their own lives, their need for medical services plummets sharply and the indicators of positive health policy rise accordingly. With growing concern for budget cuts, the economic questions supersede the social ones.

Some policy must be accepted at the national level to foster this independence and, at the same time, reduce the unbearably heavy burden of expenditures that is dictated by high-technology medicine. We accomplish both of those objectives by turning over to the people some of the functions now performed by professionals. Costs fall dramatically when real responsibility for care rests with the people themselves. By creating educational opportunities for entry and advancement in the health care system, a number of benefits will result. These include more self-determination, jobs, opportunities for pride in local accomplishments, and a delivery system that is actively responsive to local needs because it is locally administered. Some of the staggering welfare costs can be relieved. The weight of helplessness that comes with receiving too little money for doing nothing can be lessened. This helplessness engenders the cycle of welfare which passes from generation to generation, with no hope of improvement because there is nowhere to go and no jobs to be had. People who have no sense that tomorrow or next year or the next century will bring any change in their lives or in their children's lives will only know further disappointment. Being denied even their dreams is perhaps the most disease-causing element in the lives of the poor. The medical problems of the poor are more often problems of their poverty and lack of hope than of biological malfunction or injury. It is that lack of belonging, and of a desirable future, that allows many of the biological depredations to take place. Such an example can be seen in poor American Indian families in cities who are far from the life they have known, disconnected and hungry. They end up with high blood sugar

and high incidence of diabetes, further intensifying their alienation and future opportunities. It is precisely the lack of supportive networks that most affects the poor.

Health care is more than biological interactions. Human beings live in their own bodies and minds, but they also live in a society and are a part of social networks. The advances of medical
care and the benefits of those advances to the people who need
them have been substantial. But medical care is not enough and
not always the answer (H. Blum, 1976a). Appropriate technology must be applied to appropriate problems, but the mere fact
of the existence of medical care does not mean that it is the only
response we have or that it is the appropriate response in every
situation. Medical care relieves medical problems but it does not
begin to address the issue of health or of the hopelessness that
comes from helplessness.

Just as the middle class demands control of their own bodies
and access to unorthodox therapies, the poor must be allowed
access not only to the medical care that the rest of us take for
granted but also to modes that are appropriate for them and
which they identify as appropriate. Plans to allow this kind of
flexibility have been missing from proposals for national health
insurance just as they have been missing from Medicaid, Medicare, neighborhood health centers, health maintenance organizations, and all the utopian plans that we have made. All of these
have attempted to address the issue by responding only to the
symptoms and not to the real problems. Neighborhood health
centers were formulated in such a way that they existed outside
the regular medical care system; they were, in effect, "de-net-
worked" just at the time when we desperately needed networks
and connections (Alford, 1975).

Neighborhood health centers, which were the bright hope
of the late 1960s, were an attempt to bring medical care back to
the areas of our cities from which it had fled with the middle
class. Intended to be consumer oriented and locally staffed, they
sank into a quagmire compounded by poor planning, the inability to utilize consumer boards whose members did not understand medical terminology or even share the same values as the
professionals, and permanently inadequate funding.

By far their most serious fault was that they were first set up
by fiat from Washington and then administered by the Depart-

ment of Health, Education and Welfare regional offices. The treatment and referral networks, on the other hand, related either to state, county, or local authorities. Virtually no interchange of information, records, staff, or policies took place. The only things they had in common were their patients. People in need, oblivious to the finer points of Washington's intentions, used any or all facilities regardless of who ran them; when they hurt they went to the place that in their own judgment seemed most appropriate. In retrospect, we should have been able to predict this pattern. But we did not. It was a case of do *something, anything,* but do it quickly.

If the neighborhood health centers had been more integrated into the existing system, this behavior on the part of consumers would have led to health maintenance organization prototypes before the concept became fashionable. People sought comprehensive services, but they found many pieces to the puzzle, which no one had cut precisely enough to fit or to make a composite picture (Alford, 1975).

Medicare and Medicaid, after all the hope and rhetoric of the 1960s, have perpetuated the two-track system of private medical care for the well-to-do and charity medicine for the poor. This has probably been our greatest failure yet to deliver on a promise, because it came at the crest of the civil rights movement when other gains were being realized. One need only look at a system such as the one that the Kaiser-Permanente clinics devised in Portland, in which rich and poor alike use the same identification cards for the same services, to realize how little it would take to deliver on the promises.

Treating a sore throat, handing out birth control devices like candy, and offering services that focus on alleviating already aggravated conditions are not the same as getting to the root of the problem and eliminating the causes. Only when we address ourselves to the causes will we make real progress in improving the health of the poor.

THE CRISIS OF MEDICAL CARE

Health is a tremendously important concern for all Americans. It is so important that as a nation we seem to be in an almost eternal search for the healthy life. We focus so much on one aspect of health—the availability of medical care—that, in 1979 we were rapidly approaching an expenditure of $186 billion a year in that area alone. (In 1985 this was close to $417 billion, or close to 11% of the GNP.) Though the expenditures are great, it takes little perceptiveness to become aware of the fact that medical services are not available to large segments of our population and services having to do with health are not readily available to anyone at all.

It is also clear that the medical care system, for all its expenditures, is in a predicament. No one is completely certain how to deal with the problem of cost, which is climbing to more than 12 percent of the gross national product. That rate of spending must be cut. Society is slowly moving into a no-growth posture in which there will be definite limits on what can be spent in every sector.

At the same time that the general population bewails "costs," the urban poor are acutely aware that the maldistribution of medical resources has once more left them short of what the medical care system can provide. Once again we have a general crisis that is much more acute for the poor city dweller than for anyone else.

We have become aware of the inadequacies of our expensive medical care system, while slowly realizing that medical care alone does not and cannot meet all the health needs of this country. It is for this reason that we must carefully differentiate between medical care and health care. Medical care is concerned with problems that arise from the onset of disease, the treatment involved, and rehabilitation. Health is a much broader concept that is concerned with each person's optimal development as an individual and as part of the larger culture of American society. Health has more to do with the sense of well-being, the quality of life, and the ability of people to command the events that affect their lives than it has to do with illness. Health is a phenomenon which is directly related to the processes of development, nondevelopment, or distorted development.

The processes of growth depend on our genetic endowment and what we have received as "nurturants," both in food and care, from the moment of conception and throughout life. Growth and development are as related to what we learn as they are to how we learn and how we respond to the stresses, strains, and crises of life. In the process of living, learning takes place, and that learning teaches us behavior which assists or is detrimental to healthy growth.

It is clear that children born of parents who are malnourished, who are poor, or who live in environments which attenuate their total existence through pollution, noise, crowding, and illness have a diminished potential for optimal growth opportunities. It is, thus, clear that health is directly related to economic status, to jobs, and to living environments, as well as to learning both from schools and communities how to function appropriately.

If the ability to command events that affect our lives is directly related to health, then deprivations from a wide variety of causes can directly affect developmental processes and thus our health. The health of the individual cannot be separated either from the environment or from the social context within which he or she lives. The health of the household and the family and the status of its own development affects the health of each member. Each of us is born into a unique environment derived from our own culture, which sometimes makes it difficult to deal with the broader culture of American society. Adjustment across cultures leads to difficulty not only in dealing with one's own education but also in coping with the institutions, rules, and regulations of the larger society having impact upon individuals who, if they had only to live in their own family and culture, would do magnificently. This conflict between two worlds is a large source of difficulty that impinges upon health development. Ultimately, this same process may cause illness or make it more difficult to treat illness after onset.

In our perception of growth and development we talk about learning to cope, adapt, and command events that affect our lives. When those processes are not achieved, or fail us, the body tends to break down. The disease process begins due to the body's own inadequacy in coping. Disease can take many forms. The one we are most aware of is the biological, but we all know this is associated with psychological changes, which could be viewed as changes in the spirit. Emotional changes are immediate responses to the inability to cope, which may then bring about biological changes. This breakdown process may lead to disorders which, depending upon the way we learned to grow and cope, determine the pathway that our illness takes—psychological, social, biological.

Examining the growth of individuals, we find that it has many different aspects: cognitive, psychological, sexual, muscular, endocrinal, cardiovascular, or others. When development in one area takes place at a markedly slower rate than in another, the body's developmental process goes out of synchrony. It is this loss of synchronistic development that often reduces coping ability and triggers illness. Lack of social, financial or personal resources can, by themselves, contribute to these difficulties.

These separate patterns occur in our normal growth as a whole human being, but all too often they are treated by society as separate entities. We act as though we are a Humpty-Dumpty, who when we fall, cannot be put back together.

We might say that this lack of synchrony is due partly to the fragmentation of our society. A sense of commonality is what should hold the pieces together and transmit learning from the broader society to the family and to the individual so that an individual could develop in a holistic way.

Fragmented growth leads to illness. It is the kind of growth that encourages physical development at the expense of cognitive development or leads to development in intellectual areas without aesthetic development. In many minority cultures, holistic development which focuses on the community cultural patterns is a deep part of the belief system. However, as the assault of acculturation to American society occurs, what is so deeply part of one's culture is fragmented into many pieces. Deep spiritual belief becomes separated from educational learning: health practices and nutrition are disconnected; and the development processes become disjoined. Therefore, the individual becomes susceptible to breakdown.

SOCIAL BREAKDOWN OR SOCIAL HEALTH

By focusing on the meaning of health and illness, we want to stress the point that the interplay of people and institutions, as well as the total social and physical environment that we live in, is directly related to health. Though we do not deny the importance of good medical care, it is frustrating to treat medical problems if the societal systems create and perpetuate illness. There have been numerous urban situations, such as the Pruitt-Igoe Housing Project in St. Louis, which became illness factories and had to be dealt with as such. This does not deny that treatment services are also important; but there is a need for a balanced system.

Those who are concerned about poverty in American cities are part of a total strategy of health care. Concerns with urban policy, housing, pollution, transportation, jobs, political action, and legal redress of grievances are part and parcel of our concern with health. This integration provides the outlines of a balanced health care system.

Such a system involves the personal development of every individual. In this regard, those resources and energies that will make the most of an individual's development must be supported. At the same time, whatever each person can do to maximize this development must be encouraged. Thus, our own education, our own development of physical or athletic prowess, and the linking together of our spiritual, physical, and psychological being is needed. This is an important phenomenon in many ethnic groups. While the well-to-do may preoccupy themselves with jogging and yoga, the poor must focus on making sure they have an adequate diet and that they begin to learn skills to cope with and adapt to the system.

Health is related to family or household systems. We know that as the family or household is able to pull together, it assists healthy growth or meeting medical problems. The family tends to cluster its solutions and strengths as well as its illnesses. When disease strikes the poor, the illnesses tend to affect whole families because it is not just the individual but the total family household unit that is stressed. Thus we are concerned with building up the support system of households and families. Similarly, extended families, groups of friends, and mutual support systems, whether they be formed around community problems or around illnesses, are vital. For example, groups that have organized around sickle cell anemia, as well as those that have organized politically, have found that participation in such organizations increases their health capacities and, amazingly, decreases their rates of illness. Active participation seems to improve the health of the individual and the group. Once again, this is the most important lesson we have learned from the Office of Economic Opportunity programs.

In addition to these personal groups, the health system includes the total medical system—clinics, hospitals, private doctors, and, in many instances, alternative health practitioners. We are gradually becoming aware that the support of medical resources (which ideally range from the most complex and highly technical to support by a neighbor, friend, or parents) is usually directed only toward the highly technical and toward the seriously ill and away from personal services. It is critical that this imbalance be redressed. In addition to the medical system, there are related institutions, whether they are social welfare, judicial, or law enforcement agencies, that affect the medical system. There are also other institutions and factors that have a tremendous influence upon health, such as community, schools, and jobs.

Clearly the needs for each community or for each person are quite different, as we look at this wide array of activities. National urban strategy and community programs tend to accentuate the presumed similarity of program needs, while there is a need for understanding the unique balance necessary for each individual or community. Health care may be related not only to what is available in each part of the balanced health care system but also to the ability of every individual to link up to as many parts of that network as possible. The rich have easy access to the medical community, although they may have less support from family or cultural groups or be otherwise blocked in their own personal development. On the other hand, some minority groups have great strengths in the family and culture but cannot "work" the job system, the government, or the highly technical medical system. It is our hypothesis that the ability to link to as many systems as possible aids us in our ability to remain healthy and to become well when we are sick.

It is difficult to link the medical system and the personal network unless the community has resources available to permit this to occur. Indeed, most of the activities within the subsystems—medical, educational, welfare, housing, or judicial—tend to disconnect people from the system by fragmenting resources. In so doing, they may precipitate illness.

When people are ill or in difficulty, there are two classic approaches. One is treatment—an intervention to contain the specific problem at hand. The other, healing, is the process of reconnecting people to networks, communities, and to healthy development. We have looked at our medical establishment and find that medicine not only disconnects people from relevant communities, family, and other institutions, but also has focused on treatment while ignoring healing.

The medical care system as it is now constituted is a net which catches victims of social, political, economic, and spiritual illness rather than being a system geared to fostering and enhancing health. The health and medical care system has in some cases been given credit for bettering health, when other social institutions (housing, transportation, sanitation, and others) have had more effect. In other cases the medical system has been blamed for not alleviating disorders which are actually the responsibility of others.

How do we reorder the responsibility for true health? How do we reassign the responsibilities for treatment on the one hand and for healing on the other? This is a large topic, involving many complex issues. The health system itself, one example, will have to train different kinds of workers, will have to present health education differently, will have to perform mental health work in different settings. The educational system will have to teach new paradigms for health, using different means to get people to understand that health has a positive, dynamic, complex meaning and that it involves people and institutions not heretofore seen as health institutions. Individuals will have to take greater responsibility for their own health. Some kind of medical disestablishment, of erasing of dependency, of refinancing of health care will have to follow.

Individual change does not always incite social change. It is a long step from individual commitment to personal health, to the linking of individual perceptions and individual change together into networks with like-minded others.

Real health is a balance of the internal and external environments. An internal environment that is characterized by self-confidence and self-esteem can often be allied with an external environment that includes friends, acquaintances, and social linkages. Self-esteem allows for extension into the larger world and finds validations in that larger context. The dialectic between the two environments is needed if we are to be open to change and to make change.

The social context of health begins or builds on the personal context for health, the personal definition and self-responsibility for health, which leads to linkage and networking (in itself healthy and a sign of health). Through social linkage and participation in networks of change, people can together learn to effect change in themselves and in the world around them. As health is also the ability to command the events that affect our lives, those who are blocked from or unable to assume command over the events that affect their lives are, by definition and often in actuality, unhealthy.

Networks of individuals grow and proliferate new networks, new relationships. Network theory is complex and sophisticated, but there are some simple observations to be made. People in networks have different roles and at times assume different relationships toward each other. At one moment and in one context, a network member may be a leader, while in another context at another time, he may be a follower. The hierarchy within a network, if it is a true network (and not a rigid system), is fluid. But usually, also, one can find in a network some people who take on the role of being network managers. These are the ones who keep the others in touch with each other, who act to refer problems between network members, who spread the good news of the success of one network member to others. There is also another type of network member, who functions to link different networks, who has the ability to move in and out of different networks, and get them to know each other, bring about alliances, work together for common goals in local contexts.

Those who plan social change, of any kind, but also in the health and medical care fields, should begin to identify and foster networking, to identify and support network managers and those network members who can move between different networks, in order to initiate change in the health field. This is the work of making a whole. For social change, like individual change, most often comes about when one begins to achieve balance, self/group respect, impact on the external world, and normal growth and development over time. Making a whole means to work along all these lines together.

Whether these networks of like-minded individuals, working to link their small group together with other networks, are focused on health or medicine is beside the point. First of all, connection to others is itself healthy. Second, whatever the aim or goal of the group, whatever issue binds them together, can contribute to well-being. Whether the group or network works together for better education, transportation, environmental quality, neighborhood preservation, local political control, or lower taxes, the benefits on health quality can be seen. If the whole system is linked, then impact in one area can have effect in another, including the area of health. And with common engagement that is goal oriented, those feelings of confidence and self-esteem that are essential to health will grow.

Health is an outcome of purposeful activity in common with supportive others. If this were recognized by health planners, they would work to foster such networking activity in communities and neighborhoods by any means possible, as a necessary means for achieving better personal and community health. But this is a long-range attempt and is restrained at the moment by the narrow charters given to health planners and by the realities of resource allocation.

RESOURCE ALLOCATION

An urban policy that worked toward a more fair allocation of resources to the cities would be significantly reflected in personal health. Funds allotted for environmental quality, sanitation, nutrition, education, housing, transportation, and a host of other issues would go far in improving overall general health standards.

Thus any attempt to deal with the urban health crisis by

forcing a dialogue about the reallocation of resources is an important one. However, if the poor are disconnected from the policy-making process involved in resolving this national crisis, there will be no real advancement in health care. It becomes critically important for the poor not only to participate in the dialogue about resource allocation in their neighborhood communities but also to become increasingly involved in the much larger discussion of resource allocation on national, regional, state, and local levels. By being able to present a broad framework within which to understand health and illness, they have the opportunity to present arguments in the continuing debate for reallocation to meet their own needs. Canada has demonstrated in the minority communities of Quebec that such a reallocation and a change in priorities can occur (Lalonde, 1974).

The proposals for national health insurance that have been presented in Congress all fail to deal realistically with this critical area. Specifically, the proposals do not address a method for rational allocation of medical manpower so that medical care is available when and where it is needed by the people as against when and where the professionals choose to provide it. The opportunities for creating skilled jobs and training in the health care sector are also ignored. This system works to perpetuate chronic unemployment and underemployment in unskilled jobs for urban residents who must remain helplessly on welfare and outside the system.

There are many who are now talking about holistic health in middle-class suburban communities where the concern is with jogging, alternative health care, acupuncture, and the like. The fact that the middle class is increasingly willing to care for its own health is as good an argument as any to cut down on allocations for them in the medical arena. Indeed, the pressures to provide high-technology medical equipment in middle-class communities can be resisted by the argument that increased personal responsibility in self-care for the middle class is critical. These concerns with the "softer" side of medical care, self-help, and personal health are not the same as the priorities of the poor, but they can point to issues central to the needs of the poor.

On the other hand, to talk of self-care for the poor at the expense of making medical care available is one more argument leading to victimization of the poor. It is again blaming the victim. Self medical care in a balanced medical and health care network is a low priority for the poor, but a high one for the middle class. For the poor, the allocation of resources to deal with their health and their primary medical care should take precedence over high level technology. Part of the priority system should certainly go to opening real jobs, as a great contributor to self-esteem and health.

We have tried to emphasize in these remarks that awareness of the complex health and medical care networks will lead to a reallocation of resources, in part, away from highly technological medical care, with less of an emphasis on specific illnesses and more on health environment and development. In order to accomplish this, we must focus on foregoing new political alliances and on an awareness of the political processes and values involved in allocating resources. This is why it is so difficult to bring these changes about in our urban areas, since the poor are not yet politically empowered, even though they are better represented at the national level than before the 1960s. City administrators still respond most easily to the wealthy and the employed. The strategies that must emerge are primarily local ones. At the national level there is no evidence yet of a balanced health or medical care system. Since licensure and regulations are left to the states, this should surprise no one.

When we focus on the balanced health care of each neighborhood, city, and rural area, we will be able to draw upon the resources, history, and skills of the people who live in that community to create a balance with the scientific technology of modern medicine. It is in the remembrances of our own values and practices that we will find concern with wholeness and healing along with an aspiration to obtain the best of medical care. It is incumbent, therefore, to examine the health implications of all relevant actions of the nation or the local community to see how they affect the physical, social, and personal environments of people. Many of these issues are discussed in recent literature, not only by health planners but by people from other fields who see the broad picture. Participants at the Beyond Health Care

Conference in Canada (1985) and Nancy Milio (1983) have dealt with calls to limit medical care expectations and look at health issues questions as big public policy questions, for example, taxes, housing, economics, even agriculture, and, inevitably, healthy cities. Broad aspects of health care services are discussed in books such as Hawken's *Seven Tomorrows*, by Physicist Fritjof Capra in *The Turning Point* (1982), and in *Gaia: An Atlas of Planet Management* (1984). The health impact of what is done in all spheres of our cities must be understood in order to achieve balanced health care.

Chapter 7

HEALTH, WHOLE, HOLY, HEALING

That which is whole within itself and with everything around it, is healthy. To be healthy is a holy state—to be one with one's self, with our inner being, and with all that makes our world. To heal is to make whole.

Holistic health is the concern with finding that quality of life which assists in attaining these states. Thus, holistic health is not the concern alone of the physician, but of all of us facing life on this earth. Wholeness is synthesizing the pieces that get created within and outside ourselves. It is making us one with our own inner world, our dreams, and with that world in which we exist. Wholeness is growth as a person within a whole community.

Health is the *aliveness* and the security that permits exploration and accepts experience with all its fears, loves, warmth, pain, confusions—and almost total unknowns. The making *whole* is permitting all the separate pieces to exist with trust, yet without control. We know that when wholeness does not exist, something is awry. Some label this state "illness" and by so doing take away its complexity—and its meaning. We cannot accept the labelling of illness without accepting the issues of being awry.

If there is no "illness," no labelling, but only experiential existence, what we call disease becomes subjective, depending on the authority who uses the term. Failure to command events that affect our lives means not having internal strengths, giving up personal power to authorities who declare us ill or mad. Our power must be to explore our skills. But "skills to command events" sound like ego skills, and what we may be concerned with is being in touch with our own ambiguities and confusions, populating external and internal worlds, accepting and living with them—as with a flow, not being carried by the river, yet not battling it, but *knowing* it. It is the flow that can take us where we want to be, and thus command events, not by our ego, but by our whole being. Wholeness is an inner harmony of disparate selves.

Being awry, the label of illness, has meaning which we must search for. We see this "going awry" in persons and in our society and, labelled, we try to find the cure without understanding any but the most superficial of meanings. Propelled by "going awry," by problems and crisis, we are offered a chance for meaning. Our refusal to accept the chance is often the true sadness. We let crisis immobilize and make us impotent. We let it seduce us into superficially thought out and experienced senses of reality. We rush to solutions, preferring simple cause-and-effect reality to the painful searches of our very soul. For example, with the death or dying of a parent, we hold onto our childhood image of the parent and do not see the parent from the point of view of an adult—nor do we change from our role as parent to our own children. We are "stuck," not allowing ourselves the search that is the search for re-creation.

The physician attempts to undo a problem, symptom, or disease, and bring back a "healthy" way of functioning. Increasingly, however, we are aware that although people can be assisted medically, their health or sense of well-being is not necessarily augmented. Frequently, the physician and the medical care institution are concerned only with trying to remove overt manifestations of disease. All too frequently what is ignored is that contextual issues, and the individual's being out of balance, may be more central problems than the symptom.

During recent years a concern with health has focused on the body's attempt to find a new balance or homeostasis following stress and crisis. Significant in this kind of thinking is that disease is the result of an attempt by the organism to find a healthy response to crisis and stress. Often, however, the attempt to find a healthy solution results in a process which locks a person into a fixed pattern or response, labelled disease. A more healthy response may exhibit disruption and problems while attempting solution.

What, then, are healthy solutions? They might be characterized as those which do not limit the options open to an individual and thus do not limit further growth and development. But what actions are options? Options are also a function of the impact of external events on actions taken. In fact the recognition of "limits" can only be retrospective.

Health may, therefore, not always be homeostasis and balance. It is also an attempt to get ready for a new state and development, a means by which individuals prepare themselves to cope with the next kind of situation they face. Concern for health, therefore, is concern for utilization of the transition period of *crisis stress*, to redirect individual (self-healing) energy.

When people are sick they should be met at the level of illness where they can first deal with the specific damage, then return to the earlier issues and make a jump toward aliveness. To deal with illness as totally apart from life, narrows and prevents development. Much of our treatment locks ill people into an *illness world* where they have no security nor chance for growth—perpetuating the dependency of infantilism and causing the "death of creativity."

We use as our take-off point the notion of transition, the idea that individuals, at all periods of their individual, familial, or group development, are faced with moments of transition of which some are major crises and periods of stress. It is my thesis that transition and crises offer opportunities for the individual to make major changes in his own self.

There are many paths to health, yet all must be whole. In some the path is the wholeness derived from putting together the therapeutic skills dealing with body, mind, and soul. For others it is work—giving of oneself and one's whole being—to make something or someone whole. It is the act of the creation of things, feelings, and spirit: it is the act of creation itself. Wholeness can come through art, music, one's search for God, or the myriad journeys humans embark upon, knowingly and unknowingly, as they pass through life. These paths towards health are paths connected to the pathways of others; for the very environment which each creates alone or with others impinges upon and affects our own and others' health.

If we look at what are usually considered "primitive conceptions," or even at "primitive" biblical levels, we find ourselves faced with issues where those concerned with the totality of being (defined either religiously or in relation to health) take a holistic approach. This holistic approach, as manifested by shamans in primitive cultures or even in the laying on of hands of the early religious healers, is unconscious mediation between the higher states of spirituality and the more rational, and what we now call scientific—the biological and psychological approaches.

I refer to this approach of a healer to suggest what might have been left out of our scientific rational care; that is, I am proposing that health may be as concerned with levels of intuition and spirituality in the physical being as with scientific rationality. Thus, although much of the current interest in areas as diverse as the occult and spirituality is preoccupied with simplistic ideas, for example, that faith healing by itself will resolve illness, something may be involved in these nonmedical processes which those serving in the health field may mediate.

Health is classical medicine, the new alternative healing functions, education, work, housing, connections, communications, governance, and politics: it is all these functions of human existence. To be healthy is to be alive—to synthesize all the internal and external environment: it is being part of a whole community.

To *survive*, the category where most of us are, is to accept our state, to maintain the status quo, to "not rock the boat," to be afraid of aliveness and death, or illness. To survive is to control others to make them survivors too.

To be ill or dying need not be the end. Rather, illness is a signal to us that survival is not enough. To be reborn—to live again—is to permit those ghosts of our past that haunt us, lock us into survival, and force us towards illness, to be removed so we can find within us all the clues to aliveness, growth, and change.

Aliveness can be learned. It is a process whereby that seed within us, with all the potential for growth, is nourished, and skills are achieved through discipline that awakens all areas of our being. Whether this be through learning the path of Tibetan Buddhism, or for young people through a holistic school such as Magic Mountain, or with therapy, or by whatever path, it entails facing both our potentials and our demons, while experiencing, feeling, and knowing. It is using all our facilities of left and right brain: our body, feelings, and thinking. It is knowing the sun and the shadow, through a process which we each must experience, sometimes with a guide. It is integrity, strength, discipline, love, joy, and excitation. It is being: it is bearing witness by example, by every tiny movement of behavior that says, I am, we are, all of creation is a whole.

Perhaps health, as so defined, is not attainable. If not, the process toward it—the act of creating our own aliveness—that act is health.

Chapter 8

MENTAL HEALTH

A Look Into the Future

Over the years, there have been many impassioned discussions about the future of the mental health profession and how it will affect the lives of psychiatrists and psychiatric institutions. I would like to take a different approach and look at the problem of our future not from the point of view of the psychiatrist or the institution but, rather, from that of the person to whom we are giving all this care: the patient.

We can view the patient's changing problem in a way that is analogous to the growth of bacteria on an agar plate. Bacteria multiply slowly at first and then rapidly, and then the growth rate levels off.

In psychiatry we are now at the point where we are leaving the era of rapid growth rate and moving into the leveling-off era. In the first era, the patient makes it or dies. If he needs medical care, he gets it or passes out of the picture. But, in the second era, society is directed more inside the person. He needs *health* care.

Reports indicating that the country is spending $135 billion on illness should be a flag that something is wrong with our society. When we see environmental problems, arsenic poisoning, alcoholism, drug abuse, and similar problems proliferating, we as physicians must conclude that something fundamental is wrong. And we must be concerned with that and not exclusively with "medical care."

What happens if we are not? Others will step into the role that traditionally belongs to the psychiatrist. They are already on the scene, primed to be more responsive to the health needs of *our* patients, if we show by our inability to change that we cannot be responsive enough.

Psychiatry has often perceived itself as preoccupied with illness (which it has been). As a spillover, it has gotten into medical, rehabilitative, and social-control tasks—and, accidentally, into humanistic ones.

I believe it should be the other way round. The humanistic functions of the mental health movement are *the* functions (Astrachan, Levinson, & Adler, 1976). The medical, rehabilitative, and social-control aspects are just part of that responsibility.

Psychiatry has been a profession of *alienists*—those who have cared for misfits and for the people who had broken down and needed to be taken care of. I believe we must see that it should be a profession of *healing*, of *health*, of *wholeness* (Duhl, 1976a).

We cannot address ourselves to this challenge if we allow all our energies to be consumed by the current crisis, in finding a solution to ever-present problems, or in falling victim to the "system." Rather, if we are to assume our role as healers, we must learn to be mediators—to mediate the processes as they unfold on both personal and societal levels and to become bridges between what is and what can be.

What is the mediation process if not *healing*? Note that *healing* differs from *curing*. It is more akin to growth and development.

Throughout the course of history, human beings have attempted to become healed. In a sense healing is rebirth, a redirection towards fullness of life (Duhl & Leopold, 1968). In one of the major studies on health, a group of researchers working in London in the late 1930s and early 1940s observed a specific population for signs of health and illness. Following their examinations, they were able to categorize the entire population of an arca of the city according to their degree of health (Pearse & Williamson, 1938; Pearse & Crocker, 1947; Williamson & Pearse, 1965).

Ten percent of the people in the Peckham area were completely free of any signs or symptoms of biologic or psychologic illness. These the researchers categorized as "healthy" or "alive." Another 30 percent were perceived as "ill." When interviewed, they talked primarily about their illnesses. The remaining 60 percent considered themselves healthy but had many symptoms of either psychologic or physiologic illness or both. These were categorized as "survivors."

Each of these groups had a different definition of health. For the ill, health meant coming to terms with their illness so that, at minimum, they would not die, and at best they might find a way to reverse their illness. For the ill, health meant finding a balance between their inner environment (which included their illness) and their external environment (which included the things that had caused, defined, and reacted to the illness and the person). To treat an illness means that someone has to intervene in an effort to redress the balance and permit the healing process to take place.

The physician who attempts to redress this balance without dealing with both the external and internal "networks" is engaging in a futile task—that is, if his goal is to further the overall health of his patient. For to heal is to address the *balance* between the internal environment and the external. Thus, it goes above and beyond treatment and in going above and beyond treatment, the healer must become engaged in the so-called humanistic tasks. For example, if he is to restore his patient to "health," he may have to help the patient change his life-style and his behavior. In other words, he must assist at the patient's rebirth, at his redirection towards a greater fullness of life.

Does this sound vaguely familiar? It should. Both the shaman healer and the idealized family doctor performed this function, not only treating the patient for his illness but also performing the so-called humanistic tasks that enabled him to return to a life of health (Attneave, 1974). They synthesized the internal and external through their use of many instruments— ritual, music, all the senses, perhaps even magic—in addition to therapeutic intervention. Community systems were involved. Changes were stimulated, and personal systems were rebalanced with food, exercise, and change in the patient's life-style.

Nor is this too different from what many physicians are doing today. The physician who uses the patient's myocardial infarction, carcinoma, or trauma to motivate him to change his habits so that a new pattern of health may become a reality is only continuing to put into practice a venerable tradition in medicine.

So much for the *ill.* Now what about that large group, the 60 percent of the population who are *survivors?*

The survivors are those who like the status quo. To them health also means balance, but in an "as is" meaning of the term, without shifts in any of the factors previously mentioned. Treatment reigns supreme among the patients who have the survivor mentality (as well as with their physicians, if they have the same mentality). These people look upon humanistic healing practices as "soft stuff" that just wastes time. (The "survivor" mentality is not confined to medicine. In educational circles, for example, the "survivors" look askance at humanistic practices and believe that almost anything is "soft stuff" if it cannot be defined in terms of jobs, roles, or functions.)

While the survivors consider themselves healthy, they have many symptoms. They envision health as something they can achieve by the simple process of shedding their symptoms.

What of the remainder, that 10 percent of the people who are symptom free? These are the *alive,* the people Maslow (1970) calls the *self-actualizers.* They view health as a state in which one has the ability to take on new challenges. For them it is an opportunity, not to maintain the status quo but, rather, to find new solutions to problems that are continually occurring—new ways to bring a balance to the system.

The ways these two groups view a crisis situation is revealing. For the survivor, a crisis is a negative thing; for the alive, a crisis is an opportunity to find a new solution.

Physicians often reflect the group they are serving. Physicians whose practice is largely limited to treating survivors are likely to restrict their intervention to what their patients expect of them.

Our patients help us in this deception by expecting "treatment" and being responsive to "what the doctor says." I was taught in medical school that the "good" patient is the one who behaves and follows orders—the one who does not question the regimen that has been laid down for him as the best possible route to health.

If we are to be responsive to our patients' real needs, we must recognize that this is not always true. The patient who is really growing as a person may be the one who rebels and fights the system, who shows his dislike for being locked into the status quo of a treatment procedure.

The search for values in our society is a search for a context in which to do things. Our patients may be scrambling about— suing us, going to court, arguing, confronting us—but the underlying question for which they are seeking an answer often is: What is the basic value system under which I am willing to exist? What kind of world do I really want to live in?

The way we—and our patients—answer this question will determine the future of our profession. As I see it, there are three possibilities.

1. We ignore the question and continue as we have been. We continue to be survivors. We are left with the treatment jobs, while the mainstream of health care moves on without us.
2. We continue as we have been, failing to meet many of the external—and internal—needs of our patients. As a result, new professionals and new healers spring up to fill the vacuum. They may be members of an entirely new profession, or they may be the quacks (our professional term) or politicians or paraprofessionals with whom we have long been familiar, rising up to serve as shaman leaders.
3. We continue as we have been, and our patients solve their dilemma by moving toward self-care—thus following the principle of complementarity. (When functions are not performed by the community, the individual and significant others will move to fulfill the role.)

All three possibilities assume that psychiatry continues as a profession of *survivors*. There is a fourth possibility—that we become a profession of the *alive*, those who are self-actualizers.

A survivor mentality will not permit us to survive as a profession in the face of the challenges now before us and the growing needs of the patients we serve. If we merely take a firmer grip on the status quo ("This is our turf") and do nothing to develop the leadership to face new challenges and opportunities, we will deserve our fate.

But the world is crying out for something more. Victims everywhere are beginning to demand that they be victimized no longer. There is a growing demand for the *quality* of life. Environmental concerns and shifts in the processes of governance are subjects of popular interest nearly everywhere. There is a growing awareness of the need for *healers*. Healers are emerging all around us, but they are without the unique qualifications that we psychiatrists have for this role.

My concern for mental health's rebirth through the growth and development of the psychiatrist as healer is not the result of any self-centeredness about my profession or even of the understandable desire that we "protect our turf." Rather, it comes from the conviction that the processes needed can be built upon the knowledge and skills that only we possess. I say "built upon" because I believe we once had those aspects of the healing role that are so greatly needed today—the magic, the rituals, the connection with the community networks that the shaman healer had. Somehow, during the recent wave of scientism, we have given up many of these functions.

Is what I am advocating not just another name for "community mental health"? Admittedly, community health began as a dream, but it seems to me that it quickly became a matter of pouring new wine into old bottles. New programs were added, but the style remained unchanged. More emphasis was placed on medications than on humanistic concerns, on technicians than on healers.

Healers must be able to transcend the technical, whether they come from the mental health professions or from somewhere else. Certainly, the mental health professional could fulfill the role of healer; yet all too often he or she abdicates the role to others. And the others are already there—new healers are emerging all over the countryside.

Health entails learning to use all of one's being. For the psychiatrist to be a healer in the full sense of the term, he must be able to join the network of other people engaged in the healing process—other psychiatrists, physicians, religious figures, teachers, lawyers, politicians.

The shaman, at least the ideal shaman, was aware of what I call network psychiatry. In his therapy he not only focused on the uniqueness of each person, but he also helped to pull the community together. This, I believe, is one of the opportunities awaiting the mental health profession today—network psychiatry, focusing on being aware of the uniqueness of each patient and his or her relatedness to the many parts of the community in which he or she lives.

This has more than one meaning for the mental health professional today. If psychiatry, for example, is seen as a part of the network of health, those who make allocations of governmental resources may look upon our function quite differently from the way they now do. For example, the functions we have been calling "health" include far more than the concerns of the mental health disciplines. We teach people how to cope and live in a complex society. The governmental budget specialist should be told that this function should be paid for by the non-school education budget. Those who misbehave and require social control should be on other budgets.

This is why the discussion of priorities in mental health requires an *organizing concept around which developments can occur* in addition to perception of some of the critical issues.

I mentioned the way in which the shaman helped to pull the community together. Let us suppose that psychiatry continues as it has in the immediate past, as a profession of survivors intent on serving the status quo. We continue treating each group of "victims" (and by now we are all victims, battling with each other without an agreement on common governance).

If this happens, we can expect that resources (both governmental and private) will be allocated as they have been in the past—to each group. And, as each group of "victims" develops its own distinctive mode, it will also develop its own "psychiatry," determining socially who is ill, rehabilitating them, and setting up control mechanisms.

This, then, is *tribal psychiatry*, directly related to emerging traditions, values, and culture. Some of it is already going on in such forms as "black psychiatry," "gay psychiatry," and "women's psychiatry." Each "tribe," of course, is at a different place in the developmental cycle, and one can expect that all of them will by vying for resources—resources that, inevitably, will not be enough to go around. Each group has different meanings and different dreams, and these differences bring great tensions.

There is another possibility. Suppose that the "victims" eventually are all quieted down, not as members of distinctive tribes but as part of a group to which each must subscribe in order to survive. Psychiatry, in this case, would become an agent of social control within its rehabilitative and medical functions. For the "victim" would have no real choice in the matter: he would have to belong to *the* group or perish. Humanistic psychiatry might continue in name, no matter who the agents were, psychiatrists or others. However, the effect would be social-control psychiatry, using the tools of science to maintain the patients in a society where the underlying issues and values could never be questioned.

Fortunately there is a third possibility—one in which the uniqueness of the individual is recognized and encouraged to develop, not only individually and distinctively but also as an integral part of a whole. This possibility foresees the need not only for tribal psychiatry and the needs of society as a whole, but for something in addition, something we can call *network psychiatry*.

Network psychiatry focuses on being aware both of the uniqueness of the individual and of his relatedness to other individuals who make up society. It was through his awareness of both needs that the shaman was able to pull the community together while focusing on the needs of the individual. There are different networks that the psychiatrist must take into account, but the three most obvious are the family network, the human-service network, and the community network.

The *family network* includes not only the individual's extended family but also the "personal" network of interrelated, interdependent individuals with common values, interests, locations, languages, and faiths.

The *human-service network* is made up of the organizations that supplement (or at times replace) the family network. Here again, values, language, and beliefs are likely to be held in common by the individuals within the network.

The *community network* connects and interrelates many of the other networks both locally and nationally. It provides a framework in which both unofficial and official activities can be carried out.

Whether the networks grow and develop or break down depends on how well they work. Networks that become fragmented or blocked because too many individuals within them are working at cross-purposes (or are isolated, victimized, or condemned) become unable to bring health.

As Speck and Attneave (1973) have shown, the progress of schizophrenia in a person can change as a result of steps made to reconnect the networks in his or her life. Pilusek and Parks (1986, in press) have looked at the spectrum of networks that exist between people; social groups, communities, and interventions, and how, like the infant separated from its mother, people wither and die when isolated from supportive networks. Family therapy is a model of network intervention. In its ideal form it deals with governance, the whys and hows of life, and enables the individual to develop his or her own life while contributing to the collective good. Again on the ideal plane, it is concerned not only with the well-being of the individual on a psychologic level but also with the well-being of society. That includes resource distribution (economics), power distribution (politics), autonomy and the common good, and many other factors. Clearly, what we are talking about is much more than a technical set of professional specialties for the mental health of an individual. It is the mental health of the society itself. And, it is more than therapy, for therapy implies "doing something to" someone (Satir, 1975). It is *educational* since it is a program to help us learn to live on all levels. It is indeed political. (In the Greek sense of the word, we are all politicians because we are all practitioners of the skills that, we hope, will move us toward maximizing the individual good within the common good.)

Do I want, then, as Torrey (1974) once suggested, to make psychiatry political?

Not at all. Rather, I suggest that the sociopolitical dialectic is the context in which psychiatry and mental health must operate.

It is within the humanistic context that we, and our patients, will determine how well we are practicing our profession as *healers*. In the years ahead, the casualties that cause network imbalance will be knocking on our doors. We cannot solve the problems facing us if we continue to blame the victim for his problem and deal with him outside and apart from the context of social networks.

When our Founding Fathers were wrestling with the problem of a constitution for the 13 states, one of the suggestions was for a constitution based on an idealized model, a fully coherent, rationalized plan of the way our country should work. It was James Madison who pointed out that such a constitution would doom us to failure: a workable constitution would have to recognize not only all the good, but also all the baseness that is in human nature.

And so it is in planning for the future of mental health. Planning without acknowledgment of the dark side leaves no room for the "have nots." We must build a system that recognizes the diversity in individuals and respects their differences, acknowledging that they do not have to fit into prescribed roles. It will be a system based on the existing reality, based on recognition of the fact that no matter where anyone is in the system, the potential for health is there, and that we, as psychiatrists, can participate in the healing process.

Chapter 9

THE PROMOTION AND MAINTENANCE OF HEALTH

Myth and Reality

Should medicine ever fulfill its great ends, it must enter into the larger political and social life of our time; it must indicate the barriers which obstruct the normal completion of the life cycle and remove them. Should this ever come to pass, medicine, whatever it may then be, will become the common good of all. It will cease to be medicine and will be absorbed into that general body of knowledge which is identifiable with power. Then will Bacon's prediction be accomplished fact: what seemed causal in theory will become established rule in practice.

Rudolf Virchow (1849)

INTRODUCTION

I was brought up in the center of one of the largest cities in the world. When growing up, I had not the slightest question about whether that environment was better or worse than any other. I lived in the streets, went to the schools, and got to know the community in an unusual way. From the time I was very young, my father took my brother and me to every corner of the city, to all of its resources—its museums, its schools, its business districts, its ethnic neighborhoods, as well as its parks, the shores, its beaches, and to pockets of country nearby.

I had no notion that it was bad. The noise was accepted as part of living, for the "El" rumbled by our home in Brooklyn. The crossing of streets became a game as one dodged cars. The pattern of response to one's neighbors was to take and to give, to participate in the hustle and bustle. I found that the world of barter and exchange was part of my life. I worked hard; learning was a part of the experience of growing up.

I look back now to that environment and realize that much of what I am was shaped by the total environment which I experienced from adolescence on from my family and school environment. In the values, the patterns of behavior, and the style of response, a hidden curriculum was subtly learned that went well beyond the outline of my courses in school.

There was a piece of my family life which I took as the gospel of the right life, because it was part of the doxology of the family: going to the country in the summer. The streets in the city were too hot and one needed the fresh air of either the mountains or the seashore. The sun was important and it was good to have a holiday or vacation. I can remember with vivid expectations the hot, late spring days and the beginning of summer as school was just about to be let out. I looked forward to the summer vacation in the country, and each summer since birth that country was part of my life. There, too, I was in touch with the whole of that world. It was not as familiar, and it was a little more fearsome. To be in the depths of the woods in the middle of the night was much more threatening to me at first than to be in a ghetto of foreigners in a central city. I did not know the meaning of the noises of the night—the screech of the owls, the chatter of the crickets—nor the uncertainty of direction, unguided by the gridlike streets of the city.

This took a little longer to learn than city living, but I slowly found myself in touch with the world of the country in which I used to wander alone. I remember an early morning, watching some recently hatched turtles crawl across a sand trap as the dew faded away and the sun began to rise. I can remember a night at age eleven, sleeping outdoors and waking up and seeing the stars in such vivid brilliance that each star in the Milky Way seemed to implant its image in my head. I had not seen those stars before, nor had I seen the turtles or the birds, but I slowly learned about them in the country.

Nobody needed to prove to me that this world was good. Even though it was frightening, it was something I had to face. Nobody suggested that it had anything to do specifically with my health, though I subtly heard, primarily through the family mythology, that breathing open air and smelling flowers was somehow good for my growing up. Eating fresh produce, drinking warm milk fresh from a cow, and working in a garden digging up potatoes also was somehow good. Over the years since then, as I began to get deeper into concern with both illness and health, I found it impossible to separate the world of the ill or the world of a growing person from the environment. On the surface I was part of an intellectual discourse in college and university about the battles of nature versus nurture, arguments about the natural life of Rousseauist thought versus the scientific explanation of Descartes. I began to hear of genetics and its control over our development in life, and, as a physician, I began to focus on the problems of illness.

Yet somehow the hidden curriculum of my past led me more and more to the continued interplay between humans and their environment. I knew deep in my heart that it was tremendously important, and yet I also knew how little we preoccupy ourselves with it or know any of the answers.

I remember a discussion with Abel Wolman, professor at Johns Hopkins School of Public Health, who said that although we do not know why grass in open space is important, it is still important to yell and scream for it, whether or not we have answers.

It is my purpose now to begin to focus on the issues of health and environment. I recognize that the questions being posed are a result of both knowledge and analytic thought and some deep, almost instinctual awareness as well—an awareness that our environment is somehow insulting us in a way which we do not fully understand yet believe to be important.

The character of the environment that we now know is becoming more and more clear to us in a way that is not just educational, but which is having a tremendous impact on our lives. Like René Dubos, I am a "despairing optimist" in the sense that what is going on in terms of the environment and the human being's health brings me to the point of despair, while at the same time I see particular people and programs working so hard on the issue that I'm filled with hope for our ability to cope.

THE PROMOTION OF HEALTH AND ILLNESS

One must, if one is concerned as we are with the question of health, look at what we mean by that word. It may not be enough for me to state my meaning, because the word itself is used freely to convey so many different ideas. Perhaps the best definition of health is one that my mother used when, as a child, I asked her how one stays healthy. She replied that you pick the right parents, eat the right food, and get plenty of rest. Somehow it was implied that one needed to be loved in order to be healthy.

Health, however, has many definitions. Its most common usage is the absence of illness. Most people, when asked if they are healthy, would say, "I am sleeping well, I am not tired. I am feeling pretty good." Yet, when those words are reflected upon, though they are related to a general sense of well-being, the more common use of the word "health" seems to convey the absence of sickness. People are doing what they want to be doing, uninhibited by changes that have taken place within their organism which might prevent this. In recent years, as we have become more sophisticated about environmental insults to ourselves, we would say that, as long as the environment does not inhibit us through smog or other pollutants, or from being the kinds of people that we would like to be, we are healthy. It may very well be important, also, to be aware that the reality of the specific insults is not as important as whether people perceive themselves as being insulted, assaulted, or hindered from being what they wish to be.

It is easy for the analytical to state that there is no basis in reality for some of these perceptions, and yet the perceptions of internal insults or external ones may be enough to make us *feel* unhealthy. This leads to the awareness that there may be some external agents that insult us which may, indeed, insult all beings; but there are some that insult us as individuals specifically because we are unique, whether it be by our culture or experience.

A city-born person spending a night in the country can complain bitterly about the noises of the night causing sleeplessness and alarm leading to malaise. The death of a spouse who slept in one's bed for many years is felt as an absence as invasive as the removal of an organ, involving actual pain in the sense of the lack of well-being. Both are changes of environment.

Health, then, is a relative issue. I would like to suggest that health depends particularly on the question of where one is, which is dependent upon one's own physiological state, psychological and social experiences, or subtle learning through the hidden curriculum of culture or pattern of living as it relates to a specific disability which has occurred.

Health directly relates to the statement, "I hurt." If I hurt, in whatever way, I *may* state that I am not healthy. I say *may* state because the environment may define the hurt in languages that do not consider health the issue, but call it financial loss, power battles, or bring in some other question — spiritual, social, political. Health, then, for me is a synthesis of one's internal and external environment, a direct relationship to all our experiences of being, our values and perceptions. Within a society as pluralized as Canada or the rest of North America, or even the world, the question of what health is, therefore, is open to the gravest of disagreements.

I would add that the qualitative nature of the hurt may determine the definition for, if one is so hurt that all of one's life focuses around this, if one's very being is preoccupied with a disability, health may be colored by that perception and nothing else has any relevance. This may hold true of a loss by death, of the condition of *dying*, or for the severely ill. At the same time, if the insult is only part of a larger experience, health may be the absence of illness and permission to go on doing all the other things, including those that cause difficulty but are not defined as health-impairing.

I do not want to leave the discussion of health without mention of the people whom Maslow (1968) has called "self-actualizers" and Williamson and Pearse (1947, 1965) call the living or "*the alive*." These people have, as Maslow has suggested, dealt with some of the basic issues of survival, and can go on to a sense of aliveness in which they are not concerned with stability, but rather with increased opportunity for new experiences in a wide variety of arenas. Where the standard "*survivor*" concerns one's self with the returning to a homeostatic state free of pain, hurt, or illness, "the alive" person is interested in the homeostatic state as a temporary plateau before one moves onward. They are open, as are people in all creative processes, to a variety of inputs which would lead to new levels of experience and existence. These people who are alive and living do not even use the words of health. Although they reflect the World Health Organization definition of health (a state of complete physical, mental, and social well-being, not merely the absence of disease or infirmity), their concerns are with their experiences of living and the total quality of their life, and if they do become ill, they bounce back from their illness into a continued life of creativity and experience. Many of us know people who are quite old chronologically who have lived through many careers and experiences and who continue to find opportunities for their own participation. They see insults not as pain or hurt but, in the language of Chinese calligraphy for the word "crisis," as an opportunity. Crisis is both a danger and an opportunity and "the alive" people take advantage of crises for growth.

HUMAN DEVELOPMENT

With the concept of crisis, we open up a set of issues about the meaning of illness. Certainly, the notion that crisis is both a danger and an opportunity suggests the relationship between development and disease. Hans Selye (1974, 1978) has put forth major questions on the relationship between stress and the way the body reacts. He has further related those concepts of stress to the ultimate breakdown of the organism leading to a variety of illness patterns.

What is most clear from almost all the work on stress, especially Holmes's (1973; Holmes & Rahe, n.d.) development of a stress test or measure, is that the body is an adaptive organism which has a capacity to cope, up to a particular point. It is clear that the capacity to cope is based on past history, including primarily the genetic predispositions upon which all further experience is built.

The learning patterns that take place within the organism from the moment of conception on through the environmental processes of nurturance and through overt learning, set the patterns for future response. Learning takes place both within the uterine environment and, subsequently, through the birth process and all subsequent experiences. It is clear that, if basic nurturance is not provided and a variety of basic needs are not met, the individual's capacity to respond to crisis, stress, and opportunity becomes limited. Similarly, learning or the opportunity to learn, which can take place through stress and crisis, sometimes locks us into a repetitive pattern which cuts down on the range of options offered by our biological and social inheritance. Thus, during a lifetime the environment teaches us the extent of our organic adaptability and the limits within which we must operate.

One must have a view of the human organism that is akin to those of the philosophers, Comenius and Rousseau, who basically believed in the capacity of the human organism (Keatinge, 1967; Archer, 1964). For if one has that belief, one looks at the environment for what it does over time through learning and nurturance to maintain, encourage, and create alternative adaptive responses which serve the individual. Our society tends, more often than not, to limit this capacity through environmental institutions, organizations, and relationships. Indeed, the environment, through its social, political, educational, and physical institutions, attempts to mold an individual into currently perceived adaptive responses which are incapable of coping with expectable current realities rather than allow open-ended learning.

Thus, when responses are no longer capable of meeting crisis by the existing learned techniques, the organism, both in its biological and psychosocial responses, breaks down at its weakest points. The lesson, therefore, suggested by the work of Thomas Holmes is that when crises rise above a particular threshold, so that the individual can no longer successfully respond, they invariably lead to breakdown.

However, if one person's stress is not perceived by another as a crisis, that other person would not necessarily break down. Our learned coping devices and perceptions are such that we define the very crises and stresses which cause difficulty for us. In fact, many of Holmes's stress items may not be stress for people who have learned other kinds of adaptive patterns.

All of this leads to some very serious questions about the institutions that are involved in the developmental process. We must ask questions about whether, indeed, we believe in this limitless capacity of the organism from conception on, or conversely take the opposite view. This view implies that the human is an empty vessel which needs to be filled, that the environment's responsibility is to teach, and that the empty organisms must learn from the outside what they have to know in order to cope with the situation. (This is similar to the views of Skinner [1948].)

Obviously, the central values of our society are critical to our observations. If, for example, the values of the society are such that monetary returns are more important than optimal development of health, the choices made in the environment may limit the adaptive potential rather than expand it.

In all societies which must survive—and if their concern is purely one of survival—they must "brainwash" their children to cut down their creative potential for true aliveness and health. Thus, if the mentality of the environment is that it *must survive*, true health may no longer be possible except for the rare person.

This extremely strong statement suggests that our society cannot—and I underscore *cannot*—accept too much aliveness, because aliveness implies breaking down systems of rigidity, structure, and bureaucracy. Creativity requires openness. Survival requires not "rocking the boat."

Aliveness and health as learned through the developmental cycle can be hindered by the structures of our society. The basic political and social question must be, then, whether the society values issues which we relate to health more than survival itself.

This is not to state that survival needs must not be met, for indeed they must as we reach towards aliveness and health.

Think, though, what the external society believes about the creative person. Creative children have been shown to be too disruptive because they do not fit into the organized curriculum of classrooms. Rather than being locked into concrete educational patterns, people would need to be freed to adapt on an individual—as well as institutional—basis if they are to survive and fulfill their potentials as members of a society in a state of flux. The way of life that has heretofore been only for the alive and the healthy must begin to be developed across the board, even if it appears that survival itself is the goal. To conserve what we really have requires adaptive potential by individuals and society.

I will return later to the questions of what can be done in dealing with our environment. For the moment, we must take a further look at the physical, social, and political structures of our society to see whether, indeed, they fit into the developmental process.

We have observed that questions which are asked about the way we govern and the way we live affect the development of people. Because of the massiveness of our cities and institutions, we no longer can get into vital touch with the existence that constitutes human life. It is suggested that we live in smaller communities in order to be in touch again with nature, to remove ourselves from the insults of the external environment, and to permit ourselves to get in touch with both our internal being and the external worlds. This may occur through non-natural as well as natural means—touch, smell, hearing, and sight—that enable this communication to become a part of our daily existence.

Concepts of human development may be as vague as those of health. I have also suggested that *development* may be critically important to understanding our institutions. Any predetermined notion of development that denies a form of uniqueness—and thereby labels that uniqueness as illness and ill-health—precludes aliveness. By labeling uniqueness as illness through a self-fulfilling prophecy, the potentially alive behave as if ill.

ILLNESS

If, indeed, illness is caused by the inability of an organism to synthesize all its external and internal environments in order to cope with crisis or stress, it is important to understand how we currently respond to "I hurt." Our response is to treat people by locking them into the patient-dependent role which results in an inability to achieve health.

I have no doubt that the serious illnesses and hurts resulting from breakdowns of the system can be coped with by our formal health care institutions. At the onset of illness, at the crisis point when individuals are learning whether their bodies can adapt to the crisis or stress, I am not sure whether medical intervention can cause a perpetuation of illness rather than its alleviance, which could be used as a crisis/learning opportunity to move toward health.

In looking at the institutions that deal with the disease cycle, clearly almost all of them tend to lock people into a disease model. However, current trends are opening up the possibility that the perpetuated dependent situation of the ill need not be. These trends include the ability to respond to crisis at the moment of occurrence, the development of primary care programs by the medical profession, and the creation of alternative pathways for people who hurt to be responded to quickly and fairly.

Thus, the more a person is informed about his or her own body, about the processes of development of the illness, and the more that they are connected to the structure of the broader environment, through relatives, friends, tribe, or network, without being locked into the illness system, the greater is the chance that they will stay healthy and will not be locked into the ill or dying model. Self-healing through personal responsibility can occur.

Therefore, it is important to look carefully at our health-related institutions. For example, when we assume responsibility through the processes of insurance or the use of high technology, this can lead to disconnecting the individual from the sense of their ability "to command the events that affect their lives." The sense of power over one's own destiny becomes lessened. The sense of helplessness, of not knowing, of fright, confusion, of a "juggernaut," militates against one's own capacity for growth for self-healing. Survival becomes the goal, not aliveness.

Although our institutions are modeled to cope with and yet maximize the illness process, it is equally clear that the patient's model of self collaborates with models of dependency. Their images of illness, of external threats, and of danger being external, leaving one without internal power, contribute to the outcome.

Clearly, all the techniques that we can bring to bear, from education and learning to the use of the body, and the various tools we have available (spiritual, physical, biological, social, touching, relationships, as well as the medical tools) will be to the individual's benefit. It is important, therefore, that all activities which contribute to this sense of personal confidence and self-will be built in, both in personal learning through natural growth and developmental process, and in institutions that are responding to "I hurt."

René Dubos has pointed to La Fontaine, the French fabulist, especially noted for his version of *Aesop's Fables*, whose country environment was critical to the development of his works. Dubos suggests that his particular environment led La Fontaine to produce his fables. If he had been born in Russia, perhaps he would have written other fables or he would have utilized his own skills in a different way. La Fontaine was lucky, because he had the ability to turn his own internal processes into productive capacities. It would be my suggestion that his environment taught him through its hidden curriculum that he had those capabilities, and he thus was able to produce the fables.

We are all more or less educated. But most of us learn, through either the conscious or unconscious environmental social processes of our own society, only about our impotence and inability to cope. A biologically deprived organism with no food input quickly learns how to adapt to low input in much the same way as natives of high altitudes learn how to produce more red blood cells to compensate for low oxygen. Biological learning, coupled with psychosocial learning, teaches us both our capacities and our incapacities. Thus, our society trains most of us to be survivors, some to be ill, and discourages all but a few, the fortunate and the rare, from achieving opportunities for health.

John Seeley (1976) suggested that our society is based upon

a model in which some people are "haves" and some are "have nots" and some are thus "better than others." For a society to attain health means a value system which no longer requires rich or poor, healthy or ill for its survival. If our society requires some ill to survive, it cannot encourage the ill to attain health. If my hypothesis is right, that our survival requires aliveness, the old techniques of locking people into survival and illness are no longer valid.

As has been earlier mentioned, Jonas Salk, in *The Survival of the Wisest* (1973), has pointed out that our globe is moving into a new epoch (Epoch B, the second half of the S-curve), in which the techniques and the values which heretofore worked (competition, putting people down, suppressing capacities) must be replaced by healthy openness, cooperation, autonomy, and wholesomeness.

Of course, basic needs must be met if one is to cope with the external environment. These basic needs are not only involved in the learned capacity of the ability to respond, but they are associated with food, love, tenderness, caring, and the other qualities which maximize growth. As I have indicated, this basic security does not result from the "absence of stress," but stress and crisis can, in the right environment, lead to growth through learning.

I have emphasized the notion of *connectedness*, as well as the ability to command events. It seems to me that difficulties result from any environment that disconnects people from the external world of reality, that places between people and the world secondary sources of knowledge and information and does not permit the direct relationship of the individual to the things around him or her. Connectedness, as René Dubos pointed out, may very well be the ability of the individual to be in touch with the environment with all the senses and with all aspects of primitive experience. Thus, being brought up on the farm permitted Dubos to be in touch with the rational and nonrational parts of his being, and with the experience of death, growth, birth, and illness, in such a way as to make none of them foreign. Healing may very well be the process of reopening all these avenues of experience involved in holistic development, thereby integrating and synthesizing the internal and external environment.

HEALTH AND THE PROCESSES OF GOVERNANCE

In all my previous remarks, I laid the groundwork for looking at the way our society allocates its resources, to deal with our own growth development, and to deal with illness and the cry of "I hurt." It is my hypothesis that, despite the tremendous amount of money going into medical care, very little is being allocated to health and aliveness. Similarly, very little is going to assist in the understanding of growth and development or to dealing with the early "I hurt" phenomenon. Why is this so?

It has been noted that as one divides our society into the living, surviving, and dying, that the living make up less than 10 percent, the dying 20 to 30 percent, leaving the bulk of our society in the hands of the survivors. The survivors by their very presence and number set the values and the criteria against which all programs are defined. Since survivors define health as the absence of illness, and the ability to turn from a state of boat-rocking to one of stability, the survivors expend most of their health energy in those arenas which will return the people who are ill to survival states and to living and working activities in existing institutions. Indeed, the current rebellions by the have-nots and the ill are forcing a funding reallocation so that funds that have gone primarily to survivors, or to survivors who get ill, can now be reallocated to the have-nots and to the ill and dying.

We have seen over and over that reallocating these resources means a bigger "piece of the pie" goes to those people to deal with their illnesses or to raise their developmental level. This reallocation by itself does not lead to health. Only when the healthy and alive align themselves with the ill and dying do we get innovative changes that permit moves toward health for the total society, because both sense a crisis in the existing systems for dealing with health and illness. These alliances as yet are not firmly made. Our personal health may also be related to this alliance.

It means that on the deepest level we may have to change our perceptual model and consciousness about the governing processes. In order to survive, it has seemed important to allocate resources under the existing models to those perceived economic and military institutions which preserve our status.

Therefore, our notions of survival demand a new aliveness in Epoch B, in Jonas Salk's term, meaning that those survival institutions to which we have previously allocated our resources may *not* assist us to survive. The only institutions that will permit us to survive are those which maximize the individual's potential for his or her own growth as the individual defines it, *as well as* maximizing the health of even the sickest members of our society.

I suggest, therefore, something that has not been well accepted in the medical literature: we can indeed have healthy sick people; there is such a thing as a healthy schizophrenic; or a healthy poverty victim; because health is a phenomenon above and beyond the illness response.

The models of health and governance that we use come from the broader value systems "in good currency." These may, indeed, be outdated, given the changing issues and problems we are currently facing.

To sketch out some of the current problems means we have to face the transition of hierarchical power structures to newly emerging ones. Historically, royal power became elected power. Both models are hierarchical with the ruler maintaining power either by birth, military strength, or election. With power the ruler is given the license to propose and dispose and to be fair in dealing with all of the community.

It is interesting to note that many of the biological and psychological models currently used even by nonscientists of how the human organism works parallel these sociopolitical governance models. They assume that the brain is the most highly developed of any organ within the human body and with its rational ability can control all that is within the rest of the organism.

Slowly, almost nonconsciously, notions of political structure and governance have been shifting to nonhierarchical and more horizontal arrangements. As John Rawls (1971), has pointed out in his book on justice, current statements of equality are that "every person is equal." This notion is one that is being striven for politically and yet we know that it is not working. Another view of equality is that each person is uniquely different and in his or her difference is equal. The concepts of equality and of justice are applicable to health. If all people are to be treated the same, the sense of individual uniqueness is gone. Slowly we are shifting to a more biological concept that the organism is made up of unequal parts, an equality among unequals.

Rawls' theory of justice applied to health is that justice, when it is used in a hierarchical model, leads to a noblesse oblige, or a "white man's burden," helping those who are lower down on the pyramid. Justice in the equal model—all are the same—means that everyone has to be treated the same. As one gets to equality among unequals, justice and health shift. Those who are more equal than others in certain areas have the *responsibility* to assist others in the process of development toward higher states, at the same time respecting the uniqueness of each individual. Thus, justice in health is the responsibility of assisting others in the processes of growth.

If our concern with organization for health (justice) shifts in part from the individual we must begin to focus on the relationship of people within a given community. Since each segment of the community has its own personal uniqueness and development they are as equal as anyone else to define their perceptions of and needs in health. By focusing only on special group needs, what we have wrought is a fragmentation and splitting apart rather than a health program for the larger community. Our goal is to get both: local uniqueness as part of a larger system.

But does this concept of governance relate to the health of the biological organism itself? We have redefined the foci for health to include not just the individual but the community. If, as Lewis Thomas (1974) points out, the organism is not the ant but the colony, the health of the family, colony, community, or tribe becomes the focus of our concerns for health care. The specific point of health intervention may be the individual or family, but the overall frame of reference must be the community as a whole.

The human organism is a prototype of this model of organization. Each organ is uniquely itself. The liver is the liver, and yet each organ plays a role in the totality of existence. The question is never which organ is in charge. The body is in charge. The body, or the tribe, becomes the mind (not the brain); the whole is more than the sum of the parts. In the human body each organ assumes shifting "leadership." The need and the situation determine the appropriate leader.

What, then, is leadership? In the language of Robert Biller (1973), leadership may mean providing a steering mechanism, or the performance of an *education-therapeutic* function which permits the total organism to grow and to learn. Justice, health, and healing become the assisting of the total organism both to be unique and part of a whole at the same time.

The process entails that the individual has its uniqueness, but each time it makes a choice it recognizes that by doing so it limits its potential. At the time of human conception, the single cell has multiple choices available to it and its development. Thus, the genetic DNA template provides a range of options. It is the environment that limits the choices, which can have both positive and negative aspects. Governance of the whole body becomes a governance of unequals who are equal, who have to learn all about themselves, their potential, and the parts.

The concepts of Don Michael (1973) suggest that health is institutional, societal, or tribal learning. The total organism—individual, family organization, and community—must learn to be unique and whole. Health, then, is a constant dialectic between the parts and the whole, between differences or uniqueness on one hand and holding together on the other.

In the language of *living, surviving,* and *dying* there are two conflicting forces: one towards survival and one towards aliveness, growth, and creativity. The process of dialectic is to preserve and conserve at the same time that there is a move toward openness and creativity.

The question that then comes up is how one can learn these processes and create the suitable governance model. Only when one goes through experiences where one learns about life in its totality and in connecting all levels of existence by sensing through primary sources of information can one move towards this conceptualization of governance and health. If one gets stuck in a lockstep of discipline concept, bureaucracy, orientation, survival, status, or illness one is unable to deal with the phenomena of health.

Our responsibility for societal learning and change by which these new forms of equality are recognized, requires experiences on the nonconscious hidden curriculum level where concerns exist for wholeness and uniqueness. It means emphasizing the grounding in both the specific and in the abstract, and being able to continue in the dialectic between all aspects of one's own organism and with one's environment. Its dimensions are physical, psychological, social, spiritual, and communal. One way to achieve this end is through the tribe, with its culture, nonverbalized mythology, and ritual that permit the process to occur unconsciously.

In our current individual-oriented society, avoiding the tribal and common philosophy to which other things can be referred in the Western world puts increasing responsibility on the individual or on a relationship. By putting such responsibility on this small segment of the total organism, we create tremendous stress to the total organism of the whole, and we doom ourselves to failure and illness. Illness and breakdown can only be avoided if the responsibility for coping with health and governance is shared by the tribe, by the family, and by encouraging the individual's development.

Wholeness can be achieved in many ways. For some it can occur by focusing consciously on health. For others, focusing on work or play may perform the same function if the need for wholeness can continue to be maintained. From Alex Meiklejohn's work with the experimental college and the Great Books program comes the same concept—a community centered around understanding and participating fully in the issues of our age can lead to a healthy response. In his book, *The Experimental College* (1932), he points out that one does not need a psychiatrist to deal with mental health if there is a *community of learning*. Thus, our concerns are not the concerns with health alone, but rather with wholeness, by whatever route.

I was once told as I moved my focus of professional concern from area to area, as I have often done in my life, that I was really in the same business but in a new location. The reason that I moved my focus was that I reached the momentary limits of coping and societal learning and had to move to another arena to continue the process of wholeness with the environment. Some might say this is being "one step ahead of the law" if the notion of law is that it is designed to maintain the status quo and the *survival* status rather than to encourage *aliveness* and growth. To be a Protean Man, according to Bob Lifton (1970), may be the only way of truly surviving, if there is at the same time a dialogue with the "job specific" aspect of the person.

SOCIAL CHANGE

One of the basic reasons for our concerns with the physical and social environment and its relationship to health is our desire to make a change for the better. A vast number of people are concerned about what is happening to the health dollar: how we allocate our resources and whether, indeed, people are getting what they want, need, or what others say they should have.

Social change then becomes a critical issue in any discussion of health. To me social change can occur through many processes ranging from direct action to legislation or to the changing of perceptions and values inside one's self.

There is the concept of creeping incrementalism, which in part is the "art of muddling through." This is the way many processes of society continue their independent existence, interacting with problem areas, and precipitating minor changes that lead gradually to the total system adapting. Thus, as science moves forward, the tremendous influx of research money pressed on the system makes many direct and indirect changes. In part, then, social change may be considered a continuing, ecological process within a series of open and living systems.

There are some, however, who believe that social change can be accomplished by a master plan—a blueprint. I hope that at this point I have given enough reasons why such a master plan alone cannot lead to major and significant change and at the same time please all the people involved.

For me, "master planning" is a combination of two kinds of processes. On one hand it is something like presenting the results of a psychological test to a patient and asking the person, on that basis, to change. Or, on the other hand, it is the perception that the rational understanding of issues will deal with the whole of the problem, and therefore rationality itself can effect change. In this latter concept, the planner perceives that he or she has or can get all the available data. I don't believe this is so.

But what, then, is social change? I believe that social change is, in part, the ecological process previously mentioned. It goes on constantly without leadership and can lead to incrementalism, muddling through, and a symptom-by-symptom technique of action. On the other hand, social change is a process of social learning like that pointed out by Michael (1973). Such a process, with or without a leader, is a dialogue—a dialectic between all the parties, human and institutional, by which a more complete understanding of the issues unfolds. Change and learning occur on all levels. They occur through day-by-day actions as well as through longer-range proposals. Indeed, the model of social learning is similar to individual development. The society and its institutions have the capabilities and potentials to be alive, ever-changing and responsive to situations as they come up. This can happen only if the leadership is open to changing paradigms and perceptions and the leader performs an educational, steering role.

Just as easily as with individuals, institutions can get to the point where they are not alive but surviving. They become sclerosed, rigid, and incapable of responding to the new kinds of demands. Thus, institutions, like individuals, can get locked into survival, or sometimes dying, roles.

It is the surviving capacity of institutions which concerns me at the moment, because social change, then, becomes an attempt to "rock the boat" of the survivors and move them to aliveness. To do so often becomes a battle and a competition between the various survivors. On the other hand, some institutions have an ability to maintain their flexibility over time. (Some say that the survival of the Catholic Church over thousands of years has been because of its ability to bend to the wind, and to continually adapt itself to the various modalities and cultures in which it was located. Surely Vatican II showed that temporary ability through the leadership of Pope John, and with the assistance of Cardinal Bea, where a major institution was modified.)

The dilemma is that social change becomes more and more difficult the larger the system is and the less connected individuals are to it. Thus, we have to have a reorganization of both governance and technology so that our concerns can be cut down to a scale that can be handled by humans.

It is not my belief that one can fully "detechnologize" society, as Ivan Illich (1976) suggests. Rather, one may be able to shift to a level that Schumacher (1973) calls midtechnology, whose scale permits technological use for human ends, connectedness, and relationship of the decisions to the people affected. Thus, the ability to command events that affect one's life is directly related to size and to the processes in governance.

It has been said that crowding causes disease. However, we know that crowding in cultures where their governance permits coping and adapting does not necessarily lead to the same pathology as does crowding in populations which have no skills or coping ability. The process of governance becomes central to the issue of dealing with the promotion of health. It is for that reason that I make a modest proposal to assist in the process of change towards health.

A MODEST PROPOSAL

If change is related to societal learning, and social change requires a new way of conceptualizing, the development of new images and, at times, the changing of an institution's constituency, it is important for us to look at what can assist the social learning process in the health field. In so doing, when decisions are made about the design of the environment of health and non-health-related facilities and resources, we can determine what effect it would have on health.

I recommend the requirement of a *Health Impact Statement* for every proposed project within and outside the health field to see how such action would affect the health of the people.

This is indeed a *modest* proposal, although it is difficult to see how it will work. In part, it is based upon work done in the ecological and environmental fields. Through the use of environmental impact reports new questions can be raised, problems can be redefined, and the various parties involved in the community from the planners to the potential consumers can be involved. Surely, environmental impact reports have gotten bogged down in bureaucracies. They have taken endless time. People have not had an opportunity to read them. New professionals were created who merely prepared these reports. Real change, it is claimed, did not occur. Yet I believe that the concept of the requirement of these reports would be extremely useful to the social and institutional learning process.

To promote the most effective possible policy-making, calls for a dialogue between those affected by decisions and those making them. For this reason, it seems to me that we must go beyond the usual report sequence in which one expert, or a team of experts, reports to another group of experts. What is needed is a mechanism to assure *community involvement* within the process of decision making.

Although basic human needs may be universal, these needs must be met in many ways and in many environments, taking into consideration the differences in human preferences. Thus, we are faced with a two-level problem: at the deeper level are the universal human needs as a necessary requisite for health; on the more superficial level is the multiplicity of ways people experience the meeting of these needs. Thus, the way to promote the meeting of underlying human needs is to foster the expression of individual preferences in meeting these needs.

Involving the people in the planning of their own environmental health programs would serve a twofold purpose: it would assist them in gaining a meaningful connection to their government, which in itself is conducive to the health and well-being of the individual and the government, and it would also help to assure that the decisions ultimately made would meet the universal needs of people as they are variously expressed.

These *Health Impact Statements* should be prepared within the relevant human-scale community in which all the people involved could participate, and each report should involve two processes which, in fact, would be two reports: one prepared by the proposer, and one by the adversary. Similarly, in order to obviate difficulties, it would be important to maintain a short work time sequence. As noted in Chapter 4, the report and a decision on the report should be completed within a 90-day period, so that no pileup develops.

A Health Impact Statement should include three parts, such as:

1. The specific impact of the proposed activity on the health of the relevant population.
2. An analysis of the relationship of the proposal to the surrounding physical and social environment and the quality of life, and
3. The implications of this proposal for processes of governance.

The report, prepared in two versions, would be available to all members of the community, the basic decision makers, and to those people in related programs which might be affected by the activity. The short work time of the report would lead to a need for the various people involved to participate fairly rapidly in the processes involved.

As one can see, my main concern is to raise a series of questions that will assist the various people involved in a large complex health system to ascertain exactly what the issues are, and to learn in a specific way what range of concerns are included in the concept of health.

This does not mean that all must accept the same definitions. In fact, one of the more important issues will be for each report to state its specific definitions of health. There are obviously alternative definitions.

Within the total report, it would be important to include the items listed below. This is not meant to be an all-inclusive checklist, but I present it to suggest some issues that might be involved:

1. An Environmental Impact Statement should raise questions about *what* the effects of any new project would be upon the total environment. As part of this concern, it would be worth exploring the impact of the project on:
    *   The "health" of the community.
    *   The "health" of extended families.
    *   The "health" of nuclear families.
    *   The "health" of individuals.

- The ability of individuals to cope with "I hurt" independently.
- The ability of families to respond to an individual's cry of "I hurt."
- The ability of the community to cope with and respond to cries of "I hurt" by individuals and groups.

2. The measures of the health impact statement would be *economic* in nonmonetary terms, the impact of a project on human, social, physical, and environmental resources, the criteria being:

- To increase an *individual's ability to cope* with his or her own health and response to "I hurt," for example, maximizing personal, physical, social, psychological development, and ability to deal with simple cases of "I hurt."
- To detechnologize responses to health and "I hurt" needs, for example, less specialized manpower, general well-being, and lowered costs of labor, equipment, and facilities.
- An early response to "I hurt": access, speed, competence, using all of the tools available, for example, communication, crisis, and emergency clinics.
- A whole response to "I hurt"—contextual basis of problem.
- A nonlabelling of illness, unless there is no other choice of response: for example, issues can be dealt with by job, housing, etc., before being dealt with as illness.
- Construction and finance. Are these the most critical issues?
- Staffing. Is the ability of the facility to serve people and to be adequately staffed as, or more important than, the physical criteria?
- The relationship to other facilities, programs, and activities. How does this institution or facility relate to transportation, other resources, etc.?
- The development of individuals. Does the program change the way individuals develop? What is the re-

lationship to families? Extended families? Support groups?

- Exclusivity. Does it assist some people and not others?

- Holistic health. Does it deal with health as "whole," or does it segmentalize it? Perhaps dividing is important if one wants to deal with a highly important technical matter. Does it deal with a technical issue or a particular disorder, or with the needs of people, for example, families and community?

- Connectedness. Is what is being proposed connected to the broader environment? Is there a way it can be connected with people? Are people part of it or are they put on a technological assembly line? Is it connected physically, aesthetically, socially? How about connectedness in terms of a governance process? Does it have the ability to "touch"—to be in personal contact, etc.?

- Early care. How does it relate to providing care early enough after the response of "I hurt?"

- A non-lockstep. Does what is being proposed lock people into a model of behavior that cannot change over time or create environments that do not lock people into "illness" states, but encourage growth and development? Does the physical design prevent us from adapting to new kinds of techniques in medical care? Does it lock people into passive relationships? Does it allow change in notions and customs so that parents may stay with children in the hospital and change the concept of who is in charge?

- Consumer control. What does it do to people's ability to command the events that affect their lives? Does it diminish it or does it aid this?

- Change. Can the organization and facility build change over time as the focuses of problems change?

- Multigenerational issues. Does it separate the generations?

- Connectedness to the environment: social, physical, family, etc.

- "Permission" to respond on both cognitive and analytic levels as well as nonrational, emotional, spiritual, and unique social-cultural/personal responses.
- Connectedness to resources where highly technological and skilled labor are available for serious illness.
- Humanness.
- Tribal questions. Does it meet the values of some of the sub-tribes which exist in any country? Does it allow them to have links and ties to their own tribe? Does it also not lock them in so that they can go elsewhere?

In all of the above measures and questions, I have tried to indicate that I do not expect my views to hold for anyone else. Rather, the ideas I present and the questions I raise are questions that I believe must be thought about, discussed, and then worked out. However, they cannot be discussed if people involved are not informed as to the issues involved in health, especially if the questions are not clearly presented. Thus, what is proposed is an educational learning experience about health for the community, which would relate to issues surrounding health so that problems in the health systems are connected to other relevant areas.

Although it is clear that there are no answers to these questions, I believe that the following principles must be dealt with:

- "Community"-based response to health where local mid-level technology (Schumacher, 1973) can be created.
- Unique responses to groups and cultures, responding in ways that are conducive to their own ways but meeting criteria for health of the community as a whole.
- Mechanisms for creating performance specifications by the community as a whole (feeding in data by individuals and groups) which all will accept.

For the physical planner who is concerned primarily with dealing with the physical environment, the impact statement raises an especially important point because suddenly the physical planner must be aware that the physical by itself has never had a direct impact on health. We have believed that crowding by itself was important, yet we now know that the physical environment and the social environment together deal with the health aspects of the crowding problem. Thus, we are forcing people through a health impact study to perceive the soft issues that are not measurable in the usual ways of evaluation and by looking at those soft issues to fully understand what may be the real effect of their actions.

Health *cannot* be experienced secondhand. Connectedness is important for the healing process. It is equally important for the decision makers. We dare not permit policy to be determined by those who do not have firsthand knowledge of being healed and of healing. Thus, all policymakers (bureaucrats and consumers) should have direct experience in working with others in a healing and team role.

Some Examples

Let me briefly present some examples of areas in which these kinds of questions can be raised. In each of them there is a usual perception of what the issue is and, at the same time, issues that go far beyond our current concept. The examples are:

1. The building of a new coronary care unit.
2. The development of a sports movement program facility.
3. The creation of a non-public school.
4. The development of a clinic.
5. The building of a re-creation center.

In the construction of a new *coronary care unit*, the usual concern is whether this new hospital or facility needs that kind of unit in order to deal with the acute problems that come to it. However, even though one looks at the coronary care unit from that point of view, it is important to know whether there are other facilities giving the same kind of service, and, indeed, that is part of our current concept of planning. Yet, we have not faced the question of whether the unit itself, which puts people into a dependent situation and disconnects them from the broader community environment, may be perpetuating the potential for coronaries while treating the immediate episode of a threatened coronary occlusion. That is, it may be important to talk about coronaries, and potential coronaries, as a comprehensive system involving people's life-styles, their different personality patterns, their relationships in the home, their stresses, the need to have a response to people under tension. Those factors may have higher priorities for health than a care unit for when the illness is advanced. I am not proposing the abolition of coronary care units. I am asking only for the raising of questions.

Regarding a *sports movement program*, the questions may be whether the sports program locks people into an outdated concept of the body and movement; whether it is used to obtain health; whether movement can have other meanings; whether we can connect movement to imagery, symbol, and ritual; and whether movement can be the leverage point to which health can be developed. Indeed, can the promotions of health be built around new concepts of movement? For example, George Leonard's (1975) book, *The Ultimate Athlete*, suggests that physical movement permits one to deal with psychological, spiritual, physical, dietary, nutritional, and other aspects of preventive and promotional concerns. A sports and movement program may be the core of personal re-creation. How does one deal with a conventional program against a medical program? How does one deal with a changed concept of a sports program against a conventional secondary-care medical program?

A non-public school needs to be considered that is concerned with issues of human development, with integrating the social, physical, psychological, and spiritual issues. Magic Mountain in Oakland, California (Harvey, 1974), is a place where one can begin to deal with holistic issues, have regular meetings with families, focus on body awareness, on the children's physical, psychological, and cognitive development, as well as participate in learning about the process of self-government. These concerns have more to do with health than do those of most of our medical facilities. That kind of school, as compared to the standard school dealing purely with cognitive knowledge, may very well be a place to be supported when one is promoting concepts of health. Indeed, we have schools like this for the mentally retarded where we have defined the need for the school as a place for handling a health problem, but we have not, except in rhetoric, created schools for the general promotion of development and the health of normal children. Thus, the school is not the place where one finds disease early, but rather the place where one participates in the learning about wholeness, connectedness, relationship, aliveness, and governance.

Consider a proposal to *develop a new clinic*. Should that clinic be for primary care? Should it be staffed by nonprofessional manpower? Should it have outreach? Should it be concerned with all kinds of issues of "I hurt"? Does it have an available crisis response? How does it participate with the caretakers of the community who already exist? Do we need professionals for the bulk of care? Do we change our licensing procedures or our certifications as to who can give care? How do we define what is good primary care for different subsections of our population?

The *development of a re-creation center* (Duhl, 1976b) could be crucial to a community. In another context I have proposed the development of a center for re-creation for people who are in transition. In this center people faced by a crisis can begin to look at their own need for personal change. The availability of a resource for dealing with many issues without actually creating a standard medical care facility permits one to explore one's self in the fullest dimensions. A re-creation center could also set the stage to deal with personal mythologies and symbolism, to assist people in going through rites of passage, to participate in learning about one's self, one's body, one's psychological state, one's relationships and, further, as a base for social change. Again, like the non-public school it may be an institution that has health potential without actually being a health organization. Such an organization could be modeled in part on the Peckham Health Center in England which was a facility—a settlement house made of glass—available to people to use while their health was studied (Williamson & Pearse, 1947; Pearse & Williamson, 1938; Pearse & Crocker, 1947). Although medical care was given at this facility, illness diminished as a number of people moved towards aliveness from health and survival.

CONCLUSION

The organizing principle of my concepts of wholeness is not the physical environment. Rather, the environment is a tool for advancing the concerns of human beings because human development—the lives and the relationships of people—are the cornerstones (the organizing concepts) of the kind of life that I believe is central for us. Achieving it requires hard decisions. It is our responsibility to come to them. Through our policies and actions, we want to maximize the potential of the individual for aliveness, development, and the quality of life over the other values that exist in our society. You will be told that these values *are* utilized in all decisions. That is only partially true. What is different is that the priorities and hierarchy of values have changed. Our awareness of the wholeness of our society may not be more important than any achievement or creation of the parts (Salk's Epoch B).

The processes of healing involve not only the individual, but the community, tribe, and family as part of the larger social and physical environment. Although we have a responsibility for optimizing the development of individuals toward attaining their health, we have an equal one to look at the healthy development of the environment. To do so requires all our being, from science to art, from the rational to the ambiguous and emotional. Health tests our limits as human beings.

As W. H. Auden (1979) said,

> Healing, Papa would tell me,
> Is not a science,
> But the intuitive art
> Of wooing nature.

The promotion and maintenance of health is not a myth. Because of its importance, however, as a reality it cannot be left only in the hands of the medical profession.

Chapter 10

THE SOCIAL CONTEXT OF HEALTH

Common sense suggests and the data that have accumulated from years of long-term studies confirm that a dynamic relationship between human beings and their social environments can be the cause of good or poor health (Churchman, 1971; Kitagawa & Hauser, 1973). These environments may be defined as the sum of those intangible interactions that exist between people. They are usually structured by prevailing political, economic, and cultural forces and are affected by and in turn affect the physical environment—the climate, the air people breathe, the houses they live in, whether in urban or rural settings, and the roads on which they commute (Proshansky et al., 1976).

Although the relationship between the socioenvironmental context and health status is sometimes immediately apparent, as for instance in the relationship between poor sanitation and the incidence of some infectious diseases, it is not always that simple. In some settings, the lack of good sanitation may be the result of an extremely complex group of factors, including scientific ignorance, local politics, lack of constructive skills, and lack of money. There may even be some political advantage to those in power in keeping people sick and listless.

It is crucial, then, that health practitioners and policy-makers who wish to be effective keep in mind that health is embedded in a social context because people exist in a social context, that the causes of disease are not always strictly biological, and that healing cannot always depend on biomedical intervention or research (Duhl, 1963, 1968a; Somers, 1971).

TWO APPROACHES TO SOCIAL CONTEXT

There are two related, but quite different, approaches to the study of the impact of social environments on health. The first uses statistical and epidemiological techniques to correlate such factors as education, race, economic status, age, and occupation with the incidence of illness and injury (Kitagawa & Hauser, 1973). The second, a more broadly cultural approach to the relationship between social environment and health, considers the influence of "softer" factors on health and illness (Geiger, 1972). Among its concerns are the structure of social networks, the influence of the mass media on people's attitudes and beliefs, the freedom or lack of it to grow and develop normally and naturally, the effects of community politics and participation, the ways in which social settings foster or frustrate self-esteem and confidence. Although the second approach makes use of some of the statistical information provided by the first, it tends to avoid statistical analysis and must be defined in more intuitive, speculative ways. Both approaches, applied together, can help health planners and policymakers—and, indeed, individual practitioners—take action to affect the health of groups within their scope.

The analysis of social determinants of health rests on the simple observation that some groups of people are healthier than other groups. From studying these various groups and comparing them, a set of social, economic, and demographic characteristics can be derived that correlates strongly with either the absence of certain diseases or with higher mortality or morbidity.

Such studies have shown that income, age, and education are probably the three strongest influences on health, and that all are interrelated. Higher income levels and better health, lower incomes and poorer health are consistently correlated. Education seems to affect health not only because it elevates economic status, but because it allows people better access to information about health and disease and about their bodies and because it helps them make more considered choices in matters that affect health.

Age affects health in a variety of ways. Mortality statistics show that the first year of life is the most dangerous year of all until age forty. But it is old age that most often emerges as an important social determinant of health. Our society now contains growing numbers of elderly persons who make great demands upon medical services, who are often poor and ill fed, and who are prone to accidents and the effects of loneliness and isolation. Thus to be old, poor, and uneducated almost always means to be ill.

Occupation, another major indicator of health, is related to income and education. But occupation is also directly related to health because of the accidents, poisonings, and exposures to contaminants and carcinogens that many jobs entail. The effects of occupation on housing, neighborhoods, commuting patterns, intercity moves, stress, and alcohol and tobacco use are less direct but universal. In addition there are special groups such as migrant workers, coal miners, and asbestos workers who are exposed to specific and often lethal occupational health hazards.

Ethnic and cultural background are also important determinants of health (Orleans & Ellis, 1971). Health problems among blacks, Mexican Americans, Puerto Ricans, and Native Americans are of much concern to those groups and to public health workers generally. Some diseases, like sickle cell anemia, are biologically specific to racial groups. Many more are related to those general factors already mentioned—poverty, education, occupation, sanitation, housing. There are also some ethnic and cultural groups that seem to experience good health, probably because of religious or cultural factors that affect their life styles.

Other social determinants of health include geography, birth order, generation, sex, urban or rural residence, family structure, marital status, important "life events," and language barriers (Proshansky et al., 1976). Many such indicators can be observed simply and directly, but others take fairly sophisticated epidemiological study to determine. For example, attention to factors that contribute to child abuse and neglect has revealed the importance of the mother's age at first pregnancy.

Although this kind of information is valuable and necessary, my personal attention as a psychiatrist and urban planner has been drawn to the softer issues that, until recently, have been neglected. The social context of health, in my view, may be defined as the entire set of relationships that exist among people and among groups to which people belong. Health itself, rather than being simply the absence of diseaes or injury, I define more broadly as participation in a process of natural growth and development. These definitions may seem entirely too broad or vague to some, but I find they provide leeway in which to reconsider the relationship between society and health in a more holistic way (Duhl & Volkman, 1970).

THE CURRENT CONTEXT

We are going through a period of rapid change and a heightening of contradictions in many aspects of public life. Even as the economic situation is creating inflationary pressures, the threat of a major recession seems always in the wings. Demographic changes are also underway. We have seen the population of our country getting increasingly younger with fewer children, then with more older people we find that the average age is creeping upward again. Americans are still on the move; major population shifts are bringing people into and out of the cities and into the Southwest and West. We change jobs, houses, neighborhoods, and regions more than any other people on the planet.

For many, work is what orders and defines life. In many families both parents work in order to meet living costs. Yet others—especially the young and most especially the young minorities—are denied the experience of work. For some minorities, unemployment is an experience that extends over the generations.

Education is also undergoing change. The system is producing some students who know more, think faster, and command events more ably than ever, while others who graduate cannot read or write, fill out a job application, make out a check, add up their budgets, or even communicate verbally. Teachers are beleaguered and bewildered; the educational bureaucracy is swollen and inefficient; schools are viciously vandalized.

Television has had a major impact on American lives. We know all too little about its effects and can only guess at what it means when millions spend anywhere from 4 to 6 or more hours a day watching television. While audiovisual communication gets more and more sophisticated, are we too becoming more sophisticated or more dull and apathetic?

The family seems threatened and under siege by many social factors—easy divorce, easy cohabitation, new sexual freedoms of many kinds, economic realities, the impact of feminism. All the stresses and strains of contemporary life affect the family and the health of its members one way or another, sometimes for good, sometimes for ill.

Urbanization, transportation, racial strife and inequality, crime, taxes, pollution, energy—the list of contemporary social problems is long, the items on the list are inextricably interrelated, and their effects on health, particularly their contribution to the chronic diseases that beset so much of our population are profound. Within this context—this fast-moving, stressful and liberating, diverse and interlocked set of social, political, and personal changes—where do we begin to look for the signs of health or the mechanisms by which to enhance health?

HEALTH AND DISEASE

Often when I think about creating a social context that promotes individual health, I think about a unique experiment in health that took place in London—the Pioneer Health Centre. Founded in 1926 by Drs. Scott Williamson and Innes Pearse (1965) in the working class neighborhood of Peckham (Pioneer Health Centre, 1971), it really got going just before World War II. These physicians made an assumption much like one put forth by Maslow: no headway would be made into the understanding of health simply by researching the mechanisms of disease. They were aware that health itself has its own patterns of disease. To use their words, they expected the Peckham experiment to show "that health is more powerful and infectious than disease" (Pearse & Crocker, 1947).

Beginning with the assumption that there was, indeed, a state of "positive health," Drs. Williamson and Pearse built up a neighborhood center of sorts, a combination clubhouse, gymnasium, meeting room, theater, dance hall, library, and clinic. Peckham neighbors were eligible to join, with one stipulation— they would have to cooperate in an annual health "overhaul," which included an examination and subsequent discussion of its results with other family members and the doctors. An attempt was thus made to raise community sensitivity to health issues.

Out of the stipulated annual health overhauls came some interesting statistics. It was found that a little more than 10 percent of those examined really had nothing wrong with them at all; the other 90 percent had some diagnosable condition. However, more than 60 percent of those examined declared themselves to be "well," that is, they had no complaints and felt no physical restrictions on their lives. The remaining 25 to 30 percent of those examined felt they were, by their own definition, "sick." (These figures, incidentally, were replicated later in other epidemiological studies.) I would call the 10 percent or more of those who had no symptoms the "Alive," the 60 percent or more who may have had this or that symptom but said they were "well," the "Survivors," and the remaining 25 percent or more who said they were "sick," the "Ill" or the "Dying."

The Survivors are those who usually define health, who have the power to allocate resources; they are the majority and have majority powers. The Ill or Dying are those who make the most use of health resources, sometimes properly and beneficially, sometimes not. They also live their lives as if they were ill or dying and have particular attitudes toward health that are difficult to change. The Alive, on the other hand, are usually seen as deviants because they make demands for certain kinds of resources that the health system cannot provide. They demand change, growth opportunities, personal liberation, outlets for creativity and expression, significant encounters with the world and others. It seems that our society prefers to tolerate many sick people; that it is made uncomfortable by the healthy ones and their disruptive demands.

Many writers (Alford, 1972, 1975; James, 1972; Satin, 1978) have stated that more has been accomplished in the fight against disease by social and political than by strictly medical means. Changes in sanitation, housing, food, work places, population control, have led to a reduction in disease and injury that could not have been accomplished as successfully any other way. At the same time, what the Lalonde Report (1974) calls the "dark side of economic progress"—the "ominous" and medically irremediable "counterforces" of pollution, urbanization, bad health habits (including abuse of tobacco, alcohol, and drugs), poor nutritional knowledge and practice—has done much to undermine health.

The medical care system is a net that catches the victims of social, political, and economic "illness," not a system that fosters and enhances health (Roemer & Friedman, 1971; Stevens, 1971). As a result, the health and medical care system has been given credit for bettering health when other social institutions actually have done more (Anderson, 1968); and it is blamed for not alleviating disorders that are actually the responsibility of other institutions.

At present, the health and medical care system of the United States is overwhelmed by the responsibility for dealing with a host of social, political, and economic ills that do not belong to it (Conner, 1978). We are continually broadening instead of limiting our definition of illness and then telling the medical care institutions that they must deal with the growing number of symptoms displayed by Survivors and the life-denying and life-defying attitudes displayed by the Ill. Alcoholism, criminality, antisocial behaviors, drug abuse, mental retardation, anomie, fright, loneliness, stress, and all kinds of thwarted developmental issues are placed within the medical care system.

Along with relieving the medical care system of some responsibilities that have been wrongly given to it, we can begin to dispel some of the mystique of medicine and health care and some of the blind faith in medical practitioners and health professionals. A change in our dependency on the medical care system, a more realistic view of what it can and cannot, should or should not do, will lead to an increased assumption of personal responsibility for growth and development.

One way to begin is by defining health in terms of the demands that are made by the Alive, by those whom Abraham Maslow (1970) called "self-actualizing." We ought to begin to define health in terms of growth and development, creativity, and the capacity to change and make change. Then we might begin to reorder the social system to provide for the demands of the Alive. One of the goals of social policy ought to be the maintenance of opportunities for growth and personal development, while the health care system by medical means ought to try to return those who are blocked from growth back to their normal growth cycles.

In other words, let the health care system continue as it is, but let us narrow its responsibilities. We have one of the best medical care systems in the world; it does superbly at applying scientific and technological interventions in disease and injury, at research, and at discovery. If we could find ways to lighten its load we might also find easier ways to finance what it can do best. But we can no longer let the Survivors and the Dying, with their necessarily limited point of view and their great needs, have total control over that system.

SOME ALTERNATIVES

The task of creating a healthier social context and a more holistic attitude toward health care involves changes in the institutions for health and illness, in the training of health professionals, and in the society as a whole. One important concept— and my special interest—that should be considered in this process of change is networking: the examination and activation of the social dynamics that exist in families, small groups, business, and even in entire societies and countries (Duhl, 1970, 1978).

A strong body of research and conceptual studies on networking has been created by sociologists, social psychologists, anthropologists, political and social scientists, and urbanologists, among others. The interesting part of all this work is not so much that networks exist, exist so completely, or exist in so many different forms, but that they seem to foster well-being among their members. This has been borne out quite specifically by recent studies (H. Blum, 1974, 1976a; Berkman & Syme, 1979) conducted in Alameda County, California, where it was shown that individuals with relevant social ties to other human beings were more healthy than individuals without such meaningful intercourse. Common-sense observations and statistics agree: a web of human relationships nurtures and protects an individual.

It follows that a breakdown of such nurturing relationships would have adverse effects on health. That this is so seems to be the point of the Thomas Holmes (Holmes & Masuda, 1973; Holmes & Rahe, n.d.; Rahe & Holmes, n.d.) "life events" scales, which show the relationship between significant life events and the incidence of illness. People who experience disruptive life events (like divorce, death of a partner or friend, loss of a job, a move from one city to another) often become ill. Sometimes illness is also connected to important life events that would be considered positive—a wedding, a birth, a promotion. The key seems to be stress, induced by sudden major change that is not buffered by supportive human relationships or that is caused by the loss of such human relationships.

A deep human need thus seems to exist for linkage to a dynamic network of other human beings as well as some sense of linkage to the network of all living beings. Perhaps well-being is related not only to our linkage to other human beings but also to the natural world—or even to some world of spiritual experience. Unfortunately we know very little about the effect of these latter connections upon health.

The recent interest in and focus on preventive or "prospective" medicine often places too much emphasis on individual responsibility for health, leading to the syndrome of "blaming the victim." Individual change does not automatically lead to needed social change. The step from individual commitment to new definitions of health and new health practices is only the first step. The next step is to link these individual perceptions and changes into interpersonal networks in which the dialectical relationship between different perceptions and different stages of growth and development will lead to synergistic change effects. In other words, first, there must be a new understanding of what health means; next, networking must be created to build human groups to support and enhance the lives of their members.

We are a combination of the I and the You. Sometimes we live as single I, sometimes we enter into the You, the social arena. One state is not better or worse than the other—both are needed if we are to be in balance, to be healthy. And both are needed if we are to be engaged in growth and development, if we are to be open to change and to make change.

So the social context of health begins with or builds on the personal context of health; the personal definition of and self-responsibility for health leads to linkage and networking, which are in themselves healthy and a sign of health. Through social linkage and participation in networks of change, we can together learn to effect change—in ourselves and in the world around us.

The hierarchy within a network, if it is a true network and not a rigid system, is fluid and organic. As networks grow and proliferate, new networks and new relationships are created, and the people in them will take on different roles and at times assume different relationships toward each other. At one moment and in one context a network member may be a leader, and in another context at another time he or she may be a follower. Usually, however, one will find in the network some people who take on the role of managers, who keep the others in touch with each other, who act to refer problems between network members and to spread the good news of the success of one network member to the others. There will be others who function to link different networks, who have the ability to move in and out of different networks, to bring about alliances and to help networks work together for common goals.

Those who plan social change in the health and medical care field should become aware of and foster networking, should identify and support the network managers and network linkers who can initiate change. This may include helping self-help people (such as the people who would have formed groups) to gain greater independence from the established medical system by learning new skills, linking groups together for such common purposes as improving housing or decreasing neighborhood crime, and facilitating their common interactions with and challenges to the policies and practices of boards of health, drug companies, hospitals, and other social institutions.

I like to call this the work of *making whole* (Duhl & Den Boer, 1980c). Social change, like individual change, most often comes about when one begins to achieve a balance between self-respect and group respect, an impact on the external world, and normal growth and development through time. Making whole—that is, creating a true holistic health policy and practice—is more than new or alternative techniques, beliefs, or approaches to treatment. It means working along all these lines together.

Chapter 11

HUMAN SOCIAL FUTURES

I have sat through many discussions about the future. In almost all of them I have come away with a sense of unreality. The discussions, as my son recently said of my friends, are unreal because they do not deal with the meaning of life as he sees it.

I start, as he does, with those things that affect me, those people I love and care for, and those who, although I do not know them personally, speak in their own voice of their concerns.

The future is now, and now is the past redone by "who we are now" and where we want to be. We are always living in our past, and IMAGEing future. We are always affected by processes both beyond our direct control, our understanding, or our conscious perceptions, as well as by what we do know. Sadly, that which we consciously know, despite all our advances, is little indeed. Although we know a great deal, we are aware also of the infinite amount we do not know.

So much of our projections of the future are extensions of what is known. Yet what we call the known may only be that which we ascribe to rational, conscious thought. Never can that knowledge be negated but, indeed, there is and may be much more. Recent brain research has shown that for right-handed people, the left brain has become superbly developed in analytic, intellectual, cognitive activities. Though the issue is complicated, the right brain/left brain differentiation is a useful metaphor. Indeed, since the Renaissance, the Industrial Revolution, and the more recent information-computer modeling, that side of our brain has received most of our attention in the Western world.

When Sir Geoffrey Vickers (1965) discusses judgment, decision making, and change, he carefully reminds us how often we make use of a different set of functions. It is the right brain, full of feeling, intuition, and closer to the (shall we say for the moment) more "primitive states" of human behavior, that is more often than not brought into action when judgments are made. To me, judgment may be the bridging function of the two kinds of knowing. I do not propose to engage in an intense discussion of the right side of the brain, but some comments are relevant to our discussion of the prospects for man.

The recent concern in the West with the psychology of the East, as well as the repeated attempts by our youth and others to focus on a new consciousness (what they call the New Aquarian Age), are but some of the clues that there may be something worth searching for in the right brain. In several of his novels, such as *A Far-Off Place* and *A Story Like the Wind*, Laurens van der Post (1972, 1974), who was a close friend and biographer of Jung, learning of the heart, the thumping of the chest, which the Kalahari Pygmies use "to know." They are, if we wish to name it, entering psychic worlds, and the world often left to religious mysticism and the occult. As he takes us on a learning quest of a young white African man in one of his books, Van der Post shows us metaphorically how much there is to learn in this other way. Then, in a crashing final set of pages, he reminds the boy (who is the combination, the synthesis) of these two ways of knowing, that is, life. Similarly, Jung himself reminds us that to be whole is to get in touch with inferior functions (those in which we are weak) and with our shadow, or "other side" (our problems).

Nothing in my remarks should be construed as advocating the giving up of Western cognitive knowledge. I have spent enough of my life in this milieu to know its benefits and, indeed, its pleasures. Yet more and more, as I approach my half-century birthday, I see how little that knowledge helps in understanding *life*. Is it age that does this?

And with this introduction I return to *"life"*—with all its complexity, confusion, the unknown. Life is full of unresolved ambiguities, half-believed self-rationalizations, hurts, pains, and social problems. It is hardly rational. It is full of surprises: good and bad, pleasurable and painful. Somehow, it is not like the neatly planned suburbs, or the housing developments of Don Mills, Ontario or Los Angeles, California. In its best form it is more likely to be the partially planned, yet organically grown city—a Dubrovnik in Yugoslavia, or parts of Quebec.

I have used or hinted at several words: *change, growth*, and *problems*. I have not yet talked of illness or pathology, and for a physician that may, indeed, be strange. For those of you who label problems as illnesses or pathology, I can only state that most often this is apt, either in the eye of the beholder or when the involved party agrees with those who make the judgment. What may be more to the point is that what some people call pathology, I would call dysfunctional in one person while functional in another. As such, it raises a flag. I will return to *illness* later, but for the moment I would like to focus on my other three words: *change, growth*, and *problems*.

Change occurs through many processes. We watch our children change as they grow. Often we see this *change* prepatterned. My mother once said that in order to grow healthily one has to pick the right parents. Change then is in many ways partially preprogrammed, by forces of which we know little. We have called it evolution or genetics. In the East it is called karma. Even there it is not absolute control, a preprogramming, for the environment determines what part of the range of options becomes usable. This pathway ranges from the known (for example, DNA molecules, patterns of specific traits) to the unknown master plan of the great interactions that make up changes within our universe or world. What we call science is gradually making conscious rules of *process* somehow previously laid down, or just *there*. Could this process of interaction be the ultimate meaning of our concern with God?

But change is not just laid down. Yes, there is a process, and it is not completely tight and rigid, nor is it fully random. Some things do, indeed, happen more than others. And chance does lead to change. Constant new combinations and new unpredicted impacts result in switches of direction, only known or understood technologically after the fact.

Change, then, is a *process* akin to the knowledge of an iceberg which never extends beyond the small tip. We intervene consciously at that small seen tip and somewhere in the hidden energy the real action takes place below the surface. Unconsciously, I chose the iceberg as metaphor—linking it to energy—because we think of ice as frozen. In that state, how can things be going on? Ice is a structure, you might say, and I would reply that *structure is process slowed down*. Change then, in my view, is an endless, continuous, semi-free, and ambiguous process. As something occurs which is functional, at least functional if slowed down, it stabilizes as structure and change appears to have stopped. Yet even within frozen structure something is going on—a process that we hardly know, and even a frozen iceberg interacts with the environment. Too often we are stuck in our thinking and planning with structures sclerosed and hardened, ignoring the fact that sclerosing stops life and begins a process of death. For those concerned with our prospects we must respect these processes, try to understand, and yet be humble about what we can accomplish even within the realm that is *"human created."*

As the world has evolved, change has gradually become more encompassing. It is not just the explosion of communication that caused McLuhan, in the 1970s, to characterize "The medium as the message," and to describe implosions within people as meaning is message. It is also the communication of processes beyond the local. It is as if ecology on a worldwide scale had to be created, once the impact of human-created environments began to impinge on the immediate land, outward into the air, the atmosphere, and more recently into biomagnetic waves of our earth. If this is so, I now take as a given the *inability* of any human or group of humans *not to affect* the others, albeit even minutely. As I write this the smoke of a neighbor's cigarette irritates my eyes. The water I drink is hardly the pure draft of my youth. Nor can an Arab potentate move without changing the economic landscape or even the pattern of housing developments near my home.

What, then, is organic growth? Humans have existed through many stages of development. Fighting a hostile environment, weather, and other natural enemies slowly led to a world that is almost—at least where most of us live—human made.

In our creations of that environment we have done what we thought we had to do to deal with the immediate issue at hand. Slowly, in what I would call a nonorganic way, we closed our relationship with the organic world. It is not that I would or could have stopped that change. It is just that in our rational, scientific wisdom, by not being in touch with all that is life, we may, quite inadvertently, have cut ourselves off from those very things which make life. Organic growth for me is leaving open the processes so that we can still benefit from that part of our environment which, though we do not understand it, is still part of life.

Let me be more explicit. *First,* I would point to the things easy to see—the decreased air and the diminished nutrition in our foods as we take out the natural and replace it artificially with what we know should be there. We are out of touch with natural energies as we deal endlessly with the human created ones. There are all too many of these, including the taking of life in the name of protecting ourselves. *Second,* there are the more subtle changes which, in the name of education, efficiency, and profit, we slowly condition out of our children: being born with freshness and openness, being in touch with the more subtle senses of intuition and even mystic experiences and energies of nature. We teach them how "bad" that is. In the name of the future, of the common good, we take away so much that is uniquely human: the richness of linking the right and the left brain. We take away feelings, touch, and smell because Anglo-Saxon propriety said it was bad. Slowly being imposed on each of us is the making of value judgments, labelled good or bad, well or ill.

Yes, even pathology. Justice has become confused with apparent truth. Pathology may, indeed, be an organic human reaction against all these things imposed upon each and every one of us by these processes that take us away from an organic growth. Personal or social pathology may not be illness but a cry by our organism that something is wrong, that our natural energies are not working.

Hans Selye (1978), the distinguished Canadian scientist, has directed our attention to stress rather than disease, stress being interventions into the processes of individuals beyond their ability to "bio-psycho-socially" cope, and therefore leading to breakdown. Illness is a message that says, not so much "cure the disease" as "make things right again." "Bring back the human balance, the organic growth which is a dialectic process of energies between homeostatic balance, and a dysbalance which urges us to find new balances, new solutions, and change."

Stress leads to disturbance and, after a "strong fight," to illness (so-called). Consequently much of our medical scientism has been to find the specific "cause" and find a specific "cure." In the process we have fragmented life into the parts we can study, intervene with, and in so doing, leave aside the whole. Whole. Holy. Healthy. Healing. Four words with the same root. Stress and crisis as signals may indeed give us messages that some structures have to die, for in death and rebirth there is change and growth. Lindemann (1944), Marris (1974), Keleman (1975), and others have pointed to the relationship of death and bereavement to living.

Being humanly whole is not to be fragmented. It is finding growth in all spheres—physical, biological, social, psychological, and spiritual. It means not disconnecting ourselves from all our parts: our right brain from our left; our sexual organs from our feelings; our spirit and soul from our knowledge. Our world *has changed* so much that this disconnection has, indeed, occurred, and for it we pay the price that we call illness.

Humans, however, are adaptable. Scott Williamson (1965), studying health in the London population participating in the settlement house, the Peckham Health Centre, (described in Chapter 10) discovered the amazing fact that participation itself in the holistic center decreased the amount of illness in the families studied. Furthermore, as we have seen, Williamson found that the population could be divided into three groups: the *living*, the *surviving*, and the *dying*.

The *Dying* were those with discernible symptoms so great that they accepted the fact that they were ill, and behaved as if the illness was life. One might say of this 20 to 30 percent of the people at the Peckham Centre, and probably 20 to 30 percent of us, that their views are pre-Copernican, that all the world circles around their illness. Many, indeed, perceive the world in a Laing-ian (1965) way: "We are sane; everyone else is mad. We must control our world." They are "radicals," wanting more resources for themselves. They point, in the way indicated before, to the fact that the world in its way of living has gone mad, and they in their private world of illness are the rightful heirs of life itself. Their voices must serve for all of us as a signal of social crises.

The *Survivors*, 60 percent of the people at Peckham Centre and, again, probably of us, have medical, psychological, and social symptoms of functional dysbalance. Yet we deny it, acting as if it were not so. We are those who accept "*what is,*" denying what we have done to the world and to ourselves. We maintain *balance* (homeostasis) at all costs. We see health as the absence of illness. We demand stability and non-change. We "control" the world, disliking the ill and dying who are reminders that we have caused our own pain. We set the definitions, and keep control of the resources. Indeed, we are the official futurists who, out of our values, stability, and needs, program the future hoping to shape it in our image. We hire psychiatrists to label as ill those who do not conform, whether in America, the Soviet Union, or here. We are frightened by the deviants whom we call sick, and whom we label, classify, and try to ignore.

We cannot understand our children. The very things we created made our children different from us. We created Dr. Spock and he freed our children who, in turn, attack what we and Spock have done. Therefore, they prefer Mr. Spock to Dr. Spock. They live in a man-made fantasy television land of the right brain and yearn for the organic and natural. They search for the spiritual, paying a great price as they slowly affect our processes of change.

"Control all you want," they say. "Keep your planning, futurism, money, and power. We are in touch with the unconscious processes, and these are what really cause change."

In their pain of being the elite of the "have nots," they are creating the innovations that the future will absorb. As with Calhoun's (1973) rats, out of felt deprivation, change is being precipitated that will soon become part of the Survivors' world without thought of making it fully part of their lives.

For it is with the *Living*—the 10 percent found by Williamson to be free of symptoms (and which I believe to be much fewer)—that being in touch with life occurs. The "*Alive*" are whole, so busy enjoying life that they have no time to worry about health. They *are* life. They are open, live with ambiguity, and use all their being. They are creative, innovative, and in touch. And for all that, they do not have control of the world, though they contribute their being to it whether in science or in spirituality. Some of them are the true gurus, the true christs, and wise men. They walk among us as prophets in a silent way, bearing witness by their behavior. In addition, in a world where we can't control all the variables, we still use models of control (the military, models to control disease, etc.). If the model being used includes continuing learning, it is what Churchman (1971) calls "an inquiring system."

Williamson has suggested that aliveness is "the ability to mutually synthesize humans with their environment." We thus return to two interrelated processes: the individual and the *us* (the whole; the environment). Before discussion these two issues—the *I* and the *us*—it is important to show the relationship between aliveness and the developmental process. Except for genetic "sports" who are just naturally alive, aliveness comes out of maximizing one's growth. It means that growth moves from the potential in the "seed" to full flowering. The flowering in its fullest, as Comenius (1965) pointed out in the 1600s, results only by nourishment of the seed by the self and the environment.

We come then to the central theme of change for our future: the primary need to shift values from immediate need and "the present complaint" to the potential for growth and development. This means that crises and illness can serve as signals of deeper human growth issues. It means specifically that something as mundane and immediate as malpractice insurance crises of physicians, attorneys, and patients is not a money crisis but a sign that physicians and patients have lost touch. When touch (a nonrational right-brain function) is lost and there is pain, all we know how to do is sue. And sue we do!

Ivan Illich (1976) has pointedly singled out medicine as losing touch, focusing on technology, construction, and monuments while the nature of health and illness is bypassed. Medicine's crisis is that it is detached from life. Expenditures in the United States of $430 billion in 1986 are hardly adequate for medical and health care. Medicine has become professionalized, scientific, and computerized, full of certification and big business, while the patient (except in extremes) can be better helped by the laying on of hands and personally responding to "I hurt." This cry says "something has gone wrong." It does not mean fancy medicine, hospitals, or scientific knowledge as we have used it. It is a human touching a human. It is family, community, a return to a way of living where humans interact on all levels of their being. All solutions are not technological.

A mother and a child relate to each other with touch, smell, breath, and sound. It is food, sensuousness, and caring. Life is made up of these issues magnified, of issues indicated previously as physical, biological, social, spiritual, and psychological. It is the cognitive and the feeling. It is relating on all these levels.

What has happened to this organic whole life? Can it only be manifest if we try to escape to the natural—a return to the earth and community—as so many are trying to do? Can we not bring our groupings of people more into touch with these things? Must their lives be non-life, polluted by the environment? Must our rules continue to separate mother and child in hospitals, disconnect schools from families, make work a priority over living with those we love and care for?

I hope I do not sound completely like a return-to-nature person, for I am not that. I *do* feel better there. In nature I find myself in touch with a real world with a special healing energy. And yet I also love human creations: the passions, loves, and pains of living, the surprises in an organic city like Dubrovnik, the creativity of artists and poets who, out of their interactions with other humans, create worlds that are as beautiful as the world out there.

For to me life is also fantasy; it is the inner world as well as the outer. What is "I," or my *self*, is made up of continued interactions and syntheses of two worlds—the outer world (us) plus the inner (also an us) making up all the different beings that are me. I cannot live in either world alone; I can be happy only as I move from the psychological to the cognitive, to the feeling and, more recently, to the world of the soul.

The avenue to the soul is through those signals that say something is awry (Hillman, 1975). Pathology labelled (all societies label) can lead us if we search to reach the big question of life and to see life as a quest and a growth, a continuous process of mediating all these processes of the inner and outer "us," synthesizing and integrating them into a whole. And when a problem, there is the need to start again with a new look and to search for that with which we have lost touch.

I seem to be using *touch* over and over again—to be in touch, close touch. Touch is a part of living. Montague shows how touching aids life within animals and humans. Touch may be a voice, a feeling, or a contact. It is being there with what is.

I have been looking at our social problems and at the social future of humankind. We are at a crossroads—a crisis. All around us are a thousand signals, if we but listen. All of the other participants are focusing on specific issues. They are all important, but not for themselves alone. To worry about environment, energy, developing countries, food, or even the university and other resources disconnected from the basic underlying issues, which each has hinted at, is to continue (in the name of systems, ecology, and holistic thinking) a fragmentation of life or a disconnection from the processes and energy of life.

I ask you to turn to the other side of your brain and realize that the human uniqueness is the differentiation of function connected by the corpus callosum. It is the ability when used to operate at a capacity far beyond what we are now using, that we call knowledge. It is synthesis, judgment, and process.

What is the bridge in our environment, in our society? What is the bridge between the processes? It is the first unknown, that higher Self to which we are all connected, as we are to all that is.

There are two issues in that bridging. One is *governance*, or the way that we can facilitate the complex interactions that occur. Governance is not just government or politics with a big "P." It is not community or networks alone. It is the values, the rules, and the way we interact, communicate, and resolve issues. It is human interaction: conscious, unconscious, and spiritual. It is what we choose to use in living fully.

I suggest that "government" is not a problem just because it is big or bureaucratic but because it has lost touch with governance of those issues that make up life. It deals with the metaphorical "tip of the iceberg." To "get back in touch" is to govern with life and growth as the criteria. Governance, by administrating tight control, always seems to be the easiest solution to the crisis. This is the way it has always been. Our challenge is governance with a chance for difference and uniqueness. It is a "family" which, to survive, must permit each person his or her own space for growth while finding that being together leads to gains for each. We have few models of such governance. One must listen, respect, and respond to all voices.

The second issue is *planning*. Planning may be our modern form of rational prayer. For prayer, as many cultures know it, is creating an "image" of what you want, finding all those things interrelated to what you want, and calling on a "higher power" for support. Prayer deviates from planning because prayer recognizes that the middle self (the cognitive rational left side of the brain) cannot reach the higher self without going through the lower self (the right brain, or what Freud in our Western tradition negated as primitive-primary process thinking). It is this latter which we enter, through getting in touch with the mindless nonthinking state, by being with nature; for some, drudgingly washing dishes, for others, meditating. True planning, an attempt to make deliberate social change, can only result from our becoming whole ourselves in our search for wholeness in the world.

Often the guru's final word after the big search (as it was with the quest for the Holy Grail) is that the search begins and ends inside—being in touch with ourselves and by being in touch with "out there." It is the I $\rightleftharpoons$ Us dialogue. It is the ambiguities, pains, solutions, nonsolutions, the strengths, weaknesses, errors, successes, health, illness, and pathology that is life.

That holiness, wholeness, and health to which our pathologies offer a door is hope in dealing with the demons of both our environments. It is that process which is our future. The challenge is whether we *live, survive,* or *die.* To die appears to be easy: to survive is more and more difficult. To live is the facility to mediate between (synthesize) the individual and the environment. That is our charge.

We are past the academic exercises of pure rationalization. We are beyond the point of controlling others and fitting time into our models. We cannot predict structures unless we want to slow down processes toward death.

How then do we achieve a future that meets our potential? I will leave you with a potential mechanism, a process. My solution is a humble one, for I gave you a statement of where *I* am. I have suggested directions for our conscious processes and I have hinted that the path is not easy.

Although I mentioned planning and governance, I can offer you no policy or sure-fire alternative in any sphere. I will warn you that if it looks simple, I would be dubious. To anything that fixes us into stagnating institutions, as with most medical care today, I am opposed.

There may be a way—an intimation of a direction. I cannot fully go "the Illich route"; but he is asking significant questions. We must, in terms of policy, move away from the professional, technical, and rational and yet not lose what we have. We must give up institutions and let them die. We must get back to programs where people can learn to command the events (internal and external) that affect their lives, community control, diversity, alternatives ("let a thousand flowers bloom"), to open up new goals, new values, and new processes.

As one such program I suggest establishing re-creation centers (Duhl, 1976b) to bring you a symbol, a Magic Mountain (Harvey, 1974). Re-creation centers (described in Chapter 9) can focus on growth toward aliveness for people within their own traditions. This is a place where one can face the "I hurt," get an aspirin (symbolically), and redirect the energy to aliveness. Unlike hospitals and medical facilities, or schools where, to be a "good patient," or "a good student" means locked into your ill and dependent status, it is a place where the pain can open any door that is right for that quest. Staffed by those who catalyze the process and know what resources might be available, for the person it is the beginning of moving toward both the inner and outer search.

Unlike the monastery or authoritarian place that offers such hope, *Magic Mountains* are places where we can explore how free people can grow in unique ways and still be part of their family and community. In no way is it meant to be a renunciation of the world, but rather a place where we can truly educate ourselves to enter into the dialogue and processes of how to govern and participate in politics and education.

It can be a place to recharge our batteries, find meaning, and even work with a discipline which tests all parts of our being. It is a home, a community, a place to come to from the world of impersonal networks in which we live. It is a place to touch the earth and find ways to be back in touch with the self-healing energies that are life.

As you can obviously see, I deeply believe that within each of us we have that potential for health and growth. Comenius and a long line of wise men have hinted at how this can be done. Re-creation, Magic Mountains of many kinds, can help us find the magic that is within us.

I have purposely stayed away from tight meanings of words. I have avoided some but not all labels, hoping that there is a chance that what I have sent forth can find an echo somewhere within you. The voices you have heard are not mine. They seem to be the voices of many people that I have touched, heard, and felt in the past few years. They speak quietly and, as in a metaphorical but true tale, they may yet be heard.

On an island off the Philippines, a group of Marquesas monkeys were observed carefully over a long period of time. One day a monkey, who was like all the others, dug up a yam for the evening meal. Instead of directly eating it, he took it to the water and washed off the dirt. On eating it he beamed, obviously pleased with his discovery. Quickly he told his spouse, brother, sister, and his mother's current boyfriend. Each learned to do the same, but it did not catch on very quickly. On no other, even distant, islands were there monkeys that washed off their yams before eating them. Years passed. One day the one-hundredth monkey learned to wash the yam before eating it. Almost instantaneously all the other monkeys on that island washed their yams. Then on the various other and distant islands all the monkeys washed their yams. How it happened no one truly knows. A critical mass perhaps was reached by that one-hundredth monkey—perhaps a form of ESP.

The moral of the story for us is that if we learn the way, and we find our one-hundredth monkey—in the voices of the poor, dispossessed, the pained, and even in our own pathologies—the New Age we hear about may come about.

This is not a prediction but an *image*, as well as an appeal to the right side of your brain—to begin!

Part II

SOME PAST PLANS
The Golden Era Revisited

Chapter 12

NEWARK—COMMUNITY OR CHAOS

A Case Study of the Medical
School Controversy[1]

This chapter is presented as a case history, an attempt to record the events and decisions surrounding the creation of the medical college in Newark out of the seeds of the New Jersey College of Medicine and Dentistry. This issue, although often cited as an underlying cause of the Newark riots in July 1967, is also illustrative of what may happen constructively when the poor and the alienated confront the system with a series of demands, and, as such, has implications that are applicable. The Newark case indicates that the Model Cities Program, in conjunction with urban renewal and other federal programs, can be one of the

---

[1]This chapter was written in the spring of 1968 and reflects concern with the early period of the development of the medical school in Newark. Many events have taken place since this writing.

As special Assistant to the Director of Housing and Urban Development and consultant ot the Assistant Secretary for Health in the Department of Health, Education and Welfare, I tried to bring the groups together. This is, in fact, my story of working with Paul Ylvisaker and others.

mechanisms for increasing the competence of both City Hall and the ghetto to deal with the complex and interlocking problems of the neighborhood and the city. It offers insights into new levels of federal, local, and interagency coordination that can make agreement possible.

The confrontation between the poor citizens threatened with displacement and City Hall clearly showed that the "urban problem" is not only the sense of alienation felt in the ghetto community but also the capacity of a local government to solve its problems. If poverty is defined as the inability to command the events that affect one's life, both City Hall and the ghetto can be described as "poor."

This case study of the proposed relocation of a medical school begins with background sketches of Newark's politics, racial composition, health, education, and housing problems. There follows a survey of the chronology of events over a 2-year period surrounding the site choice and acreage demands of the school in the face of ghetto area opposition. Interagency cooperation at federal, state, and local levels during the school's planning phases and application for funds is also depicted. The lessons of Newark are many. It is the intent here to focus on a few acts from the urban drama.

Cast of Characters

Hugh J. Addonizio	Mayor of Newark, New Jersey
Robert R. Cadmus, M.D.	President, New Jersey College of Medicine and Dentistry, Jersey City
Manuel Carballo	Assistant to commissioner, New Jersey Department of Community Affairs
Wilbur Cohen	Undersecretary, U.S. Department of Health, Education, and Welfare
Louis Danzig	Director, Newark Housing and Renewal Authority

Leonard J. Duhl, M.D.	U.S. Department of Housing and Urban Development
Ralph Dungan	Chancellor, New Jersey Board of Higher Education
Leonard Fenninger, M.D.	Director, U.S. Bureau of Health Manpower
Richard J. Hughes	Governor of the State of New Jersey
Donald Malafronte	Director, City Demonstration Agency; administrative assistant to the mayor; Model Cities director
Warren Phelan	Regional administrator, Housing and Urban Development (HUD), Philadelphia, Pennsylvania
Robert C. Weaver	Secretary, U.S. Department of Housing and Urban Development
Harry Wheeler	Chairman, Committee against Negro and Puerto Rican Removal
Junius Williams	Director, Newark Area Planning Association (NAPA)
Robert Wood	Undersecretary, U.S. Department of Housing and Urban Development
Paul Ylvisaker	Commissioner, New Jersey Department of Community Affairs

"Today, poverty and the problems of racial transition are common to most older cities, especially in the Northeast. However, there are few cities anywhere in the nation where these and other problems extend so widely and cut so deeply as in Newark, New Jersey."

This description of Newark before the summer 1967 riot, is extracted from Newark's Model Cities Program application. In this watershed urban drama, many of the nation's problems are focused and magnified. The lessons learned from the decision surrounding the location and construction of the Newark Medical College and its relation to the Model Cities Program are applicable to the problems of many of the nation's beleaguered cities.

Background Sketches

Political Problems. Newark's problems begin with the harsh reality that Newark is land poor. The Newark Standard Metropolitan Statistical Area (SMSA), consisting of Essex, Union, and Morris counties, had in 1967 a population of 1.8 million persons, making it the thirteenth largest SMSA in the nation. The city itself, however, consisted of only 24 square miles, the smallest land area among major American cities, with 25 percent of that area covered by Newark Airport, Port Newark, or uninhabitable marshlands. Furthermore, much potentially taxable city property lay fallow awaiting urban renewal development.

In fact, urban renewal programs had been limited in results because the city's redevelopment program lacked overall planning leadership. About the time of Hugh J. Addonizio's election as mayor, the local housing authority received $300 thousand (with $150 thousand later added) to draw up a Community Renewal Program (CRP), an assessment of needs in terms of long-range social, economic, and physical planning. In January 1968 the community was still awaiting the CRP. (Later there were hopes that Model Cities planning would fill some gaps in the overall redevelopment plan.)

The new mayor's statement shortly after he took office in 1963 indicated his desire to fill these gaps quickly and yet ensure that the city would not overextend itself:

> The city has bitten off more than it can chew now, with enough problems to keep the city busy for the next 20 years. I don't want to do what the previous administration did. I don't want to be placed in the position of announcing that "this is going to be done" and then find these projects are 10 years off or even longer. We can't get to what we have now. How much can the federal government allocate to Newark?

Yet in the 6 years that Addonizio had been in office, Newark applied for five new urban renewal projects totaling $63 million in federal funds, more than three-fourths of what had been earmarked prior to his administration.

The logjam was partially broken by the State Housing Finance Agency which, through cooperation with the Prudential Insurance Company of America, was undertaking construction of 270 units of cooperative housing with 500 more units scheduled. Yet one of the crucial functions for which the agency was created—the floating of bonds to raise money—had yet to be accomplished. The tax base in Newark was constricted not only due to a dearth of property but also because the finer residential neighborhoods marking the outer reaches of most major cities fell beyond the city limits. City land taxes were double the suburban rate, in many cases enticing people into the suburbs. Those remaining in the city were those least able to pay, the black poor.

Financial difficulties were heightened by the fact that Newark had reached its bonding limit. Although state law allows a city to ask the Local Finance Board in the Department of Community Affairs for permission to exceed that limit, Newark had yet to make such a request.

Simultaneous with this fiscal squeeze, Newark spent more on municipal services but received proportionately less state aid than the wealthier surrounding suburbs. The redistributive impact of federal programs similarly favored the suburbs.

The man responsible for keeping rein on spiraling expenses while keeping pace with the city's growing demand for services was the mayor. Hugh J. Addonizio, armed with a comparatively liberal voting record from 14 years in Congress, beat the Democratic machine when he defeated incumbent Leo Carlin in the 1962 mayoralty race. The characterization of Carlin's attempt at urban renewal as "Negro removal" brought Addonizio the overwhelming support of black voters. Following the election, blacks were installed in the mayor's democratic machine and were generally welcomed to Newark politics.

Of the three blacks who helped Addonizio's 1962 campaign, and who were to be given jobs in the city administration, the appointment of Harry Wheeler hit a snag. Just before his appointment as Assistant Business Administration Commissioner, a shortage was discovered in the school milk fund of which he had custody. When this news hit the front pages, Wheeler's appointment did not come through. Some blacks charged that an "Italian plot" had maneuvered the placement of that story to the front page.

More blacks were appointed to high positions in the Addonizio administration than ever before. He named the first blacks to the following positions: Budget Officer, Director of Human Rights, Executive Secretary of the Planning Board, Director of Health and Welfare, Director of the NC-NCR, School Principal, Commissioner to the Board of Adjustment, Fire Dispatcher, Police Captain, and Chairman of the Alcoholic Beverage Control Board. However, the President's Commission on Civil Disorders noted that in "the city administration Negroes are either out of touch with the ghetto community or they are dependent on the mayor for their political lives."

In fact, election laws and procedures seemed to work against political participation of the poor blacks to Newark. A 6-month residency requirement eliminated a large portion of the newly arrived black population. It was also necessary to reregister with each change of name or address. Approximately 60 percent of the potential black voters had failed to register; Office of Economic Opportunity (OEO) amendments prohibiting expenditure of OEO funds for voter registration drives did not help.

Another institutional factor that reduced non-white representation in Newark city government was the fact that the city was broken up into five wards, each with one councilman and four councilmen-at-large. This system tended to dilute the one man, one vote principle: in this case it worked against minority groups, although it was not designed to do so. The predominantly black central ward elected one representative; each of the other four wards, predominantly white, elected one representative. This gave the black committee one-fifth of the voting and bargaining power through its ward councilman. However, overriding this, the councilman-at-large system operated with a predominantly white voting population. Thus, the central ward, which appeared to have one-fifth of the political power, actually had only one-ninth of the power.

In the 1966 race, Addonizio's opponent was a black engineer, Kenneth Gibson. According to those in the know, the Addonizio victory was again won with black support, but this time it was coerced support. Welfare clients learned that a Gibson vote would strike them from the rolls. People on waiting lists for public housing or government jobs learned that their positions were related to their vote. It was also contended that Addonizio enlisted the help of "old-line machine" blacks to see to it that new black voters were allowed to register only as Democrats. Even if Gibson had had total black voting support, the financial support crucial to a campaign would still have been a problem. Newark blacks can rarely afford this kind of contribution. Gibson believed that white votes plus white money were essential and that in the next election he might be able to count on both from the white business community.

Since the 1967 summer riot, the Italian/American/black coalition that Addonizio had counted on for his political life had been deeply shaken, if not irreparably ruptured. Although Addonizio felt that he had done the best possible job, he was in the difficult position of trying to be responsive to the voting majority (white), as well as to the actual majority (black) of the city's population, with each having very different needs and aspirations.

Racial Problems.   To understand Newark's racial upheaval, one had to see it in the context of a rapidly shifting racial composition. The black population jumped from 17 percent in 1950 to 34 percent in 1960. In 1968 the percentage of blacks was approximately 63 percent. Yet blacks did not represent that much of the voting population, due to their being underage or newly arrived or so mobile that they failed to reregister—or they were just plain apathetic. Given this emerging community, with traditional avenues to power made difficult, what would the transition to power be like? On a television program shortly after the riots, one of the Student Non-Violent Coordinating Committee representatives summed up the militants' views of transition by saying: "Nobody gives up power; it has to be taken. The Italians took this city from the Irish, and the Negroes are going to have to take it from the Italians." The form of this "taking" became the crucial question for Newark and the nation.

A study sponsored by the Governor's Select Commission on

Civil Disorders showed clearly the polarization of whites and blacks. It stated: "Attitudinally whites and Negroes are in two separate worlds. On many issues related to future relations between the two groups, Negroes and whites hold almost diametrically opposed views." The survey continued:

> The majority of Negroes believe they are denied equal job opportunities, with whites overwhelmingly taking the directly opposite point of view. Similarly, most Negroes attribute their lack of progress to white discrimination, while the vast majority of whites say the cause is lack of effort by Negroes themselves. Another unpleasant fact of Negro life as they see it is the lack of adequate police protection and police brutality, which whites, for the most part, deny exists.

There was sharp disagreement among Negroes and whites on the causes of the riots. Again the study pointed out: "Young Negroes in particular say that the riots were justified, while whites, again by a wide margin, see inadequate justification for the riots."

Professor Alfred Blumrosen, of Rutgers University School of Law, stated cogently to the President's Commission on Civil Disorders: "Some of the tensions which were created in the 1960s between Negro and white communities could be analyzed as stemming from the failure of the administrators of the legal systems to press for and achieve compliance with the Constitution and statutory mandate to eliminate discrimination."

Dominick L. Spina, Director of the Newark Police Department, believed that the riot tensions were due to the large numbers of southern blacks who had brought with them their traditional hatred of the police and to the presence of a core of unemployed high school dropouts. The President's Commission on Civil Disorders, on the other hand, found the "typical" rioter to be not a recent immigrant but rather someone who had been in the city for *over 10 years*.

Health Problems.   While the city had a series of health grants to improve prenatal and hospital services, the need continued to be staggering. Newark had the highest maternal and infant mortality rates in the country. The venereal disease rate was unmatched nationally. It had the highest rate of new tuberculosis cases. Newark ranked seventh among the 10 leading cities in total number of drug addicts. The 1966 HEW Poverty Area figures painted a picture of mass suffering shown by the following disease rates per 100,000 population: tuberculosis, 86.6; syphilis, 239.3; gonorrhea, 598.5.

The Newark City Hospital, alternately referred to as the "Slaughterhouse" or "Butcherhouse," was administered by the city, but while state law required one nurse for each six to eight patients, there were only two nurses for each ward of 39 patients. To add insult to injury, an OEO study revealed that medical services and facilities in the suburban areas surrounding Newark were some of the best in the nation.

Educational Problems.   Any diagnosis of Newark's educational ills had to be in the context of a massively transient population and severe financial difficulties. One-third of the annual school population was composed of new arrivals from outside Newark, predominantly from the southern U.S., Puerto Rico, or New York City. Twenty-eight percent of the school population annually transferred out of Newark. Seventy-four percent of all Newark's school children were nonwhite. The buildings were overutilized (108 classes on part-time) and old (over half were built in the 1800s). Although the budget was regularly increased and there now was a $51 million program for new schools, the school system lacked the resources to correct these tremendous deficiencies.

It should be noted that the school system itself was the focus of tremendous community hostility in 1967, when a black was passed over for a Board of Education position, and this has often been pointed to as one of the precipitating factors in the Newark riot.

Fortunately, the crisis in the educational system produced a candor that bid to be an important step in solving the complex educational problems. Howard J. Ashby, president of the Newark Board of Education, typified this candor when he stated before the New Jersey Commission on Civil Disorders:

> Until such time as these reading levels and arithmetic levels come up, there isn't anyone in the City of Newark, professional or otherwise, who can say we are doing a good job, because these children just can't read and do arithmetic. What I want to do is put the facts on the table without any cover-up because I think this is the time to do it. I think we are going to have to call a sharp halt to all of the camouflage that has gone on for the past 10, 15, and 20 years.

It was hoped that this openness and frankness had not come too late. As a result of growing community concern, new programs were initiated in vocational counseling, counseling and training for dropouts, work study programs, teacher training, and adult education.

Employment Problems.   The educational crisis of the city contributed to the employment problems in Newark. Forty-five percent of the population in the Model City neighborhood over age twenty-five had less than an eighth-grade education. Ironically, while the major reason for dropping out of school was the need for employment, the more educated were hired first. One result of this vicious cycle was that unemployment in the ghetto area soared past the unemployment level for the total city, which in itself was twice as high as the national average. Job opportunities for the unskilled became increasingly scarce as new industries (related to transportation, distribution, and personal services) requiring less manpower and more mechanical aptitude and literacy moved in. Simultaneously, the light manufacturing industries which employ the unskilled were leaving Newark for the suburbs, to take advantage of lower taxes and land for expansion. The poor could not follow because transportation was inadequate.

It was expected that the Concentrated Employment Program, jointly sponsored by City Hall and the Community Action Agency, would find jobs for 2,000 unskilled persons from the Model Neighborhood. Unfortunately this program became bogged down in disputes concerning program coordination and responsibility. The local people felt that they had no opportunity for meaningful participation in program planning.

The racial dimensions of the problem could be appreciated by recognizing that blacks, who represented 10.5 percent of the work force, held only 3.7 percent of the white collar jobs and 20.9 percent of the blue collar jobs. Some progress was made in black employment. The mayor called for training programs and a change in the trades unions' procedures for hiring blacks, requiring that all construction work on city projects have integrated work forces.

There were a total of 13 federally and locally sponsored employment programs in Newark. Although they helped significantly, the Newark Model Cities Program application noted that some major blocks remained: personal indifference to work after dropping out of the job market, a second-generation public welfare attitude toward jobs, disbelief in the job programs, and general timidity.

The Business and Industrial Coordinating Council (BICC) was a private effort to improve the Newark employment situation. It was a voluntary organization of 200 business, labor, civil rights, and community groups aimed at all aspects of employment. Although its vital interest was first that of employment, it became involved in police-community relations and school board affairs. According to the project director of BICC, the business community was more mature in its racial attitudes than either the police or City Hall.

These programs to improve the employment situation in Newark illustrated the city's successful "grantsmanship" and a growing sensitivity to community problems. The next step, however, was for Newark to mesh its total effort to achieve city-wide objectives.

Housing Problems. No background picture of Newark circa 1967 would be complete without focusing on housing, among the most often stated causes for the summer riot. The city's Model Cities Program application describes one-third of the city's houses as substandard, giving Newark the highest percentage of substandard housing for any city of comparable size. Public housing in the Central Ward was highrise, resulting in high density. Parents complained that in such crowding it was hard for them to supervise their children and for police to do their jobs. In these crowded conditions, any minor incident could lead to a major crisis. In fact, the July riots of 1967 were triggered by a minor incident between a black cabdriver and the police across the street from a public housing project, the Hayes Homes.

Newark had an adequate housing code, inadequately enforced. It was charged that one reason for the lack of enforcement was that the real estate interests were represented by two city councilmen who were themselves real estate brokers. Furthermore, the fine for a violation was a very lenient $50 to $60.

Louis Danzig, Director of the Newark Housing and Renewal Authority, was proud of the housing programs. He told the New Jersey Commission on Civil Disorders: "Housing conditions in Newark have now been made better in recent years by means of urban renewal and the public housing program."

Newark had the largest per capita public housing program in the country: the city received $325 million in federal housing aid and urban renewal, placing it fifth nationally in receipt of urban renewal funds. The New Jersey Commission on Civil Disorders, in its findings, stated:

> It seems paradoxical that so many housing successes could be tallied on paper and in bank ledgers, with so little impact on those the program was meant to serve. The paradox stems from a widespread overemphasis on dollars sought, money appropriated, and allocated units built. Quantitative assessments have been the measure of success. In the scramble for money, the poor, who were to be the chief beneficiaries of the programs, tended to be overlooked. For many years, the major share of the benefits of housing programs has gone to middle and moderate income people. This is still the pattern in Congress, where at the end of the last session the housing interests of poor people, in the form of rent supplements and leased housing, again got short shrift.

The Medical School

It was against this frustrating background that the decisions concerning the relocation of a medical school to Newark's ghetto area were formulated.

As early as 1962 Addonizio offered the city's municipal hospital to any medical school interested in taking it over.

In January 1965, Seton Hall College's Medical School in South Orange became a state institution. The Board of Trustees of the New Jersey College of Medicine and Dentistry had determined that the costs of maintaining quality medical education were prohibitive and asked the state to take over. Shortly thereafter, the conclusion was reached that the cost of rehabilitating the Jersey City Medical Center would be almost as great as constructing a new medical complex. Thus, in April 1966, the trustees notified the Public Health Service that the school would seek matching funds for the building of a new medical complex. The Public Health Service helped with the development of these plans.

Site Selection and Acreage Debate. The City of Newark, interested in having a medical school, brought to the attention of the college administration an American Medical Association study acclaiming Newark the city with "the most advantages and the fewest disadvantages for the development of an outstanding medical college." The mayor saw the college as part of the answer to the city's massive unemployment problems, as well as a chance for more and better services for a city which, according to its own Model Cities Program application, had the highest rate of venereal disease, tuberculosis, and maternal mortality among major American cities. The college would also give the city the chance to eradicate a blighted area that was costing the city thousands of tax dollars for police and fire protection. The charge was later leveled by Harry Wheeler, chairman of the Committee Against Negro and Puerto Rican Removal, that the real reason for courting the medical school was that Addonizio wanted to disperse black political power, which was at that time turning against him, by changing the makeup of the central ward.

At all events, in June 1966, the site selection committee of the college agreed to accept the offer of the 138-acre estate of Mrs. M. Hartley Dodge in suburban, semirural Madison, New Jersey. The decision to move to the suburbs was based on a desire to have assured control and unquestioned access to acreage for future development, as well as an uneasiness about locating in a ghetto. (It should be noted, however, that the school would have been guaranteed access to land wherever it located; as a state institution it enjoyed the right of "eminent domain" and would be granted additional land if and as the need were shown.) The committee further held that the Madison location eliminated the need to relocate hundreds of families, which would be the case if construction pre-empted only 50 acres in Newark's central ward (plus the City Hospital). All that was needed to "clinch" the case for Madison, after the site committee's recommendations, was the approval of the college's six-member Board of Trustees, four of whom lived in small suburban communities. Architects were engaged to design the complex of buildings for this very large parcel of land.

According to Donald Malafronte, administrative assistant to the mayor, in his testimony to the Governor's Select Commission on Civil Disorders, City Hall received an advance copy of the site selection committee report which recommended the Madison site. The report emphasized that Newark would be an excellent location, except for the land shortage, and that 150 acres were required.

Malafronte stated:

> We got a copy of the report and said, "We have been undone here." We all sat down with a map and looked around at the area we wanted them to go into, which was Fairmount Urban Renewal Project. It worked out to 20 acres, or if we pushed it, to 30 acres, which we felt was more than sufficient for a medical school; and we still do. It was clear that we were 'hung' on their 150 acres stipulation, but we did have this rather glowing account of all the advantages of Newark.
>
> So we thought we would surprise them in this and we drew a 185-acre area which we considered to be the worst slum area. It included Fairmount and surrounding areas, which were clearly in need of renewal—and we were going to proceed with the renewal in any case for that area.
>
> We felt that in the end they would come down in their demands to 20 or 30 acres in Fairmount, or that in a battle we might have to give up some more acreage. We never felt

they would ask for 185. We felt that it was a ploy on their part.

With the benefits of hindsight—the testimony before the President's Commission on Civil Disorders and the transcript of the later hearings—it could be seen that the city intended to use the large acreage offer as bait to get the college to come to Newark, with little intention of actually delivering it. Sensing this deception, the college was reluctant to accept the Newark site.

In November of 1966, the State Senate requested the College's Board of Trustees to conduct public hearings. At these hearings Louis Danzig, director of the Newark Housing and Renewal Authority for 18 years, testified that the land could be quickly provided for the college by condemnation. He also testified that "buffer zones . . . can be readily established to take away the fear of the surrounding areas." The Housing Authority handles public housing, urban renewal, and redevelopment. This dual role of Danzig made it possible, if not precisely proper, for him to promise the protective "buffer zones."

Part of the city's offer included sections of the Fairmount Urban Renewal Project area which had been slated for low and middle income housing. As the NAACP brief later stated, "At the time of making these commitments, the Newark Housing and Renewal Authority had not applied to change the Fairmount Urban Renewal Plan, although the plan had called for residential development of a large portion of this land and federal funds for the acquisition of land had been provided pursuant to that plan."

The pressure for a Newark site location was intense.   This pressure was generated from Essex County's 13-member Democratic legislative delegation as well as from the governor's office. Support for the Newark site had come from a wide spectrum of organizations: medical, civic, educational, religious, business organizations, and municipalities. The local papers pushed the city's case. Dr. Leroy E. Burney, former Surgeon General of the U.S. Public Health Service, stated that medical schools in general belong in the urban areas rather than in suburbia. The Regional Plan Association's New Jersey Committee urged the Board of Trustees "to choose a central city location to serve the best interests of the school and of regional development" and later urged a reduction in the acreage requested. Paul Ylvisaker, Commissioner of the New Jersey Department of Community Affairs, also called for smaller acreage in the Newark site.

In June 1967, as a result of the tremendous pressures exerted on the board, the medical college had agreed to come to Newark provided that the city would produce 50 acres by March 1968 and an additional 100 acres on 18 months notice. When the city had asked the college to pinpoint the area for its first 50 acres, the request was not for cleared land but for 50 acres in the predominantly Negro central ward across from cleared land. In reviewing this controversy, Malafronte stated before the New Jersey Commission on Civil Disorders:

> To us, this was a slap in the face. . . . It was our opinion that they were attempting to get out of the situation in which they found themselves, which was an aroused public demand that they come to Newark. . . . What they said they wanted was across the street from cleared land. This to us was insanity and enraging because they knew this was not an urban renewal area. They knew that the urban renewal process takes three years and perhaps five.

Despite the frustrating demands of the New Jersey College of Medicine and Dentistry, the city moved quickly toward actualizing the project. Title searches and appraisals of the 500 properties in the initial 50-acre site were begun. Within 3 months the legislature had passed bills which would enable the city to:

1. Float a $15 million bond issue for the purpose of acquiring property, an expenditure that would not be charged against the city's bonded debt ceiling;
2. Take land quickly by condemnation while not jeopardizing the rights of property owners to appeal;
3. Bind future city councils to any agreements made concerning the medical school by the present city council;
4. Pay part of the moving expenses of shops and other small businesses;
5. Give property owners more time to relocate.

By May 25, 1967, the city council had voted to accept the contract, and on May 26 it was signed by the trustees. It was agreed to pay $17,424 an acre, the lowest cost yet offered to a redeveloper in the city. Construction was to begin on April 15, 1968.

The "Medical School" decision incensed the Negroes, according to the President's Commission on Civil Disorders. A sense of outrage and anger about the decision spawned the creation of two important organizations prior to the riot: the Newark Area Planning Association (NAPA) and the Committee against Negro and Puerto Rican Removal (the Committee). Both wanted the size of the medical school site drastically reduced. NAPA, headed by third-year Yale law student Junius Williams, pushed for legal solutions. NAACP financed the legal brief, written with the help of NAPA. The Committee, led by Harry Wheeler, a teacher in the public school system of Newark, pushed for administrative solutions, by pressuring HUD and HEW officialdom. Neither group was broadly based. Their protest made little headway until the July riots demonstrated the explosiveness of the problem. Although the medical school issue was by no means the only volatile problem in Newark, it helped create the atmosphere in which only a spark was needed to kindle the riot fire in July.

The existence of the New Jersey Department of Community Affairs gave the state some creative points of leverage. This cabinet-level department had been created on the premise that modern community problems could no longer be met by local and county governments acting alone. The department's major role had been active support of local communities in human and physical renewal programs. The state agency designated by the governor to coordinate Model Cities efforts, it was closely involved with the OEO program of the state. In the Newark medical school issue, the Department used its funds, expertise, and "good offices" to bring about confrontation, dialogue, and finally negotiations between the warring parties.

Paul Ylvisaker, Commissioner of Community Affairs of New Jersey, played a crucial role in reestablishing communication between the city administration and the blacks following the uprising. On the second day of the riot he was sounding out black leaders to learn their grievances. He convinced Governor Richard J. Hughes that resolution of the medical school question could forge a new and healthier middle ground between the blacks and the power structure. His belief was: "We have to develop a process of collective bargaining between the present power structure and the Negroes . . ., a process not dissimilar to labor bargaining with management."

After months of talking, Ylvisaker was able to convince some of the more militant black leaders of his sincerity and of their potential leverage. Junius Williams of NAPA contacted Mike Davidson of the NAACP Legal Defense Fund, and they conducted careful research on possible avenues for a legal challenge to the medical school proposal.

At this point the U.S. Department of Housing and Urban Development (HUD) became deeply involved in the medical school issue because of its commitment to both the new national urban renewal goals and Model Cities requirements. Both were being sidestepped in Newark. HUD's newly stated national goals for urban renewal indicated that priority would be given to projects that would (a) provide housing for low and moderate income families, or (b) provide employment for residents, or (c) meet critical, urgent needs. Clearly, the medical college's project in its original form decreased the housing supply and provided no safeguards to ensure employment for residents.

The Newark Model Cities application, drafted in the spring of 1967, committing the city to comprehensive integrated planning in that area, had mentioned the medical school and its program in the following ways:

> The primary goal in improving health services in the Model Neighborhood area is to evolve a relationship with the new Medical School whereby the School will become the major stimulus in bringing about quality service, a new quantity of services, and new kinds of service previously not available.

The application continues in these glowing terms:

> It will be a primary goal of the physical development of the Model Neighborhood to provide a site so that the School may build the modern teaching and community service facilities to which it has committed itself.

The difference between these statements and the medical college's application to HEW for funds was glaring. The HEW application did not indicate a similar thrust toward the school's involvement with the neighborhood. HUD officialdom, with the prodding of an NAACP brief on the issue, decided to take the city at its word as stated in the Model Cities application.

Second, the Model Cities Program required citizen participation by neighborhood residents. The HUD Model Cities evaluation team found the input of the residents in planning extremely limited and the chances for future meaningful involvement marginal. There was little doubt that Donald Malafronte, in his double role of director of the City Demonstration Agency and administrative assistant to the mayor, could write a work program that looked good on the surface. But the needed dialogue between City Hall and the Model Neighborhood residents was tragically missing. This became clear as the interdepartmental review teams made judgments about Newark's capability to deliver. The review teams worried about City Hall's seeming reluctance to approach and deal with the real leaders of the grassroots. The citizen participation mechanism was repeatedly indicted for its failure to give target residents a role in the decision making structure. The capacity of the Model Cities Program to increase the competence of citizens to solve their problems by dealing with City Hall rather than bypassing it was being tested here.

On November 30, 1967, the NAACP wired a complaint to HUD Secretary Robert C. Weaver regarding an alleged HUD decision that no hearing was needed on the amendment of the Fairmount Urban Renewal Project (redesignating 11.5 acres to permit the construction of the medical school). HUD responded on December 8 that the review of the Fairmount project was still in process, that no decision had been made about a public hearing, and that no plans would be approved until "all outstanding questions . . . on the entire medical school complex" had been satisfactorily resolved. Counterpressure was exerted by the college's board of trustees who, on December 7, had issued an ultimatum to the city and the Newark Housing Authority to deliver 11.5 acres to the school by December 31. Pressure mounted further as the NAACP filed a formal complaint on December 19 asking HUD to reject the medical college renewal plan on the grounds that (1) the college site was unreasonably large, (2) Newark lacked adequate relocation housing, and (3) the college had not indicated an interest in meeting the health needs of the community, thus failing to satisfy the requirement of the Demonstration Cities Act.

Paul Ylvisaker's previous relationship, as New Jersey Commissioner of Community Affairs, with HUD officialdom, particularly with Undersecretary Robert Wood, played an important role here. He asked both Wood and Secretary Weaver (with whom he had worked while a vice president for The Ford Foundation) to give the complaint serious attention, and he began sounding out HEW on the matter as well. They discovered that although the Housing Authority promised the Fairmount Urban Renewal acreage to the college in June 1967, its amendatory application of September 1967 still indicated that sections of that land were to be used for residential and commercial development. The Newark Housing Authority contended that the amendment was minor and would not, therefore, require a public hearing.

A quick survey by a now alerted HEW revealed that no urban medical school on record used that large an acreage and that there was no correlation between acreage and size of student body or quality of medical education. In the face of such opposition, the college's acreage demands began to waver — then decrease to 98 acres — with a succession of deadlines stated, then withdrawn, as each deadline passed. The college, which had been reluctant to take the Newark site, felt itself the helpless victim of bureaucratic red tape and local power plays. On the other hand, the deadlines that the college delivered as ultimatums were seen by government officials as a bluff. It appeared that Robert R. Cadmus, M.D., President of the New Jersey College of Medicine and Dentistry, was not really a free man, for his career was at stake here. It became evident that decision making must not be left to peers, but required escalation to a higher level, in the face of the urgency of the problems and the magnitude of the opportunities.

It was here that I was able to play a critical role in the escalating process because, as a commissioned officer in the U.S. Public Health Service (PHS) and as a member of the Secretary's staff at HUD, I had a clear relationship with the two major federal camps. In this role I helped the departments to see their relationship to each other. I met with Philip R. Lee, Assistant Secretary for Health and Scientific Affairs, and various members of the PHS, as well as with HUD Undersecretary Wood, to brief these men on developments and to start discussions concerning the two departments' relationships to the medical college project. The new Center for Community Planning, charged with coordinating all of HEW's Model Cities involvement, also played a crucial role in the discussions that followed. As a result of this dialogue, Undersecretary Wood decided not to act on a sign-off on the Newark medical school project before consulting Undersecretary Wilbur Cohen at the U.S. Department of Health, Education, and Welfare.

Interagency Cooperation in Evaluating the Project. From January 3-5, 1968, the Public Health Service held a site visit prior to HEW's funding decision, shattering all precedent by including, for the first time, observers from HUD. The traditional purpose of PHS site visits is to allow a new college's research library, medical, and dental plans to be viewed by medical experts in these particular fields. The question before the site visitor has always been, "Will these plans produce quality medical manpower?" Each of the 50 members of the Newark site visit team reviewed a particular part of the College's proposed operation. The Division of Physical Manpower (from PHS) assessed the educational program, the capability of the faculty and student body, and the educational facilities for the medical and dental schools. The Division of Health Research Facilities and Resources of the National Institutes of Health assessed the research component. The National Library of Medicine appraised the plans for the library. There were also four observers from HUD, one observer from the Surgeon General's office, and one observer from the Office of the Secretary, HEW (Individual and Family Services). These observers were not allowed to speak, but their presence indicated a new dimension in interagency cooperation. The departments wanted to avoid the problem of one agency's deciding to fund and the other's refusing, thus presenting the college with the problem of having money for building granted by HEW, but no land relinquished from HUD, or vice versa. It was hoped that joint criteria for funding could be formulated—or at least criteria that would not be mutually exclusive. This was some of the thinking behind the decision to allow HUD observers to take part in the site visit.

The Surgeon General also recognized the unusual nature of the case by granting permission to neighborhood representatives to attend the site visit: Mr. Davidson, NAACP attorney; Junius Williams, NAPA; Mr. Marshall, Committee Against the Removal of Negroes and Puerto Ricans; and Mr. Rabin, a planner-architect.

The site tour visit included a bus tour of Newark City Hospital and the Veterans Hospital in East Orange (also run by the medical school). Although no one left the bus at any time, there was some anxiety that the presence of the site visitors might be inflammatory to the community. After the tour there were presentations by the mayor, State Treasurer John A. Kervick, and Chancellor of Higher Education for New Jersey, Ralph Dungan. All spoke in favor of the Newark site. Representatives of the New Jersey College's medical and dental schools, the library, and the architectural firm also made presentations. Each community representative also was given 5 minutes to speak. Some spoke in favor of a smaller site for the school and wanted guarantees that the neighborhood residents would gain employment during the school's construction. Others questioned whether the city would relocate the families displaced by the school. Attorney Davidson of the NAACP stated that nothing he had heard at the meeting justified the need for 98.2 acres, but that he did see a figure in the neighborhood of 46 acres justified. He wanted to know where he should go to get a definite answer to this question. After an embarrassing pause he was informed that these concerns would be communicated to HEW and HUD. The remainder of the site visit took place in Jersey City, including conferences with appropriate college officials, the Division of Physician Manpower, the Division of Health Research Facilities and Resources, the National Institute of Dental Health, and the National Library of Medicine.

To HUD observer Frank Haas, it appeared that the site visitors and consultants from distant universities and hospitals were treating the medical college as a routine request for HEW assistance ("any community problems were considered HUD's concern") with little bearing on the grant decision. The college appeared to view the criticism from the community as a threat to its primary responsibility of providing general medical education for New Jersey.

The whole question of what *is* medical education came into play here. The college perceived the function of medical education in classical terms—producing doctors. Given this perspective, the ills of the ghetto are viewed in nonmedical terms; to classical medical research, housing, relocation, and land use problems are unrelated to producing good medical men. This framework also implies that the medical profession is the only group competent to make decisions about medical education; all others, be they outsiders from HUD or the community, pose a threat to good education. The distant perspective of the community is expressed by Robert Curvin of the Congress of Racial Equality (CORE): "Nonprofessional people certainly have the ability to organize themselves; and if they don't know the technical matters, they have the ability and the insight to get adequate and competent consultants to explain these technical matters to them."

Following the site visit, a HEW-HUD letter setting forth joint criteria for funding in this case was sent to Governor Richard J. Hughes. Leonard Fenninger, M.D., Director of the U.S. Bureau of Health Manpower, drafted background material for discussions between HUD Undersecretary Wood and HEW Undersecretary Cohen and for the letter to Governor Hughes. The contents of that letter were cleared by the site visitors, HEW, and HUD. The draft was read to a group of HUD and HEW officials which included John A. Kervick, State Treasurer; Ralph Dungan, Chancellor of Higher Education; Paul Ylvisaker; and other representatives of the governor. The letter was modified to clarify responses to questions raised by the governor's representatives, and the college officials were also briefed on pertinent details.

The Wood-Cohen Criteria.   The letter required that in order for the medical college plans to be approved, certain criteria must be met.

1.   The size of the site must be resolved in terms of the Model Cities Act and of the social impact of the amount of land removed from residential use.

2. Construction and operation of the Medical School must bring about increased medical services to the neighborhood.
3. Medical school and City Demonstration Agency representatives must meet with neighborhood representatives to solve any differences.
4. Relocation plans must be developed to meet the needs of the neighborhood residents.
5. The construction period must yield jobs for residents.
6. There must be training of neighborhood residents in health fields.
7. Further long-range planning for additional facilities must necessarily be linked to the Model Cities Program.

These requirements radically enlarged the original medical college proposals, which had included no plans for training neighborhood residents and little or no outpatient facilities. Not only the plans but the college's vision of itself in the community was being altered. The college's very existence now hinged on what had previously been peripheral to the interests of medical education: housing, employment, and citizen participation.

Prior to the sending of the letter, Special Assistant to the President Joseph Califano discussed the Wood-Cohen letter with Cohen at HEW. Califano precipitately telephoned Governor Hughes telling him that the medical school proposal had been approved without mentioning the conditions of the Wood-Cohen letter. Actually, approval of the medical school project hinged on City Hall, local residents, and federal and state representatives who must reach substantial agreement on the terms of the letter. Unaware of these express terms, Governor Hughes set the machinery in motion for the execution of the project. The *New York Times* carried the story. The community was angered at what was apparently a disregard of its concerns. HUD, HEW, and state officials held an emergency huddle to straighten out the signals.

The letter was finally sent to the governor on January 10, 1968, and he immediately released it to the press, clarifying the previous misunderstanding. The letter has since been heralded as a major turning point by the governor, the city, HUD, and

HEW officials. In the words of Dr. Fenninger of the Bureau of Manpower, "It doesn't duck the issues but it doesn't promise anything that can't be promised. It simply outlines what has to be done in order to have some kind of action taken."

Community and College Officials Negotiate.   On January 26, HUD Secretary Weaver met with Governor Hughes. Also in attendance at this meeting were Warren Phelan, HUD regional administrator in Philadelphia; Paul Ylvisaker; Steve Farber, administrative assistant to the governor; and Joseph Freitas, HUD White House Fellow. The central issue was a letter that the HUD regional office intended to send to Louis Danzig, director, Newark Housing and Renewal Authority. The letter provided that HUD would approve conveyance of an 11.5-acre plot to the college following redesignation of the plot from residential- to public-use zoning classification at a January 31 public hearing, *and* provided agreement could be reached among community groups, the City of Newark, and the medical college on the conditions of the Wood-Cohen letter. The letter outlined that the second plot (46 acres) would proceed through normal renewal processes. HUD Secretary Weaver agreed to the letter.

Phelan, looking back on the medical college controversy, sees this as having been a crucial move. It forced the parties involved to start the process of working toward agreement on the seven points of the Wood-Cohen letter. It also closed the issue of whether or not there would be a medical school in Newark and set the stage for the 46-acre hearing. But it still gave HUD room to maneuver, because New Jersey State Treasurer John Kervick made it clear that no state funds would be authorized until there was HUD approval on both the 11.5-acre *and* the 46-acre sites.

Nevertheless, the Board of Trustees of the college and the community groups soon reached an impasse. The Board of Trustees and President Robert R. Cadmus questioned the legitimacy of the community "spokesmen." Three persons previously introduced claimed to be the "spokesmen" and negotiating team for the community: Mike Davidson of the NAACP Legal Defense Fund, Junius Williams of the Newark Area Planning Association, and Harry Wheeler of the Committee Against Negro and Puerto Rican Removal.

Dr. Cadmus felt that this negotiating team saw itself as bearing the "imprimatur of HUD" as the accepted representatives of the community and that their every demand had to be satisfied before the land would become available from HUD. In a conversation with Fenninger, Cadmus quoted one member of the negotiating team as saying, "We've got HUD in our hip pocket."

But Cadmus was most incensed that people who knew nothing about medical education apparently wished to dictate what the educational programs were going to be. President Cadmus and the Board of Trustees chairman walked out of an early meeting with this "community" team, alleging that they now wanted the college to limit itself to 17 acres (when the Board had agreed to the 57-acre limitation) and were demanding a position on the Board of Trustees and a say in hiring of faculty and structure of the curriculum. Adding to these tensions was the fact that Cadmus perceived that New Jersey Commissioner for Community Affairs Ylvisaker had sided with the community vis-à-vis the medical school. In the midst of this, Cadmus was getting more and more pressure from students who had decided that the wisest course was to transfer to other schools. In Dr. Fenninger's words, ". . . all the things that precipitated the crisis in December (1967, prior to the Wood-Cohen letter) were now back."

Fenninger felt that medical schools of the future would not want to locate in urban areas if it meant this kind of interference from the community. Fenninger argued that the community representatives did not have "any interest in the school as a school" but saw it as "a device to gain power and they have the backing of HUD to do so." At this point Fenninger felt that the medical school plan for Newark could fold in the midst of this "power struggle." He was irritated that no one from the medical college (no one "negotiating for the college's survival") was sent a copy of the HUD regional office letter to Louis Danzig clarifying the implications of the Wood-Cohen letter. This added fuel to his feeling that the medical school was being used as a pawn. Fenninger felt that at this point "the governor and the government of Newark had to decide who was the community that was represented by whom and transmit that judgment to HUD." Fenninger argued: "The governor is going to have to make the judgment as to whether or not the school is more important in that location or other factors in that area are more important."

Fenninger believed that the crisis could have been avoided by requiring some additional information when the New Jersey College of Medicine and Dentistry originally applied for building money to relocate in Newark: for example, what planning groups had been used, what kinds of information had been exchanged, what were the expectations of the community relative to the medical school, what understanding had the community been given about the role of the medical school. Such changes in the application then were brought under consideration. A second step toward avoiding the slipshod, Newark-type plan first proposed was the Health Professions Educational Assistance Act providing project money to plan medical schools with a view toward total community needs.

Ylvisaker, concerned about the impasse between the Medical School and the community's negotiating team, suggested to the governor a series of public meetings to hear other elements in the community. Many local groups, feeling that nothing could be done until agreement was reached on the Wood-Cohen letter, had not participated in the public hearing on the 11.5-acre site. It was advisable to get the pulse of this larger community regarding the seven points of the Wood-Cohen letter. Representatives of the responsible federal agencies would be asked to assess this feeling and to make judgments on the issues of agreement, approval of the 11.5-acre and 46-acre sites, as well as the PHS application. The state had to trigger a mechanism for agreement soon or the college's Board of Trustees would be likely to recommend that the college abandon the Newark site.

However, at the first community meeting held in the second week of February 1968, the community reaffirmed Williams and Wheeler as its representatives in the negotiating process. Also delegated by the community were two men from NAPA; two more from the Committee, Reverend Sharper of the United Freedom Party and the Abyssinian Baptist Church; Duke Moore, UCC Director of Technical Assistance; and Oliver Loughten, the Newark Legal Services Project (OEO-funded). The question of who was to represent the community had finally been answered. Nonetheless, as pointed out by Ylvisaker's assistant in the New Jersey Department of Community Affairs, Manuel Carballo, the question remained as to *which segment* of the community this group represented.

That HUD representatives were not present rankled with the state, for at this first meeting the community had questions about HUD policies and plans for Newark. In Carballo's words, it was "rather ridiculous for HUD to insist on community participation and yet not be a part of it." HUD's Region II director Warren Phelan had refused to send a representative from the Philadelphia office because he did not want the Department put into the position of having to make decisions on the spot. Phelan later remarked, "I like to be where I can fend and think. I like to put staff out on the front line so that they have room to maneuver by saying, 'Let me check with Phelan.' " It should be noted, however, that a HUD official was present at all subsequent meetings.

The parties involved in the subsequent negotiations were: (1) the *"negotiating team"* of nine blacks determined that the black community have leverage in the planning; (2) the college, represented by *Dr. Cadmus*, who had reluctantly chosen the Newark site and now faced the prospect of losing his faculty and accreditation because of delays in the negotiating process; (3) *Louis Danzig* of the Newark Housing and Renewal Authority; (4) *Ralph Dungan*, acting as mediator in his capacity as Chancellor of New Jersey's Board of Higher Education. The mayor did not attend the sessions but was represented by his assistant and Model Cities Director, *Donald Malafronte*. Last, always in the wings, were the *HUD* and *HEW* officials who provided technical and procedural advice and counsel.

In negotiating agreement over the Wood-Cohen letter, community meetings followed informal technical meetings. Here the community, state, and local people met with experts in housing, medicine, Model Cities, and labor and hammered out issues and positions to be presented at the open community meetings. Using this procedure, the group approached understanding and agreement to a degree that Carballo felt there was sufficient accord on acreage, health services, and employment to schedule public hearings. When advance notice requirements would put off the public hearings for 17 days, Carballo suggested that the interim period could be used to further resolve issues. The state was anxious to have the hearing as soon as possible because of the medical college construction schedule.

According to Carballo, the main obstruction at this point was HUD's apparent unwillingness to commit itself to anything, specifically relocation. Carballo said that the state knew through informal channels that HUD had, in fact, finished its relocation study and that they were "sitting" on it until Secretary Weaver could review it. Carballo realized that Danzig was ready to agree to a reasonable relocation program with staging and rent supplement provisions, but HUD was not there with the relocation study. Thus the momentum toward final agreement was slowed.

The perceptions of these events by NAPA's Junius Williams, a member of the community's negotiating team, differ drastically from those of Carballo. Williams saw Danzig as the person tying up the relocation report by not making all the necessary information available to Charles Beckett of the HUD regional office relocation staff. Williams also felt that the state was attempting to rush them into public hearings prematurely. He insisted that he and the community needed more time to digest the information on community health programs submitted by Paul O'Rourke of East Palo Alto and Alvin Conway of Knickerbocker Hospital in New York City. Williams felt that he had finally convinced the community that the proximity of a medical school did not necessarily mean good health and that it was imperative to have guarantees from the college concerning its relationship to the community. For example, he demanded assurances from Cadmus that there would not be a situation like that at the Veteran's Administration Hospital in East Orange where the hospital was run by the medical school with very few blacks on the staff. Cadmus denied the possibility.

There were more tumultuous meetings, with the fate of the medical college, the community, and the Model Cities structure hanging in the balance. Sometimes the tumult grew out of the frustration of trying to make governmental structures responsive and responsible to the central ward residents. Junius Williams summed up the lack of communication and clarity neatly:

> It seems that throughout this process . . . there is never
> anybody to blame. We come from the community and we

> ask a specific question. You, who are supposedly represent-
> ing the powers that be, always say, "Let's be reasonable."
> We make a specific request; then the people who are sup-
> posed to be representing the power structure say, "It is not
> our fault that such and such exists."

Sometimes the crisis was the result of one black community
member's anger at the militance or lack of it in another:

> We have been fighting for houses and schools, all of us,
> a long time and not one of you came out and said one word
> for it. Why come tonight and say something?

Sometimes Dr. Cadmus' view of the medical school vis-à-vis the
community was the focus of angry outbursts. On one occasion
Cadmus exploded:

> There is no argument whatsoever that vertical con-
> struction (of the medical college) is recommended, includ-
> ing Mr. Danzig—if he knew what he was talking about. He
> is not the expert, so don't get your authority from that
> source. The experts have said that the planning we have
> presented to the federal government is one of the best
> plans they have seen, and I don't think that they would like
> to see it packaged so that quality education and quality per-
> formance . . . can be ignored.

Danzig responded in kind:

> So long as you got personal, I have to respond in a
> somewhat personal nature. This whole issue would never
> have arisen if these people had stayed out of my business,
> which is land and its use in the urban scene—about which
> Dr. Cadmus knows nothing.

Pat Girders, architect and city planner from Yale University,
commented further:

> . . . it would be a mistake in this kind of session to treat
> experts . . . as if this were some kind of magical or holy

thing. . . . I know enough about the medical profession to know that there is a jargon; it takes a while to learn a great number of things about it, but there is nothing holy about it. The policies for these kinds of decisions . . . can be made here. Policy decisions don't need to be made by experts. . . . The medical center can be done on less acreage than we are talking about.

Sometimes Malafronte, in his role as director of Newark's Model Cities Program, inspired the wrath of the community with his proposals for a community task force on Model Cities. One community member bluntly stated:

I'm not too sure I'm satisfied with Mr. Malafronte as the head of the Model Cities Program. I go a step further than that. I am not sure the community is going to accept you.

Reverend Sharper carried the criticism to all of City Hall:

In spite of the fact that the governor of this state would appoint a reasonable committee of individuals . . . they (Malafronte and the mayor) come up with the recommendation that undermines (our confidence) . . ., if there was any confidence on the part of . . . this community in the administration of this city. In fact, we have no respect for City Hall at all. It is just there. It is not even a shell of anything that has any integrity in it where we are concerned.

When tempers flared around the housing relocation issue, the anger of ghetto residents was directed at Danzig by spokesman Junius Williams:

For those of you new in the session, you are getting indoctrinated in the whole process. Number one, you can't talk because Mr. Danzig talks; number two, he has been successful in making something that is very simple into a confused mirage. (We say) 54 acres of land is necessary to house the people that are going to be dislocated and somebody is going to have to find all that land. It is just like that. Until that happens, there shall be no medical school.

Sometimes a confused community resident living on the proposed medical school site, bewildered by it all, did not know which person to believe:

> We have been told all last year from June up until October from City Hall that they would be prepared to pay us for the property so we could move out. Now, we don't know who we are to believe."

Yet out of this chaos came agreement. On March 1, 1968, what had seemed impossible 2 months earlier was, in fact, accomplished. All parties involved in the negotiating process agreed that "substantial progress" had been made toward settling the issues of the Wood-Cohen letter and that this "progress" was sufficient to permit the scheduling of public hearings. The hearing would be canceled if progress did not develop into "substantial agreement" prior to the hearing date. By March 15, "substantial agreement" had been hammered out, the hearing proceeded, and the resulting agreements were heralded by HUD Secretary Weaver as a "beginning solution to a highly complex and controversial situation."

The areas of agreement emerging from these hearings were as follows:

I. *Acreage*

The blacks had wanted only 17 acres for the medical school, hiring architects to back up their point. They eventually agreed to 57.9 acres.

II. *Health Service, Employment, and Training*

The medical school agreed to upgrade the services and facilities of City Hospital and to implement a comprehensive community health services program subject to review and recommendation by the community health council.

III. *Relocation*

The State of New Jersey pledged that demolition and construction on the 46-acre site would be staged in a manner not to displace any individual or family until satisfactory relocation accommodations could be found. Those families who could not be otherwise relocated would receive rent supplements through the New Jersey Department of Community Affairs.

IV. *Medical School Construction*

A major objective of all parties was the assurance of employment opportunity for minority group members on the construction site. It was agreed that there would be significant representation of minority groups in each trade, with at least one-third of all journeymen and one-half of all apprentices in each trade being drawn from minority groups.

V. *Model Cities*

The federal regulations relating to the Model Cities Program would be rigidly adhered to by the Newark City Demonstration Agency. An ad hoc committee of community representatives was formed to serve as the catalyst in developing a broad-based community group to serve as the vehicle for community participation under the Model Cities guidelines. The composition of this group was to be decided through community elections. They would have a joint veto over the programs developed and administered by the City Demonstration Agency and would have the power to call for public hearings.

VI. *Housing Construction*

A Citizens Housing Council, representing the community, was named to work with a task force in planning for Newark's housing needs. The Newark Housing Authority agreed to convey 52 acres of land to nonprofit community-based housing corporations for housing.

These agreements were cheered by all parties involved. These are some of the reactions:

Paul Ylvisaker

> If this becomes the procedure to be followed by the rest of the nation, we're going to be able to lick the problem of the cities.

Donald Malafronte

> If we can continue this we will be able to hold this city to-
> gether.

Harry Wheeler

> It is the Magna Carta of Newark. . . . For the first time the
> people had a voice in making policy that affected them . . .;
> it gave the black community a feeling of being somebody.

Dr. Cadmus considered the blacks' demands reasonable and is reported to have said:

> We got clobbered. The summer of 1967 changed the
> rules. Before, we simply looked at our goal as building a
> medical school. We said the problems of housing, jobs, and
> relocation were the real problems but we can't do anything
> about them. Then we learned we could involve those peo-
> ple who could do something.

Behind the Scenes

How, given the complexities, the tensions, and the distrust,
was agreement possible? It appears that a contributing factor
was an informal network set up among key decision makers in
HUD, HEW, Community Relations Services (CRS), the New Jersey Department of Community Affairs, leaders of the central
ward, and City Hall. The Wood-Cohen letter set the stage for
this network of players. The fact that some of the players had
worked together previously facilitated the game. No figure
emerged as the protagonist; the network remained more important than any of its members. Each player had his own
sphere—housing, relocation, medical care, citizen participation—with the boundaries set at his city, his agency, his department, or his office. At crucial points, these spheres intersected
and linkages occurred. HUD worked in tandem with HEW, co-
ordinated closely with its own regional office (which served as a
primary funnel for information concerning state, city, and com-

munity efforts), and kept tabs on the needs of City Hall. The community groups established links with CRS, Ylvisaker's Department of Community Affairs, Yale University students and faculty, and HUD's Model Cities team; from each of these came technical assistance. The City of Newark found its fate intricately bound up with that of the medical school, the residents of the black central ward, and the Departments of HEW and HUD. In sum, as a result of the negotiations, people and institutions became aware that the welfare of the "turf" of each was dependent upon the welfare of the "turf" of all.

Later Scenes

The story did not end there, however. The real tests lay in implementation and follow-through. Several problems remained:

A frightened white community organized vigilante groups to "protect our families and homes."

The Advisory Council of the U.S. Public Health Service elected to defer a decision on funding the medical school until June 1968.

The Department of Transportation had not worked out highway plans in the neighborhood consistent with the HUD-HEW conditions for funding.

The black community itself continued to bicker about who represented whom.

City elections to choose the permanent citizens' participation structure were held amid charges of fraud. The elections were not accepted by the city and proved embarrassing to HUD. Since HUD planned to make Newark a second-round city of approvals in the Model Cities Program, the questionable elections could be thrown out, with the city still to work out a viable relationship with the Negro residents of the Central Ward.

Although the stir of crisis no longer charged the federal bureaucracies and the tendency in retrospect was to view the whole crisis as a clash of conflicting personalities rather than of unresponsive structures, the Newark medical school story illuminated several important areas:

1. The interrelatedness of federal programs operating in a specific case.
2. The importance of cooperative relationships between the federal agencies (HUD-HEW) and the state officials.
3. The importance of meeting social needs in a community as a prerequisite for land utilization under an urban renewal program.
4. The usefulness of a program such as Model Cities as a coordinating force to pull together diverse activities in a given area.

The events in Newark outlined in this case study continue to have relevance within a much broader context—that of major social change within the United States. Although the focal point of concern was a medical school, the issues of blacks, the poor, and all others who have not participated in what Hylan Lewis (at an April 1968 conference on Blacks and Minorities and Mental Health in Asilomar, CA) calls "the democratization of the spoils" serve to point up the inadequacies of many of the social institutions in our society. Confrontation with the poor has become an essential part of program making in the fields of health, education, welfare, and housing. These programs must be made more responsive to human needs, justice, and equality.

ANATOMY OF A CONFRONTATION, 1967-1968
COMMENT ON THE PRECEDING REPORT
BY ROBERT R. CADMUS, M.D.

A View from the Other Side of the Aisle

As I read the Duhl-Steetle description and interpretation of the events surrounding the decision to relocate the New Jersey College of Medicine and Dentistry to Newark and compared their account with my own observations and experiences, I was both pleased and greatly distressed by what had been written.

I was pleased because Dr. Duhl has described his own participation and the participation of other federal bureau personnel in an insightful and candid manner. This is an important contribution. It provides some necessary information and perspective for understanding both past and present events in Newark which have not been available generally. To my knowledge, this is the first time that some of the activities that occurred behind the scenes at the federal level have been stated so explicitly and publicly. At the local level, of course, we were aware of movement behind the scenes, and certainly we felt the impact of such decisions and manipulations; but often we could only *infer* the rationale of those persons who were pulling the strings at national and regional offices of HUD and HEW.

In the same context I was distressed by Leonard J. Duhl's presentation because he seems to assume that his role as a participant observer at one end of the network of decision making and interaction enables him to speak with equal authority and inside perspective about local activities, interaction, and decisions. In many ways his discussion is like the report I would expect to receive from a jet plane traveler who tries to describe what America is like after having traversed the country at 35,000 feet. Admittedly, he has had a significant view of the terrain and, if provided with binoculars, may have seen a narrow band with greater clarity. *But only on his side of the plane.* He must rely on his companions from the other side of the aisle to describe to him the other half. I regret that Dr. Duhl, whom I in no way wish to criticize personally since I wish to continue in his friendship, unwittingly has made a somewhat unilateral presentation. Nor can this be compensated adequately by a unilateral presentation from my side of the aisle. What is needed is the kind of integration which might emerge in the give-and-take of discussion, with a full sharing of experiences and a careful fitting together of a three-dimensional chronology of events. I have never really had an in-depth conversation with Dr. Duhl and have had only two very pleasant but brief chats with him *subsequent* to the preparation of his manuscript; but as this history was unfolding and as he was doing some of the things he describes and was gathering some of the documentary materials on which his discussion is built, we had no personal contact. He never talked with me, either face to face or by telephone, nor did he communicate with me in writing. I understand that he had a staff assistant visit Newark to gather some firsthand information. Unfortunately, the assistant did not contact me, either.

Much of the material he uses to describe and explain local events and local people is drawn from newspaper and news magazine sources. Since such articles generally are written under time pressures and to satisfy an employer who must sell newspapers, they are likely to be colorful and interesting to read but ordinarily are not regarded as an altogether unbiased or fully accurate source of information. Moreover, newspaper coverage extended over a long period of time is apt to be irregular, fragmentary, and crisis-oriented. This accurately describes the coverage in our case. We were in and out of the newspapers, and much interstitial material never received a wide airing. Finally, much of the newspaper commentary used by Dr. Duhl comes from persons who were committed to vested interests or who were campaigning for their own point of view.

In retrospect, I have become aware that the college probably helped to foster a one-sided and somewhat unfavorable newspaper view of itself. Rightly or wrongly, the college believed that it should not take responsibility for informing and/or convincing the citizenry of Newark of the desirability of having the college in their city. It was felt that this would be presumptuous because this was the prerogative and the task of the elected officials. It also was felt to be premature since the college was not yet located there, and, in fact, the decision to go to Newark was contingent on land availability. Furthermore, the trustees felt that the college could not win acceptance via the newspaper but rather that acceptance would come only as a result of deeds and actual performance. On principle, this position seemed reasonable. Subsequent experience, however, showed that avoidance of involvement was not altogether practical.

Probably one of the best examples of a myth which has been perpetuated because it was not challenged publicly is the myth of the so-called "demand" for 150 acres. It has been a matter of considerable sadness to me that this "paper" issue, which started with a somewhat visionary and generally structured estimate by experts of possible land requirements 50 years from now, was reified into a "demand." To both sides of the controversy it became an unfortunate battleground which often prevented rational discussion of the real and present needs for land and program.

When the decision was made to consolidate the scattered units of the college and to build a new campus somewhere in New Jersey, a variety of offers of land were received from many places throughout the state. In the early fall of 1966 the trustees held a public hearing in Trenton. At this hearing some 11 of the 21 counties presented proposals.

When the need to relocate the New Jersey College of Medicine and Dentistry was first broached, the trustees recognized that the new medical institutions in other states had not done uniformly good planning and therefore called in a panel of experts to give the board advice. The expert testimony, including references from federal publications, repeatedly stressed the fact that most urban or suburban medical programs had become landlocked and had, in effect, raised the value of the surrounding property. Then when additional land was needed, the school had been either unable to obtain it or unable to afford it. It was projected that perhaps in 50 years some 150 acres might be necessary in order to accommodate the college's space needs and to permit the building and tearing down of units, within the confines of a single tract, so as to keep current and modern. Our *immediate* needs, however, were for a site of approximately 50 acres.

From the outset, Newark was one of the most vigorous competitors. In fact, the record will show that Newark's offer kept changing so as to counter any other offer. The original offer by the City of Newark was to give the college a small, somewhat triangular piece of property in the Fairmount Urban Renewal Tract and, at the same time, to require the takeover of the Newark City Hospital but with no commitment as to the financing of indigent care. This site seemed unsuitable to us because heavy traffic boxed in the site on three sides and because there still existed in the center of this property a city school for the deaf and a church school, both of which would have been difficult to move rapidly. Newark kept raising its offer and reducing its demands. Finally, they matched, in essence, what would have been offered in other settings.

It was obvious that if we were to locate in Newark we should pivot around the Newark City Hospital. The site we asked for was adjacent to the hospital: a 46-acre superblock, chosen because of its size and location in one of the most deteriorated areas, near a limited-access federal highway and adjacent to the other state-owned academic institutions (Rutgers, Newark College of Engineering, and Essex County Community College). It also was free of some of the major traffic constrictions and building problems presented by West Market street and the Fairmount tract. At no time in our negotiations did we suggest an *immediate* need for 150 acres. There also were several alternative ways in which future development could be handled. During these discussions, Corporation Counsel for the City of Newark came up with the idea that the college was not unlike the Airport Authority which had freedom to expand *if and when expansion* were shown to be necessary and suggested that a similar provision be written into the contract.

On the surface this appeared to be a simple way of handling the problem. We agreed and passed on to what we saw as being more difficult issues. To poorly housed people in the community it appeared as a monstrous power grab. To black men and women concerned with political power it loomed as a potential for destroying a unified voting bloc. The city justified its action on the basis that it was necessary to match the suburban offer to ensure securing the college for Newark. This was publicized as a "demand" by the college. Our public silence confirmed a growing fear in the minds of many people. Our silence or, more accurately, our inability to get the newspapers to fully comprehend and to set the record straight gave credibility to the misunderstanding.

In the early days of discussion with the City of Newark it appeared that the college was talking with a government that was in contact with its people. The groups who appeared before us to present Newark's case were always a cross section of all ethnic, lay and church, business, labor, and government groups—by usual standards, apparently a representative group. Later, of course, it became quite apparent that the "establishment" did not represent the true feelings of a significant sector of the community. New spokesmen appeared, and a different pattern of communication and new working relationships had to be worked out.

Nationwide influences as well as local influences also must be considered if one is to have a truly balanced perspective on what has happened in Newark. Newark cannot be isolated so easily and precisely as Dr. Duhl seems to suggest. In the same period that the Newark riots occurred, other major cities suffered similar consequences. Protests about poor housing, inadequate health care, discriminatory practices in employment, law enforcement, education, and so on, were common issues in all these riots. History was being written rapidly. Indeed the whole of American life was changing. Confrontation coupled with demands for rights of self-determination and participation emerged in many places. A year later another round of cities felt the same social impact. Newark was not among the repeaters. Many people have asked why Newark did not riot again that second summer. Several black leaders have suggested that the "Agreements" hammered out by the community and the college were a major factor contributing to a relatively cool summer. Without question the direction taken earlier was right. That summer was still a tense, anxious time of watching. Even so, particularly in Newark, people were adjusting, learning, and growing at a fabulously rapid and joyful rate. But it would be naive and egotistic for me to suggest that the now-resolved question of the location of the college was the major difference.

Anyone who participated in the marathon public meetings and numerous caucuses that culminated in the "Agreements" rapidly became aware that spokesmen for the black community and their supporters were using the issue of the college to open for consideration such citywide and broadly political issues as housing, relocation, employment, participation in Model Cities, antipoverty planning, and wider issues. As I have indicated earlier, for a variety of reasons the city administration wanted the college very badly. One city administrator, for example, quite candidly pointed out that "when the college is relocated in Newark, it will be the fifth largest employer in the city." Furthermore, as many cities across the country also are discovering, the problems of managing a municipal hospital are tremendous. The spokesmen for the black community and their supporters saw this dilemma very clearly and simply took advantage of it. In essence, they said, "If you want this college in Newark, you are going to have to give us what we want—an opportunity to open all these issues to discussion and allow us to participate in determining the way they will be handled in the future."

When a baby is born during a thunderstorm, his birth should not be ascribed to the thunder. Social crises do create storms, thunder, and pressures. But when the storm has passed one should be very careful in deciding what is cause and what is effect. Important as the decisions directly affecting the college were, I honestly cannot say from a human point of view that they were the most important decisions being threshed out around the negotiating table. Practically, of course, all the issues and decisions were interrelated. The point is that some of the issues were more critical than others. In the same context, I also must recognize that while the college was the *focus* of tension it probably was only the most recent and dramatic symptom among many symptoms that led to what the black community in Newark has called the *rebellion*.

During this period I saw a tremendous growth and change on the part of the faculty, the trustees, and certainly myself. Although we were untrained for the tremendous social problem that was going on, we were willing to learn and to listen, to give and to take, and to have compassion. As a result, we have learned a great deal. It also was a very painful period for us. Certainly, at several points the continuity of the college was in doubt. Many leaders of the national scene felt that we could not weather the storm and would fail. In all sincerity many felt that the best solution for medical and dental education in New Jersey would be for us to fail and to let a proper, deliberate, and perhaps sheltered growth of Rutgers become the pattern for the state. Many of these leaders voiced the thought that the entire role of a health education institution was being misunderstood and that only a mediocre quality of education could emerge from the wreckage. Because the health needs of the community were so great and because of the insistence that the college would have to agree to respond to these needs it was feared that the demand for service would entirely crush educational objectives. Although many of the nation's health experts recognized and agreed that special attention had to be given to some of the sociological imperatives that were involved, they did not believe that the community or the state and federal bureaucrats who were urging the college into service roles had a real appreciation of the costs and mechanisms required to accomplish these new objectives. Many of these experts, with no experience in community affairs, confused delays in decision making with inaction or incompetence. They set deadlines convenient for their purposes but unrelated to the human needs of the people in the ghetto. Meanwhile, the processes of participatory democracy ground slowly and were harmfully tardy. In working with problems of this sort, it almost comes down to having a day shift and a night shift. Most of the people representing poor and disadvantaged groups in the community can meet with us only at night or on weekends, on their own time. Those who work in post offices and as school teachers, clerks, contractors, and so on can rarely attend a meeting before 6 or 7 o'clock in the evening. Human limits have to be respected and so progress was slow. We found few in the medical establishment able to understand and to work within this constraint.

No one should underestimate the value of confrontation, nor should it surprise anyone to find when the heat of confrontation has passed that the participants are fused in a symbiotic relationship and joined responsibility. Confrontation can be the first step to meaningful courtship. I think Dr. Duhl tends to ignore this aspect and instead has emphasized the conflict in confrontation. Perhaps I may be asking too much from him since he is writing from a distance and ended his observation and collection of data shortly after the close of the meetings which developed the "Agreements." I am sure that whenever an historian undertakes to do the case history of any true love affair he finds many little quotes, actions, reactions, ploys, and, at times, contradictory emotional human reactions which are difficult to blend into a logically consistent and constructive piece of writing. Nevertheless, a meaningful marriage often results from such a give-and-take courtship.

Although the college was in distress, there was a tremendous amount of handwriting on the wall for its future. The actual choice of Newark was neither mine nor the mayor's but properly came from the Board of Trustees. They made the choice deliberately, with understanding and vision. Duhl says at some point in his report that my "career was at stake." This phrasing misses the point. The point is that this *is* a career! A high public health official once asked me, "Bob, why do you want to go there? I wouldn't touch it with a 40-foot pole." Well, I chose this college; I welcomed its move into Newark, the home of my forefathers since 1666. My grandfather had been a carpenter in Newark and my father was born in the very area in which we were to be located. I knew its history and was distressed by its difficulty. But, knowing something of the past I also thought I could sense something of its future. Challenge as well as risk clearly were involved.

No one stayed at the college or has since joined it without recognizing that, in part, he is not only a missionary for a cause, but also that he must be sufficiently emotionally secure and dedicated so that he will not worry about his career.

There remain a few sequelae to the events reported in this case study which should be noted in assessing its value. Among these are important lessons to be learned about the role of government bureaus in social action.

I have mentioned already that many participants in these events in Newark seemed less interested in resolving problems of health and health education than they were in forcing a confrontation to change patterns of civil rights in areas such as housing, employment, education, police protection, availability of health care, and opportunities for increased participation by ghetto residents in planning programs to help the poor. I have come to believe that these issues motivated many persons holding appointive offices in various government bureaus, as they did Dr. Duhl himself, to cause them to interject themselves in our problem. To these persons the initial controversy evidently seemed to be an almost "heaven-sent" opportunity to manipulate social forces to achieve their desired social ends. Quite deliberately they used the college as a pawn.

The role of the federal government in this entire matter was one of private diplomacy and intrigue. Never were their plans or dreams discussed forthrightly with the college. It now seems clear that this kind of careful, behind-the-scenes action was required because they only had partial power. They could indicate desired goals and could stimulate initial action but they did not have power to carry through in an executive sense. They could act as gatekeepers, but once the threshold they guarded was passed, their influence was sharply reduced. In order to provide themselves with a more extended power base they needed the public confrontation nearly as much as did disadvantaged minority groups in the community.

The letter mentioned by Dr. Duhl which was signed by Secretaries Wood (HUD) and Cohen (HEW) carefully outlined the issues that would have to be opened to discussion and the nature of an acceptable resolution. It also suggested that if matters could be settled in the indicated way, it was "reasonable to assume" that favorable action in funding would be forthcoming from HEW and that HUD would be able to approve the release of land.

I do not know what tomorrow will bring in the complete evolution of the Newark scene, but there is an important lesson to be learned from this multilevel complex of interaction. To benefit from these experiences in planning for the future, one should be very much aware of the way in which decision and/or indecision may affect action and attitudes at different levels. The negotiations which led to the "Agreements" were completed in April 1968. We felt that we had accomplished what had been required by the Wood-Cohen letter. It took 14 more months, however, before our application for construction money finally was approved. This, despite the fact that our plans and application had been submitted in November 1967, 6 months before the Agreements. In the meantime, most of the land had been cleared, and some of the good feeling in the community that had been generated by the Agreements began to be lost. When hope is raised and allowed to dangle it can breed bitterness. Resentful, suspicious comments began coming from the community. There were complaints that people had been hurried needlessly from their homes and that the need for having the land had been misrepresented. Some readers may be inclined to dismiss our insistence on this point as "sour grapes," since ultimately we did receive approval. It may be instructive, however, to ask whether the brief success of the negotiations that led to the Agreements and their subsequent distribution in mimeographed form to a narrow segment of the community could be expected to offset previous attitudes and expectations about official promises, some of which had contributed to the Newark "rebellion" in the first place. Our social credibility depended on keeping our promises in timely ways, and the delay undermined our position. Although the federal personnel who played a part in this social evolution justifiably can feel proud of their accomplishment—since the construction grant, when it came, was the largest award ever made—it should be recognized that much of the social value was vitiated by the time lag.

At the present time in this country, particularly in the field of federal grants for construction, it is peer review which sets priorities and determines what shall and shall not be done. The peer review council, acting on the New Jersey College of Medicine and Dentistry's application for federal construction funds, approved the application, but felt that other schools and priorities had a legitimate claim to take precedence. In this situation two branches of government—HEW and HUD—set demands upon this college never before or never since made of others. When we accomplished what many thought was impossible, one part of the government said *yes*, and one part said *no*, and again the poor were left dangling in the middle. If bureaucrats are to use federal money to manipulate society, they should have the authority and the ability to do so along with public responsibility for the outcome. If, on the other hand, they live within a structure which uses selection by peers, then they should recognize the inflexibilities of their own system.

It is obvious that the case history of Newark is not fully written. Some of the darkest and, hopefully, some of the brightest days may still be ahead. It is of considerable note, however, that much of the current history of Newark is being written in an understanding environment of cooperation between the black community and the New Jersey college of Medicine and Dentistry. My travels in the central ward of Newark bring questions regarding jobs, housing, police, government administration, and so on. I do not pretend to know how to solve these problems. Sometimes I find I am not even competent to understand all their ramifications. I do know that it is necessary to continue to

seek for understanding. As a result, the college has become involved in more of the social and cultural activities of Newark
than has any other medical program in this country to my knowledge.

The title of the Duhl-Steetle report should not be "Newark:
Community of Chaos" but "Newark: The Birth of a Flower." A
flower indeed must come from a seed. We had that seed. It also
must come from the dirt. We had that dirt. There was need for
much fertilization, much cultivation; there were many fears for
drought, many predators, but we now have the flower. In succeeding generations the flower can become a more perfect hy-
brid, but today it is a flower.

As the Duhl-Steetle report stands, I have to question their
writing of this case history. The presentation is incomplete, the
dynamics and plot of the story are more complex than reported,
and I think the possible alternatives are quite different.

DIALOGUE, 1969
REBUTTAL TO THE CADMUS COMMENT
BY LEONARD J. DUHL, M.D.

Epilogue

The presentation of the Newark case study of the medical
school controversy was originally written more than one-and-
one-half years ago in order to point out to the staff of the U.S.
Department of Housing and Urban Development how complex
the issues are in any one case and how extremely difficult it is to
accept the viewpoint of any one observer. It clearly is presented
from the viewpoint of someone in the federal government. I
present the Cadmus response to the study and respond to
it here not only to present ideas about events from different
points of view, but to underline the import of dialogue in matters such as this.

In order to gather the material, Nancy Jo Steetle and I went
through records of various agencies involved: state and federal,
local and regional, in addition to newspaper and magazine articles. We interviewed various key actors—some of those listed in

the "Cast of Characters," as well as various other individuals involved. We did not interview Dr. Cadmus, since we were in the service of HUD and could not cross into the domain of the Public Health Service. PHS officials felt that collecting data there would have confused the action. This limitation was accepted in preparing the case study and submitting it to the *Journal* (*The Journal of Applied Behavioral Science*, Vol. 5, No. 4, 1969).

Various persons have since commented upon the study. The participants, including Dr. Cadmus, saw the problem from their vantage points. What he adds in his comments is an important and relevant addition. Indeed, Demetrius Iatrides, director of Boston College's Institute of Human Sciences, ran a seminar in 1968 in which numerous participants presented their own views of the events. A book may be forthcoming from that endeavor. Various articles in *Architectural Forum, The City*, and elsewhere have presented additional vignettes about the case. With each statement we get a different view, additional facts, and different judgments as to the validity of the decisions made and of the various actors in the drama. As Dr. Cadmus points out, we are not ready for a final case study. Like a medical case report for a clinical conference, this paper was written at one point during the diagnosis and treatment procedure.

The case as presented is not the last word, nor is it exhaustive. Obviously it reflects my own judgments as to what the critical issues were from where I sat then, in the office of the Secretary of the U.S. Department of Housing and Urban Development. Let me outline more concretely how these issues and results appear to me:

- Most federal agencies and collections of many separate programs, disconnected from one another and oftentimes antithetical to one another. Though this is ostensibly a medical school problem—and is thus concerned with education and health care—it is also a problem of civil rights, housing, citizen participation, community control, land use planning, city governance, resource allocation, decentralization, new federal roles, politics, and, above all, values in decision making.

- Programs in communities, such as medical schools, housing, education, and psychiatric facilities, tend to have "lives of their own." They operate independent of community and consumer needs, desires, and priorities. They are often more capable of answering needs of the past, rather than those of the present, or needs anticipatory of the future.

- In most decision making—federal and local, public or private—concern with user needs is usually given low priority. The usual urban renewal criteria, including that of hospital construction, have given more concern to money and bricks and mortar than to the people involved. The original proposals for the central ward area in Newark ignored the people and put buildings above program.

- The presence of confrontation—even riot—forces existing institutions to make changes. The "usefulness" of confrontation is that by provoking a crisis it leads to disorganization. In the process of trying to regain equanimity there is a potential for change. At the same time, crises can be resolved negatively—by external controls—with rigid adherence to past modes of behavior, and with the resulting "backlash" preventing even incremental change.

- In the Newark case the confrontation led to change and growth. This occurred, I believe, because various actors chose to negotiate and to work out differences, so that gain-gain rather than gain-loss situations would result. The trade-offs led to a resolution where almost all the participants were relatively satisfied. The users, as well as the suppliers of service, played a part in the process. This occurred despite the fact that none understood "the whole" nor fully comprehended or accepted the views of others. However, almost everyone believed that he had learned from the experience. Dr. Cadmus gives much evidence of this in his comments. Similarly the black community gained increased sophistication and competence.

- That agreement could occur was due to two important facts: several persons (e.g., Paul Ylvisaker, Robert Wood, and I) agreed that maximum energy would go to find a solution; a set of rules was forged by which people who disagreed could work out their differences. The Wood-Cohen letter served as a "constitutional" framework within which all the decisions were subsequently worked out. When there are no rules to deal with complex issues they cannot be resolved. That the decisions have not yet been implemented by this new administration is one of the real problems that all endeavors of the Kennedy-Johnson period now have to face. However, HUD did approve the proposal.

- The current state of community problems is such that no one institution, organization, or profession can contain the problem so that others will not be involved. Indeed, everyone seems to be in everyone else's problem, forcing changes of perception, "rules of the game," and priorities. Since we do not have rules for the new complex games (old governmental games have failed), we need to find new rules. The Newark case is an illustration of how one can go about resolving issues which seemingly have no solution by bringing all the parties together to the negotiating table.

- Problems obviously cannot be solved by local decisions alone. New combinations of people must be put together. However, *institutions cannot* negotiate; *individuals can.* Thus, people with power to negotiate are essential to any resolution. Yet, most often those people who have the power are least able to offend their own constituencies. They must protect their organization and power. An alternative solution is that key persons—not necessarily in power or in positions of authority—can join an informal network of like persons from various organizations, and together they can try to make the changes required. Elsewhere, I have called these groups "floating crap games," or "invisible colleges." These groups, formed through long association, are concerned with being on the "cutting edge" of problems rather than with preserving institutions. By attempting to understand the whole, the trends, and armed with the power of information—intelligence—they have indirect power.

In the case of the medical college, it was this informal group of outsiders, representing all the critical areas involved in change, who set the broad conditions that led insiders in the community and in the college to a resolution. Setting the conditions is not control. *The real solutions were worked out by community and medical college people themselves. To imply that setting conditions is manipulation ignores the fact that freedom in a complex society does not result from laissez-faire.* Freedom must be planned for. Freedom also takes action. This case describes one type of action that can take place.

- There are in our society few "perfect," unalterable solutions. What has been reported here is only a part of complicated processes. Changes in medicine are occurring concurrently. The medical school faculty and trustees did indeed learn, and Dr. Cadmus has become a leader in this change.

- New directions in housing construction are evolving in Newark itself. No one claims that the Newark case is solved or has caused other change. The city is far from solving its problems—economically, socially, or politically—but Newark *is* moving ahead.

As indicated, this case was presented at one point in time to aid in understanding. Even without completeness and without setting down every viewpoint, it can serve as a teaching case for those of us who are involved with *training people to assist in dealing with current community problems.* I hope that others who have data will contribute more to our knowledge of this case by contributing their observations. I am thankful to all those who educated me—as they agonized through to resolution. And to Dr. Cadmus goes my great admiration for having learned through crises and for having led an institution through a sea of ambiguity toward a healthier role for a medical college.

Chapter 13

THE JOBS CORPS

Proposals for Redesign

If administrators and politicians are going to play God with other persons' lives (and still other persons' money), they ought at least to get clear what the divine intention is to be.

Daniel P. Moynihan (1969)

We believe that new institutions for learning are needed in America. This article reviews the results of an experience in educational redesign, to illustrate a style of analysis that may be useful to others.

BACKGROUND

In the early summer of 1969, the Job Corps requested the services of the Organization for Social and Technical Innovation (OSTI), Cambridge, Massachusetts, to evaluate and to develop techniques for evaluation of the Job Corps Mental Health Program (Contract B99-4892). In discussion with the Office of Economic Opportunity (OEO) personnel and in reviewing the terms of the contract, it was felt that a comprehensive study of an evaluation system could not be made at that time. Rather, an evaluation of the Job Corps and the support systems provided by the Mental Health Program would be attempted.

Dr. Harold M. Visotsky and I, serving as staff consultants to OSTI, visited selected Job Corps sites in almost all geographic locations in the country. The many Job Corps camps, men's, women's, and conservation corps, with their various styles, different goals, procedures, and methods, were visited and studied. We also visited the central office in Washington, D.C. and worked extensively with members of the Job Corps staff, reviewing their manuals and documents for policy statements, for evaluation methods and statistical reporting techniques, and to determine the decision making mechanisms at central and local levels. We also investigated the methods and modalities of communication at central and local levels. At the local level, all staff, ranging from the director to counselors to Job Corps enrollees, were interviewed. A written report of each evaluation was prepared on site. This incorporated the organizational analysis, methods of communication, policy implementation, decision making, self-evaluations of effectiveness, and the varieties of statistics for transmittal to the central office.

The final report, compiled with assistance from Jonathan W. Brown, a systems analyst, who also visited one of the sites, was written to present alternate models for design of a Job Corps program which would incorporate mental health concepts and philosophy as an integral part of the policy of the Job Corps. It reviewed the difficulties of assessing the ambiguous variables of the functioning Job Corps programs. In this instance, it reviewed the methods by which the Job Corps was evaluating its programs within its own system. It did not attempt to review the literature by Levitan, Purcell, Gottlieb, and others on the evaluation of the Job Corps program.

Dr. Visotsky and I submitted our report from OSTI in late October 1969, and copies of that report were furnished to all Job Corps directors in November 1969.

William Mirengoff, Acting Director of the Job Corps, U.S. Department of Labor, invited us as the authors of the OSTI report to discuss our findings with members of the Job Corps headquarters staff who had a direct interest in the subject matter in a meeting in January 1970. At this meeting, the essence of the report, as well as the methods used for evaluation, was discussed.

THE JOB CORPS CENTERS: SOME ILLUSTRATIONS

As of September 1969, the Job Corps was operating a large number of Centers located in a wide variety of urban and rural settings, ranging in size from 100 to 3,000 corps members and functioning in a variety of organizational and training styles—with considerable differences in both staff and corps member attitudes and behaviors.

To give some flavor of the variety in Centers, impressions of our team's visits to several Job Corps Centers (JCC) are summarized.

JCC A is located amid the small farm towns and light manufacturing areas of the Midwest on an enormous deserted Army base dotted with the architectural relics of World War II. Forty miles from the nearest major urban area, the Center's overall rural serenity is disturbed only by an occasional bomb blast or flare illumination provided by the local National Guard at its seasonal observances. Generally, the camp's neighbors are racially intolerant, adhering to their Fundamentalist views. In this setting live 1,500 to 1,600 corpsmen, of whom about 70 percent are black and the remainder are members of other disadvantaged minority cultures. There is evidence of severe tension among staff and inadequate organizational communication. These conditions both contribute to and precipitate inadequate staffing and the presence of diverse, even contradictory, goals. Seldom are there executive staff meetings to share significant information or to solve problems collaboratively. Difficulty in recruiting and retaining competent key staff minimizes the training job that can be done. Interracial conflict is rife. There have been major disturbances at this Center, and more are predicted. The use of disciplinary procedures is frequent, and two dormitory areas are segregated to isolate disciplinary offenders. At the time of our visit, 370 (24 percent) of the camp's residents were either AWOL or under arrest. One informant noted that his figures indicated that 78 percent of those who came to the Center leave prior to completing a course (the official figure is given as approximately 50 percent). A psychiatrist appears about once a month and "evaluates" patients. The staff members in the counseling section have infrequent contact with him, although they feel he is sympathetic. The organizational form is one of task specialization, with consequent gaps in service areas and divisional rivalries for resources. The corpsman's apparent primary reference group is his dormitory floor group, which usually consists of roughly 120 corpsmen and additional staff counselors, dormitory managers, and others.

A contrasting Center is JCC B, located in the wilderness of a western state, with only 300 corpsmen in residence. The surrounding population is hostile to black people and the Job Corps. Despite this—perhaps because of it—the morale is high; there is a feeling of connectedness between the staff and the corpsmen. The camp's goals focus on the needs of the corpsman, with less attention directed to specific task accomplishment in organizational divisions. The language of the camp reflects psychological awareness, with an emphasis on understanding behavior as a form of communication. The mental health program is handled internally by the counseling staff, with occasional consultation from a local psychiatrist on particular cases. All staff members are seen as counselors operating in a problem-solving and therapeutic way. Staff recruitment is largely local and the longevity is high. The Center functions as a community, perhaps without realizing it.

The women's JCC, with 400 corps members, is located in the black section of a major midwestern city, housed in a former women's residence of the Salvation Army. By design, the Center operates as a therapeutic community, with much decision making shared by many levels of staff and corpswomen. These areas include curriculum within training programs, discipline, and residential and recreational affairs. Groups and group formats are used often. The director of the Center is a prominent person who lends a charismatic glow to much of what goes on. The counseling staff, in addition to the routine one-to-one corpswoman counseling, is involved heavily in the total administration of the Center and staff training. The intake program, in addition to the normal testing and assignment procedures, deliberately attempts to affect the corpswoman strongly, thereby minimizing the probabilities of dropout before completion of training. Most of the staff interviewed seemed to have a better-than-average knowledge of therapeutic communities, group behavior, racism, program development, and other sociological and psychological areas.

Another women's Center, JCC D, is located in a major midwestern city in a former YMCA building. The staff, largely recruited from YWCA programs, brings experience in working with adolescent and young adult populations from lower-class minority culture backgrounds. This program, like the preceding one, was designed consciously as a therapeutic community with the collaboration of the mental health and health program consultants. There has been intensive staff training and consultation in organizational behavior. The mental health consultant is reputed to spend 90 percent of his time on overall program consultation; needs for his services on individual case consultation are consequently less. Much of the staff has remained with the Center during its 3 years of operation. Although there is seemingly less control by the corpsmembers of program decisions than in JCC C, staff decisions can be and often are affected by their expressed wishes. There is a high level of communication among key staff members at both regular and informal meetings.

Diagnosis

These four descriptions underscore the diversity—and unfortunately the divisions—within the Job Corps Center operations. From the site visits resulting in the descriptions above, from interviews with the central office staff, from documents provided by Job Corps offices, and from interviews with former corpsmen and staff members, we made the following observations:

1. Despite a shared rhetoric and vocabulary, there are no discernible shared goals or program objectives toward which staff can focus their efforts.

2. There are many Job Corps—men's, women's, conservation corps—with different goals, styles, procedures, myths, and measures. There are varying patterns of selection, placement, management, evaluation, and health services. This results in a greater preoccupation with one's own "piece of the action" and a lesser concern with the program as a whole.

3. The Job Corps is currently an organization in the process of change, including the difficult process of becoming part of a larger organization, the Labor Department. New goals are being established and ways of measuring effectiveness have yet to evolve.

4. The lack of goal congruence and clear communication within the Job Corps is sorely felt. Explicit goal development can be accomplished only by unblocking clogged channels and by opening new ones able to operate in the future. Probable outcomes of increasing information flow are a healthier overall program, increased and meaningful evaluation, and increased productivity in meeting program goals.

REDESIGN: SOME ALTERNATE MODELS

Based on these observations, we see at least three potential models of organization and redesign of the Job Corps which vary in their conception of program goals. Given these goals, we then propose some probable outcomes and evaluation measures for each model.

Model I: Vocational Skill and Jobs

In this model, the chief function of the Job Corps is to train corps members in the vocational skills needed to obtain and retain a job.

Certain key *presuppositions* are essential to the operation of this model. They are:

1. Skilled training is the primary deficiency of the corpsman. If achieved, all else follows automatically.

2. Adequate vocational training prepares the corps member for a position in an open job market in the geographic area and social system to which he returns.

3. The real problem is external control. Thus, regimented activity focusing on skills to be learned for later use can develop internal discipline and control which will serve the corpsman in the future.

4. It is less costly—with any enforceable contract—since you do not have to pay for "soft, woolly-headed programs" like mental health.

The *evaluation* measures for cost-benefit analysis (as well as performance) in this model are simple. They are:

1. The number of corpsmen who successfully complete a course and are employed.

2. The lowest cost per corpsman per training.

3. Submeasures: For example, cost accounting of individual pieces of the whole can lead to trade-offs.

Probable Outcomes

1. There will be a high rate of rejection at input points, up to and probably including orientation. In other words, those who receive training are likely to be those who can be trained in nonresidential (and less expensive) settings. It is even probable that under this system a number of accepted corps members could survive without training.

2. The vocational skill training will bind itself more closely than is now the case to areas of occupational opportunity and need.

3. Health services, mental health services, counseling, recreation, and other divisions within centers will have the primary function of ensuring the corpsman's retention in the program or his early rejection on "technical" grounds (i.e., psychosis, severe aberrant behavior), for which the program is "not responsible."

4. Contractors operating centers will ask for (and need) strict, enforceable contracts with selected corps members.

5. Recruitment of high-level professional staff may be difficult.
6. There is a fair potential in this model that people who might otherwise complete training in existing public educational systems may "drop out" to join the Job Corps, where the skill training may be much better and concrete rewards for being trained are constant (living allowance, regular meals, terminal allowance).

Critique.   This model is simple and allows for unequivocal evaluation data. Unfortunately, such a program may have little effect on an expanding poverty culture. While it rescues a few, it trains many more who are probably capable of succeeding by themselves. Unless there is enormous expansion of the Job Corps, this model also has little substantial impact on anything, except for the people going through the program. However, it is probably the model of choice for profit contractors, since it allows "unambiguous" profit estimation and contract performance. It has the clearest definition of product goal. The model also has a certain appeal to hard-nosed legislators and administrators. The trade-offs and costs can be most easily evaluated.

Because of poor internal communications which result in center staffs' having limited and differing conceptions of their *raison d'etre*, this model is currently the implicit but dominant general performance standard within the Job Corps. As we present other models, we hope that the deficiencies of this model will become clearer. In brief, its only advantage is that of being easily grasped by those inexpert in the study and evaluation of social welfare programs.

This model is also unsatisfactory because enrollees will not be attracted to the centers; the selection process assures that the "unreachables" remain unreached. Its social goals are mixed, despite the apparent clarity. We simply cannot prescribe how to implement this model with real effectiveness.

Model II: Acculturation and Employment

In this model, the chief function of the Job Corps is to develop in young people from poverty, minority, or disadvantaged minority subcultures a wide range of vocational and social skills which will enable them to make an easier transition into the broader social environment. The Job Corps serves as a kind of intensive Ellis Island. This model *presupposes* the following social views:

1. There are ways of living which cannot survive in the complex modern world.
2. An intensive training program with young adults is an appropriate intervention to learn new patterns of living.
3. The federal government and its contractors can provide not only vocational training and an environment but social training, which will enable the corps member to become part of the broader society.
4. Behavior patterns in young adults are not internalized and set. They wish to become, and can be trained to become, self-respecting members of the (national) community.

Evaluation. Evaluation measures for this model are complex, but not impossible. Their chief disadvantage is the delay in feedback between evaluator and staff operations personnel, with a consequent delay in responsivity of the overall program operations to change. Change can be effected with the aid of evaluation data, but more slowly than may be desirable. Evaluation measures of acculturation and vocational improvement would include:

1. "Fate" studies of cohorts, to establish overall success of the intervention program.
2. Studies of social and economic costs of training corps members, measured against social and economic productivity within the same group.
3. Individual measurements of adaptiveness and social competence, including such variables as marriage rates and qualitative analyses of adjustment to marriage; ability to function within authority structures; promotion rates; proportion of corps members entering programs for continued education and training; studies examining whether

corps members widen their patterns of association after exposure to the Job Corps; studies evaluating corpsmen's involvement with community and social projects after exposure to the Job Corps; and so on. In general, such studies and evaluations look at the social competency of the corps member in entering the dominant culture. Job holding as such becomes only one measure of Job Corps success, albeit a potent one.

Probable Outcomes

1. This model offers the potential to cope with a more problematic population than does the first model.
2. Recruitment of such a problematic population, however, will depend upon the program's presentation to minority subcultures.
3. Given workable budgets, this kind of approach can recruit and retain a highly skilled and creative staff.
4. The health and mental health services in this program will bear primary responsibility for preventing dropouts and facilitating retention of corps members. These services probably would have much to do with overall program design and control.
5. Programs stressing both vocational and social competencies demand high inputs of staff training. A much higher proportion of budget will necessarily be spent in developing cohesive and total staff involvement in the overall center operations.
6. Larger camps following this model would probably decentralize much internal decision making to corps member units of 300 to 400, led by the staff assigned to that unit.
7. Considerable differences must be anticipated in terms of unit direction and programming. These differences will not only vary from unit to unit but may be expected to vary considerably over time within the same unit.
8. Output measures, however, can be relatively consistent.
9. By comparison with the first model, internal management difficulties can be expected to develop much tension. This

will occur primarily because a key operating tool in this model would be social systems data collected on a continuing basis. By contrast, in a jobs-only-oriented camp, only task-performance data are needed by administrators. Social systems data are utilized at present only when the center has a major disruption and they are used sparingly to resolve the crisis after the fact.

10. The program is person-centered and humanitarian. It calls for some legislative show of social commitment to disadvantaged people.

11. Success of the program will depend to a large extent on conditions within the social system to which the corps member returns.

Critique.   This model of viewing the corps members as an unacculturated resident has had a good deal of currency, particularly among social scientists and liberal government administrators. Another version of the same theme is to view the corps member, or potential corps member, as having an "atypical" or "abnormal" developmental pattern, which the serving agency is attempting to put to rights. Regardless of the validity or falsity of such views, a program making such assumptions today (or assumptions approaching them) will receive scant support from the minority cultures from which it wishes to recruit. The political ethic in the black community (and increasingly in the Hispanic and Native American communities as well) is to view any efforts toward changing their life-styles that are not controlled by the client population themselves as another white man's trick. This attitude is clearly reflected in the internal affairs of many of the Centers, although it is doubtful whether evidence of it has been documented publicly. Much of the resistance to training and social competence development occurs quite clearly in Centers where there is a predominantly white or white-value-oriented management. If this training model were to be implemented, it should be subcontracted to predominantly ethnically identified organizations, probably nonprofit in nature. The question is whether there are enough such organizations, with developed staff competencies, to take over the number of centers contemplated.

MODEL III: JOB TRAINING AND COMMUNITY CHANGE

So far, we have discussed two models which concentrate on individual training and/or behavior change. For both models, the success of the program is a function of the geographic area or social system to which the corps member returns. The placement branch must locate appropriate jobs; social conditions must be open enough for the corps member to use his new-found coping skills. In our analysis of the Job Corps, we have also noted a breakdown among the selection, training, and placement sections of the program. The third model to be presented attempts to deal with some of these existing and potential difficulties, while providing increased linkage and support to other federal programs of assistance to poverty areas.

The chief function of the Job Corps in this model is to serve as a center that can develop and implement training programs of varying lengths and kinds to meet the manpower requirements for various other programs being mounted in economically depressed areas, urban and rural. A training program in this model can be initiated only when a community group or agency such as a Model Cities board, Community Action Program (CAP), Small Business Administration (SBA) program, any Manpower Development and Training Act (MDTA) training program, or an industry group such as the Urban Coalition, a tenants' organization, or other has commissioned such an endeavor with the Job Corps Center. The overall objective of the Job Corps in this model is to develop and expand a competent manpower pool in disadvantaged areas among the young adult population. The community agencies' responsibilities are four-fold:

1. To identify and plan for the manpower needs of the community client system.
2. To identify and recruit the potential corps members.
3. To collaborate and assist actively in developing the appropriate training program within the available resources.
4. To provide appropriate jobs and follow-up services to the corps member upon return to the community.

The Job Corps responsibilities are:

1. To develop programs that meet the needs of the community and the corps members with whom they have contracted, in both vocational and social competency areas, as identified and agreed upon.
2. To assist, with the Department of Labor, communities and their agencies who are of special interest to the national government, in identifying needed skills within the community structure and potential populations and methods for recruitment into Job Corps operations.
3. To conclude formal contracts for service with responsible agencies, with evaluation and performance measures to be agreed upon contractually as appropriate to the training task.
4. To work with other federal agencies to identify potential areas of need where Job Corps resources can be maximally employed.

The first model presented can be conceptualized as a "technical training institute model; the second can be seen as a "transition school" model. This third design can be usefully thought of as a "university of the poor." At a time when state and local educational systems are not only overloaded with their conventional clients but also face budgetary restrictions which prevent them from taking on specialized training programs in poverty areas, this model represents a powerful tool for both culture change and economic development of disadvantaged and minority areas.

Evaluation.   Evaluation at a national level is a simple computation of the number of successfully completed contracts. At a more qualitative level, conventional economic indicators of community functioning can be used with a fair degree of success— i.e., reduction in unemployment in target areas, increase in economic productivity, decrease in economic dependency, and so on.

Probable Outcomes

1. Necessarily, the Job Corps will become enmeshed in and committed to other federal programs aimed at rural and

urban ghettos. It may shed its organizational air of anomie that is currently noticeable and troublesome.

2. Contracts will provide clear, time-limited goals for all levels of staff, both within the Centers and in the central office.

3. Implementing such a change in functioning is liable to meet with resistance from second- and third-level managers within the Centers, who will under this model be deprived of some decision making powers they currently hold; they will also be subject to closer evaluation.

4. Second- and third-level managers will need more discretionary powers over resource disposition (money and manpower) than they are currently allowed by the central office of the Job Corps.

5. There may be more difficulties at the time a contract is negotiated than during its life. Fewer problems in running the Centers may be anticipated, since there will be a close liaison with the contracting community organization and active collaboration on their part in training.

6. Budgeting in the Job Corps may be assisted by contracting for matching funds from the community agencies involved for certain components of training—including health and mental health services.

7. Dropouts from the program become a responsibility and problem shared with the community involved.

8. The fate of various components of the present Job Corps is not clear in this model, particularly the mental health components. However, if they serve a useful function they should be able to present a case and sell themselves within the framework of contract negotiations. Staff anxiety levels are liable to run somewhat higher than they already are.

9. This model is congruent with at least two expressed tenets of the current federal executive branch. The program provides for increased local controls and is directly involved in overall community and economic development. It has the further advantage to the executive that the evaluation, although having differing specific measures, is firmly based upon consumer satisfaction. Thus the Job Corps might be more palatable than it is currently.

10. Job Corps members in a particular training sequence from a particular community can be held together and expected

to develop a more stable reference group with healthier norms and outputs than is currently the case. At present, the corps member goes to a Center, becomes a part of a new group, and then leaves it when the training is complete to enter into a usually unstable or unsuitable social system in the community. Under this model, the Job Corps has the potential for forming class groups from the same community whose members can form some meaningful and cohesive dependencies which can continue in the back-home situation. This has the added advantage of reducing potential follow-up costs that are needed in an individual-centered program.

Critique.   Although this model is currently "good" from the point of view of both the corpsman and the community, it may further threaten those who see community control of programs as undermining the legitimate, established political process. Further, it is not likely to be attractive to Job Corps administrators at any level who see themselves as losing power in the model, or who currently perceive their performance as inadequate. Nor is the model likely to be popular with profit-centered market organizations, since they must meet and negotiate with client groups who are often difficult and seemingly irrational in their demands of formal organizations. Under current conditions, and in the other two models described, the transactions involved in service contracts take place between people who perceive themselves as equals or near equals. In dealing with community organizations, transactions are not likely to pervade with the same amiability nor conducted with commonly shared procedural rules. However, this is perhaps a necessary confrontation for both parties, given the current state of affairs.

Further, it is likely that evaluation of any component of the current Job Corps under this model will turn up a good deal of disturbing data. It is only because of the lack of clearcut program objectives that the current evaluatory data seem to conceal or distort a number of problem areas. In respect to evaluation, the Job Corps has one of two alternatives at this point: (a) continuation of the current inaccurate assessment of ambiguous variables which gives an "optimistic" picture of the functioning, or (b) collection and confrontation of data which quite probably will not make anyone feel better but will delineate how "tough" the training issues are in the populations with which the Job Corps deals.

In conclusion, in view of the current situation in education in general, and in the urban ghetto in particular, we feel that new institutions for learning cast in different forms than we now know may unlock some of the problems. The problems confronting educators and trainers for deprived groups of citizens require programming which must incorporate class differences and differing social and cultural backgrounds, motivations, and communication patterns.

Chapter 14

MEDEX PROJECT EVALUATION[1]

Introduction

The Director of the MEDEX Project, Richard A. Smith, M.D., described the purpose of the MEDEX (*medecin extension* = physician's extension) Project in a special communication published in the *Journal of the American Medical Association* (*JAMA*) on March 16, 1970 as intended "to develop an extension of the physician—another pair of skilled hands under his supervision." Dr. Smith cited the shortage of medical manpower, especially in the rural areas of the State of Washington, the decline in physician-patient ratio due to urban migration of physicians and replacement failures, and the increasing age of those general practitioners who practice in outlying areas.

---

[1]The MEDEX Program is at present (1986) still functioning in the U.S., notably in North Dakota and Washington state, and the project operates a training center at the University of Hawaii School of Medicine, which trains personnel to work in many parts of the world, particularly in Lesotho, Micronesia, Pakistan, Guyana and other developing nations.

"Thus efforts are needed to be directed," he said, "to increasing the capacity of practitioners already in the areas, as well as making general practice more attractive to physicians seeking new work settings." He described MEDEX as "A model of nonphysicians extending primary medical care transferable to rural, suburban, and urban settings. It is anticipated that this model will demonstrate that former military corpsmen with additional practical training can perform many tasks, performed at present by civilian physicians, which do not require the extensive and sophisticated education obtained in medical schools."

From this general statement of purpose, we defined three interdependent objectives against which to evaluate this project:

1. To introduce the concept of paraprofessionals substituting for highly-trained professionals in performing the more routine functions of health care.
2. To support desperately short-handed medical care subsystems.
3. To bring about the necessary organizational changes in the health care system that will permit high-quality health care to be conveniently available to all Americans.

Method

Three physicians with public health training and previous concern for the problems associated with the organization and delivery of health care made frequent visits to the program from outside the Northern California service area. Members of this evaluation team were present during the initial selection process. They visited 13 of the 14 physician-preceptors before the MEDEX trainees were assigned to the field portion of their training and again after 10 to 11 months' experience with the program in the field. The evaluators interviewed the physician and his wife, key office personnel, especially the chief nurse, and often accompanied the physician during his actual treatment of patients. All MEDEX trainees were interviewed during the selection process and again at the end of their field training period, whenever possible, to obtain their impressions about the strengths and weaknesses of the program.

Analysis

If the first goal is restated simply as an attempt to demonstrate the practicability of assigning former military corpsmen to the civilian medical force and, accepting as a measure of success the willingness of the physicians to continue the relationship by hiring the MEDEX personnel and the MEDEX' willingness to continue in his position as an employee, we rated eight successes, four who had a "modified success" and two which had to be rated as doubtful. Of the 14 MEDEX trainees involved, this was a 57 percent success rate and a 29 percent rate where there were questions. The "modified successes" were those who have left their original preceptors, although, interestingly, three of the four continued to work as physician's assistants and two within the general area of the program. Only one left the program completely and he did so because of major personality problems after a total of only 2 to 3 weeks in the field.

One of the "modified successes," who continued to work in the MEDEX Program, was hired by the preceptor of the trainee who left after only 2 to 3 weeks. He had been working with a group of four physicians in a small town. This group was characterized by a covert conflict among the partners and jealousy about the increased financial advantage that might accrue to the one physician-preceptor to whom the MEDEX trainee was assigned. To equalize this advantage, the MEDEX was assigned to each one of the four doctors 1 day a week. While he obtained good teaching from at least two of the doctors, he was ignored completely by a third. He had no opportunity to develop an ongoing relationship with any of the physicians and, as a result, was used almost as an afterthought to suture minor lacerations and to write up histories, physical examinations, and discharge summaries on hospitalized patients of one member of the group. His preceptor was in some ways relieved that he accepted an offer of employment in the neighboring town.

Another MEDEX left a partnership of two physicians where, again, there were personality conflicts between the physicians. He accepted a position with the Group Health Program and continued to function as a physician's assistant.

The last "modified success" was one of the most experienced and amicable of the trainees. However, he found himself covering an office in a town at some distance from the physician's primary office. He did not feel he was prepared to accept major responsibility in the physician's absence and the presence of two newly arrived physicians in the town left little demand for his services while his physician-preceptor was away. He left his preceptor to work with a group of orthopedic surgeons in Spokane.

Of the two doubtful cases, one was registered as doubtful because, in August, a decision had still not been made about this trainee's being retained in the practice. The potential for his usefulness was great, but very little medical responsibility was delegated to the MEDEX. Rather, he remained in a strict apprenticeship relationship to his preceptor, a very dedicated, conscientious if somewhat rigid physician. The obvious demand for assistance in extending this physician's capacity and the willingness of the MEDEX trainee to work under close supervision made this a potentially very positive match.

The other case registered as doubtful belonged to the Group Health Program. The MEDEX trainee was assigned to the chief of the general practice section who believed in the program but who, himself, had considerable administrative responsibilities. A shortage of office space and the physician-preceptor's preference for seeing all patients and providing most of the care himself made this a good training experience but of little real benefit in extending the physician's time. In fact, the physician complained that it took more of his time to train the MEDEX than it would have taken to provide the service himself. When one physician in the group was assigned to take full-time responsibility for the emergency room, this MEDEX trainee was assigned to work with him in the provision of emergency care. While the MEDEX did not leave the system, he left his direct relationship with his preceptor.

Sociodemographic Characteristics

Those cases registered as failures were examined for what MEDEX and physician characteristics might have been related to their inability to continue with the program. On the MEDEX' side, there was no clear relationship to *age* or *education*. One MEDEX who transferred from a group to a solo practice setting was acutely sensitive about the fact that he had not completed high school except through a general education equivalency certificate. He was noted by his physician-preceptor to be rather loud and unprofessional in his approach to patients so that some social status discrepancy was apparent. Nevertheless, his reason for leaving the practice did not seem related to his education, but to the setting in which he found himself. The sample was too small to test the importance of *marital status*, but the only unmarried MEDEX trainee left his placement after only 2 to 3 weeks, in part because of unprofessional social behavior. The evaluators did not have enough information to examine the question of *urban versus rural background* but noted that many of those who left their rural settings had grown up in rural areas. One key factor seemed to be the actual *clinical experience* the military service had provided. The man who left after only 2 or 3 weeks had been trained but had then been assigned to other nonmedical activities in the service. While he spoke convincingly about his abilities, he was simply unable to perform even a simple laceration repair without the patient complaining about his nervousness.

Independent Variables: Physician

The more significant variables seemed to be related to the physician-preceptor. The first seemed to be *the relative supply and demand* for physicians' services. One physician worked as a member of a group covering a relatively small population area. This physician felt that the patients had a right to see the physician and the MEDEX was called only when needed. In another setting, the MEDEX was competing with two new physicians in town when his physician-preceptor was not immediately available. On the other hand, in those areas where the physician was in solo practice and was the principal source of medical care in the community, the importance of the MEDEX increased tremendously.

The physician's ability to delegate seemed critically related to success or failure in its extremes. Those physicians who attempted to delegate too much responsibility too soon and provide less than adequate supervision for their MEDEX trainee either lost their MEDEX or allowed questions to develop about the quality of care delivered by their assistants. Those physicians who could not delegate responsibility to the MEDEX person to any significant degree made little use of their assistants and might have done as well without them. Viewed again on a *flexibility-rigidity* continuum, one would characterize those physicians who could not delegate or who delegated excessively as the more rigid. *Communicativeness, willingness to supervise, conscientiousness* of the physician preceptor, and whether the placement site was a *solo or group practice* did not seem to be factors definitely related to success or failure.

Intraoffice Relationship

In at least two or three practices, major problems developed between the MEDEX and the chief nurse. These seemed to be related questions of status and role relationship to the physician. In many instances, the MEDEX displaced the nurse in routine office tasks, such as assisting in minor surgery. This led to the actual laying off of a nurse in one practice and to grumbling and criticism in one or two others. In some practices, the problem of acceptance of the MEDEX by the rest of the staff seemed to go quite smoothly. This would seem to be an important area to emphasize in future training.

Changes in Quality of Care Delivered

There was some evidence that care was actually worse in three practices because of lack of supervision. For example, one evaluator observed a bite wound in the leg of a girl that had been closed with a continuous running suture. This treatment of a potentially contaminated wound left no possibility of opening one section.

There could have been more consultation provided by the Project staff to the preceptors of those MEDEX trainees who were having difficulty in the hope of salvaging strained relationships. This became much easier with models for successful and unsuccessful practices than was the case during the earliest, exploratory stage. It may have helped in the practice where the one MEDEX trainee was assigned alternately to each of four physicians and, therefore, primarily responsible to none. It may have helped in another practice where the MEDEX found himself working primarily with a physician other than with his assigned preceptor. It may also have helped with the three MEDEX who were left alone and unsupervised much of the time. It may have helped the one physician who had difficulty delegating even minor problems if he could have seen how others found they could successfully share routine responsibilities. Because of the wide dispersion of the preceptors, travel to provide consultation would have been difficult but perhaps should have been required as a condition of certification.

Selection

In the initial selection, great care was taken to ascertain that 11 candidates had extensive medical training in the military service. Unfortunately, some of the applicants had completed their training but had then gone on to other assignments in the service and so had had little or no actual clinical responsibility. More attention might have been given this factor as well as to the quality of the letters of recommendation.

Training

Some preceptors complained that the MEDEX person assigned to them was not properly prepared in areas which they felt would have been the most vital use to them. For example, one preceptor felt that the MEDEX should have practical experience in taking X rays, doing simple laboratory work, such as CBCs (complete blood count) and blood sugars, bacterial cultures and Gram's stains. He should have some training in physical therapy such as the use of microwave and ultrasound and whirlpool treatments, he should know how to take electrocardiograms (EKGs) and, perhaps, some training in drop anesthesia for simple, brief procedures such as D and C (dilation and curettage). This would argue for involvement of the preceptors in the design or at least in the review of the curriculum prior to the inception of training.

Certification

The California law, as passed in the 1970 legislature, requires certification of the physician before he may qualify to have a physician's assistant and for the periodic recertification of the assistant every 4 years. This law seems eminently sensible because it requires that the physician's assistant be allowed to practice only under the direction and supervision of the physician who takes full responsibility for his work. Further, because certification of the physician is required, this may give the training institution additional leverage to consult on the actual organization of the practice and the relationship between the preceptor and the MEDEX than has been possible in this early demonstration phase. Decisions about the degree of supervision required seem to have been entirely determined by the preceptor and ranged across the board from almost none to almost total delegation.

Even among the evaluators, differences existed in conceptualizing the future role of the physician's assistant. One member stated categorically that the physician is wasting his time in triage. The other two felt more conservatively that, in this most affluent country, where the physician to population ratio far exceeded that in Britain or Sweden, everyone should be entitled to treatment from the best available source and that each physician's assistant should be clearly responsible to a single physician except in very isolated areas where supervision by way of closed circuit television or radio were the only way of making care available. Some believed development of a second-class system of care possible, much like the Russian feldsher program. A comment of Eugene Stead, a physician at Duke University, who, in a letter to me, said "the physician's assistant can learn to do anything which a physician does routinely" was borne out in large measure by the MEDEX Project and has been especially well demonstrated in those practices where supervision and the degree of responsibility to be delegated were clearly defined.

Conclusions

Of the objectives listed at the beginning of this evaluation, the first was accomplished. In the majority of cases studied, the paraprofessionals were able to substitute for highly trained professionals in performing the more routine functions of health care. The second objective, to support short-handed medical care subsystems in medically deprived areas, was achieved in a small and selected sample by utilizing paraprofessionals. Objective three, to bring about the necessary organizational changes in the health care system so that high-quality health care would be conveniently available to all Americans, was not achieved by this program. There was never a significant change in the values or relationships of the system into which the MEDEX assistant was placed. However, the accessibility of medical care steadily declined for those deprived by economic circumstance or cultural bias as Medicaid cutbacks increased. The inefficient use and lack of coordination of myriad potential health-care resourced remained as before. There was no change in the medical care system to turn it outward and to direct its technology and skills toward the environmental factors influencing the course of illness.

In summary, despite the criticisms of selected practices, the MEDEX project clearly was a major success. It demonstrated the feasibility of applying the military model of assigning trained paramedical personnel to work with physicians to extend their capacity. This applicability was especially well shown in areas of rural practice where the demand far outstripped the supply for medical care. There was evident the need for a continuing central, organized authority in the development, distribution, and continuing consultation with the practicing physician to ensure that the quality of care remain high. Further, refinement of the training and the continuing education of MEDEX assistants would be necessary to ensure that they keep abreast of their preceptors in their ability to utilize new knowledge as it becomes available. Concerns continued regarding the applicability of a MEDEX Program under a fee-for-service system: What relative unit value should be assigned to the MEDEX assistants' services?

Finally, enlargement of the program would need to be gradual and carefully gauged so as not to exceed the capacity of the trainers to provide continuing supervision of the project in the field.

Part III

SOME PERSONAL INSIGHTS

Chapter 15

THE UNIVERSITY AND
THE URBAN CRISIS

My concern in this chapter is with the university, but it is also with our society and where it is now going. To try to separate the university or society from myself, and the changes that have taken place within me, is a difficult and almost impossible task. Thus, I ask you to bear with me, as I relate something of my own education, and try to point out where I am today, as a professor in a major American university.

The pathway to professorship, for me, was through medicine, psychiatry, and psychoanalysis. Out of this educational and professional experience grew concern not only with the individual who needs help, but a commitment to the needs of population groups who are only partially provided for by our human services, either out of lack of knowledge or power to get what they want and need, or because of basic inequities in the system. For many years, as a Washington bureaucrat, I helped support universities, in research and training, while faced all too often with their inability to meet the needs of the society. How futile it was to ask for help from universities on major social programs. How distant from policy issues, and how unrealistic was their reaction to social change and the needs of new students!

When I entered the university as a faculty member in a program in social policy planning I had already served as a national planner in mental health, fought battles in the Office of Education Research Advisory Committee as a member, worked with HUD as a top level staff person, and had participated in the creation of numerous "Golden Era" national programs: Peace Corps, War on Poverty, Model Cities, Mental Retardation.

With this background I became a professional educator, and I asked myself as I began the new role: What is education all about? A tremendous influx of new students inundated the university with mixed backgrounds and experience. Those who "knew where they were at" went to and found the established departments. Those looking for a moratorium—or a chance to find their identity—went to the new programs. An emerging new program is one where the identity is not set. City Planning, building on past physical planning and economic analytic bases, was in turmoil over social planning and advocacy and thus an ideal department for searching students with varied psychological and career profiles. Public Health, in the midst of similar changes from epidemiological laboratory to medical care, was wide open, and students with varied concerns for ecology, social health, medical services, and social reform entered in large numbers.

Similar programs fared in the same way. In schools like Berkeley, torn by the torments of student rebellion and reactive conservatism, the massive cafeteria of courses overwhelmed the student who tried to put together a personalized "gourmet" meal. Surely the same question of integrating the vast number of pieces and parts which make up knowledge has always been with us, but the input of students or users was previously a more select sample of our population. By select I mean the student was able to know exactly where he was going, what slot he was aiming for, what was needed to achieve his goals. He arrived with an ability to synthesize these parts into what he felt was a relevant whole.

Consider, then, the dilemma of a university:

1. It receives a vast input of variously prepared, motivated, and directed students.

2. The goals of its products are unknown, since the world for which the university has prepared itself is changing faster than the university's capability to deliver.

3. Great numbers of students need "processing" in an institution where faculty-student ratios have been declining and the faculty and the administration have been unwilling or unable to assist in the role of helping the student find a unique path for himself and a future role that would contribute to society's search for new solutions.

4. The university as an institution, quite naturally finding it as difficult to change as any individual faced by inevitable truths about himself, searches to find new patterns of behavior. People and institutions are inherently conservative, less by choice than by biological, social, and psychological processes that lean more easily toward "sclerosis" than toward innovation.

5. Crisis upon crisis afflicts the university which confronts piecemeal the varied parts requiring changing, leading to adaptive responses but not to critical or major reorientation of structure and process.

What I have noted about the university can be seen in the society at large. The university is the city in microcosm. It is no longer a contained, hierarchical organization with clearly defined purposes but a former "multiversity" faced by hundreds of independent parts each doing their own thing subjected to the whims and vicissitudes of all political structures, and to the power fights, turf battles, patronage, and vicious infighting we see in cities (perhaps more openly because the stakes are smaller).

The city, as Webber (1968) pointed out, is no more. It is a noncity, a collection of homogeneous places connected together by a web of arbitrary rules, freeways, and governances into a thing called a city (Los Angeles!). Where are its boundaries? Who is in charge? Is there coherence, control, or leadership?

University administrators are buffeted like mayors by the whims of riot and confrontation, the press and TV, and major decisions affecting its life are made arbitrarily without concern for the whole or the long run. How easy it is to pick a university president who is low profile, will not rock the boat, and who will not face the realities of the world but will only hold together a rocking (sinking) ship (Bennis, 1971).

The "non-university" contains the important remnants of the past: the preservation of knowledge, science, and objective analysis of the world, pieces we can not do without. Yet it is also faced by new demands "to be relevant," meeting the flood of new "immigrants" ill prepared for "citizenship." The A + universities can face this demand two ways. One position is "We are there; thus we can attempt to test ourselves and try new roles both within and outside the walls" (as Brewster at Yale). Another position is: "We must pull back and protect our flanks, because our life blood is dependent on not disturbing the source of our funds" (state universities).

The aspiring universities can only face up to their image of the "top 10" (real or imagined) and take few risks, while the bread-and-butter colleges (and some urban universities) are faced with torment and can only grow or succumb to mediocrity and the past.

These varied pressures—the demands of the community, students, faculty (sometimes), and administration may add up to change despite themselves. The external form remains the same while the quality of the courses and programs almost unconsciously transmit a new ethos.

As a psychiatrist I am so often struck by the need to "save face," to remain the same with new interpretations (the same old U.S. Constitution), and even to maintain an antichange mentality which nevertheless communicates "silent covert messages to the viewers." The television stories and news coverage which attack radicalism and confrontation nevertheless communicate a new ethos and value system that is far beyond our ability to control. The effect of the "music of the young"—censured by FCC regulations about mentioning drugs—with its complete (and impossible) suppression can only stop the communication of a new ethos.

The university is in this same situation. No matter how its official structure and curriculum communicates, a vast new competitive education system (wall newspapers, the underground press, music, and the word-of-mouth communication by rumor, telephone, travel, and informal get-togethers) is affecting the minds of those students heretofore the private educational precinct of the university machinery. Rather, it argues for changes in the unconscious while the conscious remains unchanged but tormented. It portends change in following generations who can not help but hear the covert as well as overt message.

One of the university's roles is to transmit knowledge and to assist in preparing people for the immediate future. Therefore it must create an environment which supports (1) the search for knowledge about who and what we are, were, and are becoming, and (2) the need to face problems, rather than disciplines or professions. This role is not new to the university for it has done just this in agriculture, medicine, business, and national defense. What is new is a reordering of priorities, with issues concerning people becoming more important than things.

In the move towards problems, classical positions of the university come under attack. Even though universities realize they can never destroy what already exists in program and curriculum, they nevertheless fight the added programs which may meet new demands. (The orthodox faculties, I'm sure, fought the inroads of science. Some, I know, in the not too distant past, preferred not to have practical programs such as medicine or even law in their orbit.) The arguments are diverse and polarization results.

My concern is not the abolition of what is, nor the systematic institution of control (for example, a budget control solution), for in either case we limit the number of options. Any fixing of the question "What is the university?" cannot help but limit the future options and choices. I am, thus, against either pole. Rather I would encourage the maximum number of options (mini-universities) within the whole, which would assist the student in putting together the diverse training unique to his own needs and the community's requirements.

To divorce the uniqueness of the student or, indeed, my own perception of who I am and what I need, from the question of the *roles* of a university would be a sad state of affairs. Not knowing what the future will bring, since our projections for the future always fail due to constant value and ideological shifts, it is hoped we will create a true non-city of learning, a university of diversity and dispersion, where new patterns of education will be attempted and no model will be fixed in perpetuity (Freedman, 1971; Meyerson, Rabkin, Collins & Duhl, 1969).

This, then, becomes the moment for advocacy—a statement of what one sees as being needed and an attempt to claim "one piece of the pot" in the large university universe.

Since our society is in flux and there are *no* answers to our pressing problems—only a muddling towards possible solutions—we must open ourselves to experiment. Our focus must be directed toward how our society operates and how to change it. By simplifying our needs we can see levels of concern about human behavior independent of current disciplines in the individual, in families and groups, in organization, public and private, and in government and politics.

In each we must truly begin to understand (not theoretically but by translation into action) something about the realities of society's current behavior. It is neither good nor bad: it operates pragmatically with a veneer of ideology, with patronage and corruption, with "white collar crime," with "ins" and "outs" that vary with ascension to power no matter what the ideology, with fear, selfishness, concern for private turf, with the need to preserve what is, and, finally, with the apathetic acceptance of all this as a way of life. No matter how hard we sell new images of the world, ordinary citizens (even professors) are harried by short-run concerns and bread-and-butter issues, whether they be money, happiness, accomplishment, or "kicks."

Against this knowledge of what is (raw, anthropolitical muckraking in the style of Lincoln Steffens and Albert Deutsch) must be placed the knowledge we have about change. How difficult it is to admit that active interventions may have little long-run impact and only momentary diversion of the stream of societal and individual change. How many of us "world changers" see how unimportant our role was in the nature of things. How sad is the result of psychotherapeutic evaluation which like radical and reform movements operates more on faith and input measures than the result of outputs.

We can say for sure, however, that people who participate in their own salvation—fighting for changes in things that affect their lives—feel better, have a sense of integrity and worth. We know too that those who feel they belong to family, tribe, collegial "floating crap game" or invisible college have a security which permits identity to form and an integrity to develop.

Thus the knowledge of change, its theories and techniques, critical to knowledge transmission, is also central to the structure of the educational organization itself. Whether the problem is change or evaluation of change, the focal issue may be man's relationship with man. The central question may be the infrastructure of governance and rather than the pieces and parts, the linkage, the synthesis and integration instead of individual disciplines and skills (Duhl, 1967).

What does this suggest for the university structure itself? The non-university university may well become not a purveyor of pieces of knowledge but an integrator and synthesizer. This role may be performed inside the university, or in the new non-university university, by individuals, institutes, consulting firms, and knowledge factories. What happens in these groups? People (perpetual students) within the non-university draw upon ideas, courses, and people from a variety of places located either within or outside the university proper. Faced with real life tasks (performed for better or worse) they pull together, independent of discipline, whatever is needed for the job. Ideas are integrated, people learn to synthesize, use analog thinking and develop creative innovative approaches to old issues (Schon, 1963, 1967). Unhampered by tradition, free of the security questions plaguing tenured and untenured faculties, they can produce irreverent and nonexpected responses.

Indeed many new approaches such as zero-based budgeting, block funding, cost cutting, and decentralization, among many others, have come not from established universities, but from the new think tank, consultation organization "universities." Such questions as hierarchy versus collegial models become easier. The nature of scientific research, for example, can be tested.

It is my strong belief that the critical issues of research are within the context of man's interrelationship to man, institutions, and even machines. It is the processes of interaction, the linkage questions, both formal and informal, that are critical. The nature of research shifts, especially when the variables are unclear and when values change. The appreciative system of man (Vickers, 1965) becomes unable to comprehend in old ways, and he requires new techniques for governance and integration of what "he knows." Research may require more anthropolitical incursions into situations, permitting theory to emerge from rather than to control studies (Blumer, 1969). The more standard scientific inquiry techniques may not hold in this situation.

What then for structure? A shift towards education rather than training would acknowledge our inability to predict the future. A form of integrating basic knowledge with experimental knowledge recognizes that *in vivo* and *in vitro* experiments are both needed. Educating people from multiple disciplines together reflects real life issues. Linking psychological with social and cognitive learning reflects an understanding of human behavior.

It is on this last point that I would like to dwell. The students I have seen, who come not with prescribed notions of what their role is, but with a need for a moratorium where they can find their unique future, require help which often is not forthcoming. Often their personal solutions are fortuitous depending on the faculty member with whom they work. They are lost in the "cafeteria" and the implosive demands of diverse societal inputs and they need assistance.

I have called for "therapeutic communities" as education models, knowing that the word "therapy" has negative connotations. Rather my concern is with "intentional communities" who gather for the moment (a new tribalism) to share, transmit, assist, and educate each other on mutually shared problems (Marris, 1962). Old definitions fail. Who is teacher and student? Where are the walls of the university? Are the consumers teachers or clients? All these questions and concerns and others challenge us.

By proposing this model I *do not* condemn the university as we know it to obsolescence. Rather, I'd like to use its offerings and resources in a new manner. To do so, however, requires a new notion of educational experience. In my mini-university (and there must be others with different goals) people concerned with problems (sociologists, doctors, planners, psychologists, economists, and many others) must be blended with integrative "specialists in generalization," and those concerned with bringing out the psychological best in people (Burn, 1956), as well as social experiential learning. In *Freedom to Learn*, Carl Rogers (1969) suggests that the encounter group movement, and even the communes are not models to be followed *in toto* but that they *suggest* the components of a system of learning which encourages diverse student input and output and which can produce *usable* products in assisting social change in our institutions and government.

I can easily be accused of trying to create change agents and not scholars. I can only respond that the scholars and researchers I want are those who are concerned (in my proposed mini-university) with societal change and can give us answers not to basic research but to action-oriented issues. The clinician model in medicine, with its research base is one model, focusing on issues of diagnosis, intervention and evaluation, despite limited knowledge (heresy?). This is said despite my own critique of "the medical model," which in its classical usage is unaware of the human ecological issues of man and his environment. This issue aside, my push is closer toward the professions as models rather than toward academia.

The days ahead of us seem to me to offer three options:

1. A continued nightmare (Bourne *et al.*, 1971);
2. A tight rationalized systematic control system where we think we "know" what the outputs are; or
3. A new system of planned diversity which permits nonrationality (not irrationality) and multiple attempts at solution-finding for society.

Since the University is a reflection of society and indeed reacts rather than leads (as some think it has and should) it is in the process of great change. If it resists change, it may be our twentieth or twenty-first century dinosaur. More likely it will maintain its label but give up its function to newly emerging parts of our society which uniquely are the new education institutions.

In sum, our search is for competence in the individual and in our institutions (public and private) to be able to command events that affect our lives. The basic poverty of our society (Seeley, 1976) is in our failure to meet either the pressures for change in ourselves or in our organizations by coping, adapting, growing, or being "self-renewing." Since our societal crisis, our urban crisis, is also our university crisis, it may be ludicrous to ask a crisis-ridden individual to create the conditions for his own salvation. But indeed we must, for whether it be university, community group, or government, that is the only place that salvation lies.

I turn to the university (perhaps unjustifiably, since my respect for learning and education was bred into me long ago—indeed it was culturally conditioned) in hopes that it can perform a unique role: critic, leader, educator, even therapist. I am advocating that its members and its products be part of a bigger search for solution in the broader society and in new educational institutions: an awesome challenge to the reader and to myself.

Chapter 16

INTERDISCIPLINARY TEACHING
IN HEALTH

For many years I have been concerned, almost exclusively, with interdisciplinary issues, and for 10 years with the process of graduate education in health and planning. I am left with a deep frustration which cannot be dissipated despite some insights that I believe I have achieved. To illustrate, I would like to refer briefly to an interdisciplinary program for the training of health personnel, medical doctors and others, at the University of California in Berkeley, The Health and Medical Sciences Program (UC-HMS).

The Dream

Our original belief, that is, the belief of the dreamer-planners, was:

- That health has become a euphemism for medical care and that this is a relevant area of concern for the university;
- That both health, a kind of optimized human development, and medical care relate to issues way beyond the scope of the physician;

257

- That to educate people for both of these worlds requires that they learn together, both cognitively and experientially;
- That one could use existing resources if an integrating and synthesizing experience were made available and that the disciplines involved are broad and relate to the full questions of human existence;
- Finally, we believed that a university and its surrounding community could provide both the teachers and participants a mutual learning experience (Duhl, 1973).

The program began with the first 2 years of a medical school, a mental health practitioner program, and a genetic counseling program, as well as a dual degree program where students would get two concurrent graduate degrees, in their basic field and in a hand-tailored experience in health sciences.

On the surface the program is a success, for students attracted to it have been exciting, vital, and well prepared. Some learned from the interdisciplinary courses to work together, share common language, and develop a less hierarchical model of health and medical care. However, we did not get to issues of health because:

- Vocational priorities predominated with emphasis on professionalization, preparation for licensing, and accreditation issues;
- University faculties have maintained fixed notions that physicians are the core of medical care and health, putting priority to their education and depreciating interdisciplinary education;
- Bureaucratic priorities of meeting legislative and administrative expectations overruled the issues of the original goals and expectations;
- The concept, "interdisciplinary," most often meant to people putting A and B together in a package and not synthesizing or integrating A and B into something else;
- Interdisciplinary perceptions and skills are assumed to be qualities anyone can have, the basic disciplinary skills be-

ing the important ones, the interdisciplinary, icing on the cake; and

● Protecting of turf predominates in almost all discussions, unless there is money to be obtained.

The successes of the UC-HMS Program cannot be underestimated since the students are of high caliber in their fields; funds have been obtained to fully legitimize the program; FTEs—the bread and butter of academia—have been made available; and the presence of the program is noted on and around the campus.

Interdisciplinary Ways

All this has led me to some questions about "interdisciplinary" ways of being. I have concluded that:

● It is a way of being, of perceiving and organizing reality, and the creation of new ways;

● It often comes as part of developmental growth in a person's life;

● Some people seem almost "born with it," in much the way immunologists talk about genetically different response patterns;

● It is not a cognitive function alone, but one which arises out of right brain, nonanalytic abilities;

● There are multiple levels to interdisciplinary being;

● It can be learned early in life in totally reinforcing cultures;

● At birth all persons' potentials are great but we (at least Westerners) delearn this through the education and vocational process;

● Those who are in that place of "being" most often have a specialized skill as well;

● No matter what the basic training, those who arrive at a truly interdisciplinary place, a place where vocation is transcended, are more like each other than like those of their own discipline; and

- In some forms of interdisciplinary being, learning to live within the cracks, with ambiguity and risk-taking, is a central attribute.

In general, we have also found that people who think, conceptualize, or feel in wholes, even within a systems-oriented, postindustrial society, maintain a notion of their own difference, strangeness, and sometimes expressed craziness. In the process of education it may be less important to educate for this sense of wholeness and interdisciplinariness than to give support (being a mentor) while going through the vocational disciplinary education—for example, medicine. By laying on hands one gives strength to maintaining a perceptual reality which is in conflict with dominant reality.

Interdisciplinary Learning and Teaching

Over the years of training it becomes important to link these developing students to others who, as one of them expressed it, "are one of us." Belonging to such a network, they are supported by maintaining at least two identities: the "holist" and the "specialist." Belonging is the recognition that others perceive similarly and can obtain rewards. Such support permits living with the ambiguity and risks of true interdisciplinary life.

All too often there are those who pass for interdisciplinary either because they are skilled in two or more disciplines, or they have a systems orientation. Neither can truly support a developing interdisciplinary person since the former does not have the ability to synthesize and the latter lacks a multidimensional ability to synthesize. These latter are as "vocationalized" as the specialist since they do not integrate the multiple levels of interdisciplinary experience.

Often, too, there is the academic comprehension without the experiential. It is of the latter that teachers can bear witness by their own behavior to a way of being, often more poetic, than academic or scientific. For, as we know, true creativity in science has both components.

One also hears the criticism that interdisciplinary synthesis is soft or undisciplined. It is neither, for true interdisciplinary

experience in health, medicine, or any field has a rigid requirement of discipline, which often goes unrecognized. Medicine often calls it clinical judgment; science, the beginning of states-
manship, or wisdom. Often it seems to be the ability to call upon
multiple levels of experience, knowledge, and resources by intuitive, cognitive, and other means. Can this be taught? Perhaps it
can only be evoked, but often it requires a kind of teasing out of
the creative process (Vargui, 1973; Koestler, 1964). Such work is
indeed disciplined, though not disciplinary.

All this process of learning is difficult within a discipline-
oriented university and in a field such as medicine. It constantly
amazes to see how the words interdisciplinary or holistic, for example, are accepted and mouthed, and how the process and
program that evolves follows a more standard model.

Difficulties of Change

The pressures to change come from a few dedicated people
called "one of us," from the impact of emerging problems, and
from the awareness of student and client, as part of their non-
knowing state, questioning established ideas.

The maintenance of status quo is easy to understand as a
protection of turf, but less so as holding on to a particular view
of reality. For, unless one experiences a new reality, one cannot
comprehend its existence, except in old reality terms. Progress
towards new realities interfaces with active maintenance of the
familiar, or essentially shuffling the cards of the status quo.

Because medicine and health are fields that are in great
transition, they are full of every problem that one can imagine:
values, costs, priorities, emphases, all documented elsewhere by
others. Both fields are difficult areas with which to deal. It is as
if the diagnosis of the problem is possible, but the action for
change improbable. It is as if this cannot be done unless there is
a sense of hope and a set of images showing how it might work.
These new interdisciplinary images do not truly exist except for
pieces of the problem.

I have used the words "new reality" several times, suggest-
ing that interdisciplinary is not an adequate term to express the
issues involved. For in health and medicine the words "interdis-

ciplinary" and "systems" have a strong recent history but have made little impact. New reality, therefore, means more than a Kuhnian (1970) paradigm shift. It is almost, in the terms of science fiction fans, a parallel universe where everything is the same yet completely different. To "understand" requires our whole being: one must experience it before fully knowing. The university by itself is not the place for such concerns. As yet we do not have, except as noted previously, institutions that do so in very narrow problem areas.

The Challenge

What, then, will result in change? Change will take place only when a critical mass of a new view, not a majority, is available so that the field itself is not responsible for its own change but reflects the changing "realities" of the society at large.

The dual degree program at the UC-HMS is the closest metaphor for the issues being discussed. It could be considered just two parallel degrees, for example, law and health sciences. To manage such a program would require an interested professor to assist a student in developing the parallel programs. To truly synthesize a holistic, interdisciplinary approach means a program on the interdisciplinary level as strong as in the disciplines, with experience, cognitive learning, multileveled awareness and the support for a new consciousness. The dual degree program has, as it became formalized, taken the former course, as such, keeping the outer form but losing the essence. That indeed may be the fate of our concerns until the critical mass is readied and change in reality occurs.

The field of health and medical care is a challenge not only to its practitioners, but to the society as well, for it serves as a metaphor for the larger social problems. The real question is how to seek and to find the organizing framework; and the questions of value, end results, and means are all wrapped up in the question of what is a holistic, interdisciplinary way of being. Our quality of life is at stake.

Chapter 17

PARTICIPATORY DEMOCRACY

Networks as a Strategy for Change

The purpose of this paper is to sketch on a broad canvas the significance of the rallying cry "participatory democracy." From university students in the classrooms and in the streets, from businessmen in the meeting rooms of corporations, from medical patients, welfare recipients, and urban renewal relocatees, we hear cries of people for a greater say in their own destinies. What I suggest is that these demands offer an opportunity for this society to effect the changes it so desperately needs.

Participatory democracy can be seen as a new form of democratic coalition politics and, as such, it can function as a strategy for change. For this reason it is important to understand the phenomenon. Participatory democracy rejects the traditional hierarchical structure and its values and instead embraces the decentralized power of dissimilar equals. Fundamentally, participatory democracy is a leaderless form of political organization since leadership is provisional and power is widely dispersed. Because it is leaderless, loyalty is transferred to the organization, idea, issue, or value. Thus, participation reflects allegiance to a cause which, in turn, fosters self-contained, closed societies. Because the supporting psychology is one of equality, horizontal movement becomes the new upward mobility. Within the democratic network or unit, a wide range of options are available which do not require the achievement of status but only the development of effectiveness or competence in new roles of equal status.

Why then does participatory democracy become a vehicle for social change? If one views the situation as an integrated whole, social change consists of a series of interplays among and between the many levels—individual, family, institution, business, government—where changes at any one level affect all others. A change anywhere and at any place thus reverberates throughout all systems. For example, changes in health care delivery systems affect medical, social work, and even legal subsystems. Ordinarily, most people are closed off from many of these effects and can respond only within the narrow constraints of hierarchically structured social units. Participatory democracy implies a broad range of participation, in different coalitions, allowing the mutual influences of social change to branch out in many different areas.

Participatory democracy is not a new phenomenon. The elite have always participated. Among royalties and aristocracies, birthright meant human rights. In administrations, the top echelons have generally shared decision making. Scientists traditionally have worked together, sometimes openly in societies and projects, but often in invisible colleges. So too, the intellectual elite have gathered together in their own coffeehouses, which, in eighteenth-century England, accommodated both members of the Royal Society and the East India Company. But as we move down the scale of prestige and status, smaller and smaller proportions of the population have ever participated in defining their own life situations. And, they have had only the most minor impact on larger political or social processes, mainly through threats of violence.

However, the model of the "extended family" has provided other institutions with means of allowing broader and often democratic participation. The Mafia even uses familiar terms such as "the family" and "godfather" when describing itself. The Spanish Opus Dei is a network of intellectual, technological and bureaucratic elites. The Catholic church functions in radically different ways, nearly autonomously, in its various geographies.

The Jesuits and the Mormons have operated in a similar net-work style. But even extended family forms have been useful for achieving participation only at higher levels of prestige and power.

What has changed, therefore, are the participants. Formerly, and in some societies still, perhaps 1 percent of the population participated. I estimate that we now reach 40 percent participation in some capacities in one or more of our ecological subsystems. How this has happened—why more people are allowed to play the game—is the promise of participatory democracy. What I described above are *closed* participatory democracies with very exacting admission fees. Participants are born with either the right religion, fanaticism, parentage, IQ, money, or luck. Yet these models suggest to us a structure upon which to build *open* participatory democracies responsive to our needs.

Needs and Values

And what are these needs? We are growing. There are ever more of us. And our lives seem to us ever more complex. It would seem logical that our institutions would necessarily become more complex and larger. That has happened, but instead of making the larger systems run more smoothly, the increased size of institutions seems to have had the opposite effect. The size and complexity of our institutions have increased their distance from us. This, in turn, has increased the feelings of impotence that fuel the fantasies (and realistic perceptions) of nonparticipation. This is intensified because institutions have a propensity for self-perpetuation. When maintaining a traditional institution and its power structure becomes a primary goal, an institution becomes discontinuous with the purpose for which it was erected. It becomes rigidified. It ages badly.

The distance, complexity, and unmanageability of our institutions combines with the directness, proximity, and immediacy of our communications to intensify alienation. Thus, when basically nonbureaucratic institutions develop bureaucratic hierarchies, our ordinary and natural means of communication and exchange become useless for reaching the centers of institutional power or responsiveness. We have a front row seat in war, but most of us could not find our way from one office to another in the Penta-gon. This results in the inability of people to define themselves, as they once did, by their participation in one of the local games. The political party, the union, the corporation have all lost, for many people, the particularity necessary as a prerequisite for abiding loyalty. As a result, participation rarely gets beyond pro forma activity or conformity.

This leads many people to question the values upon which our society has rested. People are increasingly recognizing that all answers do not lie within mathematical probabilities, systems theory, and the ability to provide hardware, technology, or even material goods. They look toward interpersonal relationships and humanness for answers. Many people turn toward the dis-advantaged, who, like themselves, they see as the objects of the inequities of the system. They are concerned that society does not seem to care about the individual. They recognize that there are needs for childhood, growth, and development. They see the potential availability of food, of love, and of education for all. Yet they see that these basic human needs of the life cycle are not being met. They see the very existence of our present social institutions as devices that perpetuate past inequities rather than cure social ills or promote normal human development. They see that they want changes and that they need to make these changes themselves. But it is hardly surprising that those who see this most and best are those who have not developed unques-tioning commitments to traditions and institutions: the young, the explorers, the disenchanted, and the underprivileged.

What results is a new coalition politics concerned with the process of change as well as with the product. No longer does it suffice to build a day-care center. The architectural and organizational plans must represent the shared work of the potential consumers as well as the suppliers. A group of medical professionals can no longer design what they perceive as an adequate health care de-livery system. Patients, as well as the suppliers, purveyors, and regulators, demand participation in these plans which affect their well-being, or, as it often turns out, their ill-being. Al-though this may not yet be the dominant pattern in our society, all the signs point toward an increased sensitivity to issues of par-ticipation in the events and structures that will influence one's destiny. This movement is expanding at all levels and among all groups, pressing for a new definition of democracy and involvement in our society.

Social System Responses

In response to these demands, the "new" model of the extended family emerges. *We are witnessing, on a very small scale, yet perhaps prophetically, the emergence of families of colleagues, informal networks, floating universities, groupings with open memberships.* Such groups function in the academic university setting as well as in the utilitarian ghetto milieu. What binds the members of these groups together are shared concerns and values. Many of these subsystems reflect the revolution in values, the antimaterialistic, humanistic approach to problem solving. In reaction to a closed world, they stress in their titles, their equality and openness— collaborations, cooperatives, communes, coalitions. Often, while a spokesman may represent the group on an ad hoc basis, no real leadership emerges. For example, who is the president of an invisible college in science? Who is the leader in the vast social changes we are part of? Who is leading the student revolts, or the demands of the blacks, of welfare mothers, of parents of school children? If a leader arises in one area at one time, he is hardly likely to be the same leader in another movement elsewhere. It is a swelling, sporadic tide that tells us of a new movement grounded in a widespread popular sense.

Some consulting firms have been at the forefront of organized groups desirous of transforming themselves into open-ended, loose cooperatives. Theoretically, the organization works without rules and laws, with information freely flowing to all members. The purpose is to build an institution whose internal dynamics create a series of relationships between a series of innovative groups so that the whole is greater than the parts—in other words, a university. The aim of this structure is to provide an institutional response to the need for educating for change. Yet what is supposed to be a learning network more often is a "school." Politics and financial rewards, to name just a few impositions, interfere with the infrastructure. Yet success can—in fact, *must*—be achieved, for the creation of learning networks is the essence of a viable coalition in politics. All closed subsystems must be opened to allow adequate interface for interaction.

Fundamental Changes Needed

This is all to say that some fundamental changes are essential to the functioning of this society, and that participatory democracy—an ecology of open networks—offers us a means to effect these changes. Because we live in an ecological system, a change in any subsystem can be experienced throughout if we do not create artificial barriers. Thus, the techniques for change are plentiful. The individual still can make a difference. And, increasingly he *must* make a difference. So too, group and institutional action can affect the infrastructure. One need only reflect on the antiwar movement and the 1968 presidential election to realize this. But this, unfortunately, leads us to question what the change is toward. My position, I hope, is clear.

We must decentralize to permit a maximum of pluralistic responses so that individual needs can be met differently by specialized groups. To this end, I offer the conceptual model of an ecological system of open-ended participatory democracies that permit the leverage to effect change. *But we must know what we want.* We must define the problems and secure the minimal data. Only on the basis of a clear understanding of the issues and facts can these open-ended networks, uncommitted to traditional values or organizations, form new and meaningful coalitions. Widespread change will require flexible coalitions at broader levels founded on smaller networks with more limited goals.

My model imposes great hardships on the individual. Leadership is virtually up for the asking, which means that we are all leaders, either good or bad ones. The problem, then, is how best to educate ourselves for this new kind of leadership thrust upon us.

Peter Marris (1962), in research on entrepreneurship in Kenya, hints at the necessary educative processes in his discussion of an African nation's abortive takeover of the economy after the exclusion of the British. In the customary manner, the British and others provided the blacks with adequate capital and sufficient technical assistance, yet their businesses failed. Marris believes that the failure lies in a poorly conceived "educational" system. That is, instead of blacks being taught the skills necessary for directing businesses, they were exercised in the rote motions of second-level managers. In contrast, the Harvard University School of Business prepares scores of young men and women to take over the reins of the economy. The success of the business school is not a function of a heretofore unpublished text on the secrets of Horatio Alger, but rather reflects a concept of education. Students at the business school spend their years making contact with one another and with other members and future members of the business structure while problem solving. For them, and indeed for all of us, reaching the top is easy when the steps are so visible. Thus, *what the Kenyans needed to learn in a business school was not economics, but rather how to reach and rely on one another—what I call "network learning"—as a technique of problem solving.*

The essence of network learning is the realization that success equals the setting of conditions for success. To begin with, network learning entails a recognition (that is, a re-perceiving) of "old" systems. For example, communication is a critical aspect of network life. The telephone can be used as an instrument linking together scores of disparate (in both geography and ideology) people. So too, transportation and money are systems with untapped potential. These are tangibles—"real systems," as I choose to call them. *But the core of network learning is the intangible, the human.* In fact, a network person must be defined as one who "doesn't keep book," who has no records of IOUs. He is not concerned with the quantifiable, the statistical, and the technical, but rather builds his web of relations of personal and human ties, imitating the style and structure of the extended family. Elite groups have always utilized a network approach to sustain power and control. Peasants and poor working people have used it to compensate for their lack of power and control. In the 1960s the concept of networks that brought people in crisis or with similar problems together, became more common. People learned to rally together in neighborhood or family crises and hospitals and communities established more formalized ways to deal with such situations as suicide, bereavement, alcoholism, illness, etc. The spread of networks and coalitions, devoted to issues rather than existing groups, expands enormously the potential of effective, goal-directed action that is founded on shared ideas and human interactions.

Because he recognizes the unmeasurable aspects of human nature, the network person is uniquely capable of dealing with the complexities of modern life. Unlike the Kenyans in Marris' work who failed to understand that technical, measurable plans are not adequate, the network does *not* assume that the peripherals will follow automatically once the hard data are set down. The network person understands that what we need is precisely the reverse. *We must plan the peripheries—the values, the networks, and the invisible colleges—and then the technology and the hardware can be plugged in automatically. The reformation, the revolution we all talk about, is just this. The nonrational systems of human ties must become our building blocks. Social and cultural values must take precedence over technology if indeed our hardware is to work.* And they must have new forms to avoid the excessive stability and hierarchies of traditional organizations. This, of course, brings us into the realm of governances, rules, laws, or the "game of games"—that is, politics. What I have described as the reformation is the New Politics, the politics that takes cognizance of the importance of human values and relations.

The question now is how to effect change in this new politics. The old party politics of majority rule and party loyalty, where if A is greater than B there is change, no longer works in a society without predictable loyalties, hence majorities. Instead, we must turn to "pragmatic radicalism," dealing with each issue separately and sacrificing ideological considerations for the issue at hand. Since majorities can no longer be secured across the board, we must work for ad hoc majorities, thereby changing situation A, then B, and then C. Fortunately, these ad hoc majorities are easily secured, indeed, participatory democracy is the demand of individuals who want to affect these concrete situations. Ultimately, the real task will lie in our ability to form coalitions of effective majorities, for fundamental change represents the sum of these effective majorities. And by educating ourselves in learning network schools, we will develop the requisite abilities to cope with our complex society.

Chapter 18

DYSLEXIA

The pattern of learning and the pattern of work that I have worked out for myself over the years is related to dyslexia. The realization of my condition came about in an interesting way. I had been told that my son was dyslexic when he was in the second grade. A reading difficulty emerged at that time which, after careful evaluation, was diagnosed, and special tutoring was provided for him. His reading improved markedly and there were few difficulties through many of the years that followed.

I did not consider the diagnosis again even during the time in high school when he began to have difficulty with foreign language and with his basic English composition. His grades were beginning to suffer but I assumed that this was due to the particular period of time that he was in school (in the 60s) and I thought his difficulties were probably because of a distress due to a family crisis in which parents who up to then had been in a stable marriage were now divorced. He received psychological and psychiatric help, but little change in his academic ability occurred except that he was certainly much more comfortable with himself.

When he went off to college it became clear for the first

time that he was having tremendous difficulty with writing, spelling, and with a foreign language. This time he received tutoring which helped him slightly and he arranged for his own psychological help.

He did, however, drop out of college after 2 years, during which time he became a hot-dog skier and began to run a restaurant. Noting his increased capabilities in math and basic management skills, he began talking of going into business as a career.

It was then that I became aware for the first time that through his activities in high school, wrestling, running, and handball, and now skiing, he had increased his physical coordination. This was my first clue that perhaps the dyslexia that we had noted earlier was still interfering with his learning.

Dyslexia is a broad catchall diagnosis which includes a variety of disabilities of mind, eye, and physical coordination. The areas most easily noted are difficulties in reading, the reversal of letters, spelling inadequacy, the reversal of numbers, difficulties in mathematics, and the inability to deal with foreign languages.

It was at this time that I myself recalled that I had had these difficulties all during my childhood. I had been "blamed" for messy math papers and, although I had always gotten the answers right, there was a threat of being flunked for this sloppiness, all of which resulted in a top grade but a failure to continue in the field of mathematics. I also had particular difficulty in learning French and found it necessary to memorize an essay on riding a bicycle so that I could pass the New York State Regents examination. This essay had been corrected by my teacher and I remembered it perfectly. When I got into the exams, the essay question was, "How did you spend your last summer?" I replied that I had spent my summer riding my bicycle in the park and then proceeded to write my essay. By using this technique, I passed.

But more important, I realized that I had learned how to read, courtesy of a librarian, when I was about eight or nine years old. She taught me how to scan and speed-read. I read voraciously until my first 2 years in medical school, when memorization was critical: I could not remember word for word and I almost flunked. Soon thereafter, when my clinical work began in earnest, my grades improved markedly.

These are but a few of the situations with which I was faced.

My son returned to school and proceeded to do extremely well with courses. The work that he had done as an athlete and in his restaurant job certainly helped him. The fact that he was in his early twenties also helped, because dyslexics seem to improve with age. However, he still had difficulty and proceeded to have himself tested at a major university medical school. There it became clear that although his dyslexia had improved, he had tremendous difficulty with spelling, writing, and situations that involved learning a foreign language. His intelligence was obviously more than adequate and the school officials recognized that he should be excused from foreign language and be assisted with writing.

He received tutoring and was able to do extremely well.

About this same time my own personal awareness markedly increased and I became acutely aware of students on the graduate level who were having great difficulty in writing their papers and with subjects such as statistics. Very quickly I did a rough screening of some of these students and realized that they, too, were number reversers and had difficulty writing and reading aloud.

I might say parenthetically that my own experience in reading aloud was such that I had given up reading speeches and primarily talked off-the-cuff without notes. This especially occurred as my own nearsightedness got worse and I required glasses. I found my own writing very hard to read and this, coupled with the process of reading aloud, became laborious. I encompassed this by engaging a secretary who not only typed up my material but corrected it.

In the students' cases I found that they had acquired some ingenious techniques. These included: making sure they took courses that emphasized discussion, classes in which true/false or multiple choice examinations were given, courses that allowed them to take home papers that were to be written (which they would do and rewrite three or four times), avoiding mathematics and statistics courses, and moving to the softer subjects.

These strategies gradually lead, as they did in my own case, to the development of a life-style which includes a secretary who edits one's papers, an assistant to help on proposals and letters, and joint editorship of books and articles with someone competent in the demanding editing required of professional and academic work.

The many students I saw revealed a range of difficulties that included both writing and mathematical skills. With tutoring they improved their work measurably. The tutoring included those activities which emphasized techniques having to do with comparisons, dealing with textures, shapes, and forms, as well as learning ways to read which do not use the standard eye-hand or eye-mouth coordination.

As for my son, it became clear that the notion of balance and also physical coordination are critical. It is interesting that dyslexics have trouble coordinating fine movements. They must learn, as did my son, with gross movements—wrestling, running, and sports that are big-movement oriented.

In the developmental pattern of dyslexics many turn out to be people who had not learned how to crawl as infants. Many of these children were "scooters" who coasted along, pulling their legs behind. This suggested a technique for learning methods of cross-crawling or swinging arms and legs as one does in walking and running which assists in balancing the body. It seems that those who have this difficulty also have problems of dominance mix. Many, like myself, were dominant in the left eye, but utilized the right hand in writing. Simple tests can show this mixed dominance to be present in many dyslexics.

Dyslexics in society have been estimated to number as many as 20 percent, with males revealing an incidence rate almost four times that of females.

An interesting experience of my own fits into some of these issues of physical difficulties. In my own case, my malcoordination manifested itself in my being inadequate in sports, a stumbler, a person incapable of dancing or learning how to dance, or of playing tennis. In my late forties, when I decided that I was going to learn how to play tennis at all costs, I did so only by returning to my instructor once a week for almost 3 years. Fortunately this instructor emphasized only the positive aspects of my performance, not focusing at all on the negative. He was also a person who spent time creating the positive image rather than breaking down the movement into its critical parts. It became clear fairly soon that I had learned some of the imagery of movement, because I found myself able to fantasize the movements that had to be made. In about a year and a half, I found that my ability to play was fair. My swings were good, although there was really very little power behind them.

One day, quite incidentally, my right arm was hurting and instead of letting me leave the court the instructor encouraged me to start playing with my left hand. I have since done this on a regular basis. I found that not only could I play, but that the strength of my right-hand strokes improved markedly. If one were to speculate that there is a balancing of the body, one could suggest that this technique, reflected both in my tennis playing and in such sports as running and skiing, would enhance the ability to play tennis. But more important than that, the transition of the physical to the psychological skill was also evident. My son's critical comment after he learned to ski was to state that he now felt he could transfer this competence from the physical to his cognitive learning.

One of the most interesting aspects of understanding dyslexics has been that most of their lives they are quite convinced that they are stupid or lazy. Teachers tend to urge them to try harder believing that if the person would only try harder and if they would prove to themselves that they could be able to do the work. In many instances, they are treated as if hearing-impaired, with instructions being delivered in a raised voice.

Those of us in a culture where cognitive learning is given high priority over emotional and physiological learning, find it especially difficult to deal with our own dyslexia. The reason this seems to be so is that the inner-voice and inner-image has never focused on physical movement and only focuses on the cognitive. Often we have cognitive fathers who push the cognitive side. They are tremendously forceful and we tend to be overwhelmed by their push towards these kinds of activities. They deny the kinds of problems that we have. We, ourselves, then pick up these perceptions in dealing with our own children. Students manage to focus on this and the result is that they are not open to the possibility that the difficulties and solutions lie in another realm.

One of the people involved in my son's admission to university suggested that he work on improving his ability in a variety of ways. This counselor seemed quite insensitive to the dyslexia, claiming that it was less important than my son's ability to work on his problems. A telling incident occurred in which the adviser suggested that if my son were able to demonstrate his ability in subjects such as English composition and language, he could get into the university, and then, when he got in, would probably not have to take these subjects. This became a double bind, and created a situation that was particularly difficult for my son. The university official believed that to label my son dyslexic would be to stigmatize him for the rest of his life. It is my impression that the reverse is true. Many people who are dyslexic tend to consider themselves "crazy"; therefore the label "dyslexic" permits them to isolate the problem—and in knowing the diagnosis they find that there are ways to cope with the conditions and related issues.

The need for sensitivity in schools, colleges, and psychological institutions in this area is great. Very often the difficulty is translated as a psychological one rather than of malcoordination and dyslexia. The need to deal with these students as if they had a handicap is basic. It is interesting to note that many institutions are willing to accept physical handicaps, but psychological and psychophysiological ones preclude admission. However, under the Handicapped Act, schools and institutions may not discriminate against handicapped people, and these include dyslexics. Of course, in entering schools, and in the curriculum, they must be given special help. The handicapped who are in wheelchairs require special bathrooms and ramps. Dyslexics may need techniques using tape recorders, editors to assist them, and the development of new ways to learn subjects like language. Allowances may also have to be made at first because dyslexics' inability with certain aspects of learning cannot be corrected by "hard work," but by developing entirely new techniques.

It is particularly important for universities, colleges, and schools, as well as businesses, to look very carefully into these invisible handicaps, because the number present in our society is much greater than is realized. This may also require a review of the techniques available to us for both teaching and work, since the patterns that fit for the majority of the population do not work for the dyslexic.

Such have been the indications from long personal experience with a disorder that seems to run in families, and also from experience with a number of students, children of friends, and many of my patients.

I conclude by recommending the book *Reversals* (Simpson, 1979), the autobiography of a dyslexic woman who sensitively reveals her personal difficulties and speaks to the strange sense of differentness and oddness that one has because one does not know that one has capabilities that are of value. She was diagnosed as dyslexic at the age of twenty-two, not by a physician or teacher, but by a poet.

In my own case, it has been my good fortune to find a job and life-style that have enabled me to meet the problems of work in ways that bypass my dyslexic incapabilities. The fact that I can use a secretary, that I can talk at meetings and use seminars, and that I can avoid specifically focused writing has been tremendously important for my own sense of well-being. Furthermore, I've learned to create a world for myself that does not entail being measured in the typical manner and, if one learns to be an expert in a field that nobody else is in but in which others necessarily reflect, one need never have his or her own inadequacies or dyslexia uncovered.

There have been many dyslexics of note, ranging from Leonardo da Vinci, Gustave Flaubert, Thomas Edison, and Woodrow Wilson to Nelson Rockefeller. Outstanding examples, however, are not those for whom we need feel concern. It is on those who have not developed the ability to cope that we must begin to focus. Until we do, we are losing segments of our population that could be highly productive and that loss, as much as theirs, is ours.

Chapter 19

ON LEARNING DISABILITIES

A Proposal for the Office of Technology Assistance[1]

Some handicaps are not as immediately observable as others, and because of their subtlety, they are difficult to address. Learning disabilities, occurring in otherwise normal individuals, are among such handicaps. The learning disabled are unable to learn in conventional classrooms although their difficulty is not attributable primarily to mental retardation, visual, auditory or motor handicaps, emotional disturbance, or socioeconomic disadvantage.

Estimates of the extent of these handicaps in the school-age population vary, reflecting differences in the definition applied, the types of assessment tools, and the background of the estimators. Most estimates fall between 3 and 16 percent. Problems of accurately identifying the learning disabled population also involve a lack of agreement concerning the type and number of syndromes and subcategories involved. People attempting to assess the extent of this disability cite inflated estimates relating to financial and commercial aspects—a fast-growing field of pro-

---

[1]This study was completed by the Office of Technology Assistance of the Congress of the United States in 1983 (Cousins & Duhl, 1983).

fessionals, publications, programs, and materials. Drake Duane, President of The Orton Society (established in 1949 to educate professionals and the general public on dyslexia), has stated that even if one accepts the conservative estimate of 5 percent of the school-age population, it would mean that "reading retardation constitutes a greater health problem than the combined occurrence of mental retardation, cerebral palsy, and epilepsy."

The figure most commonly quoted for dyslexia, the figure given out by The Orton Society and corroborated by other English-speaking countries, notably Canada and England, is that 1 person in 10 is dyslexic (Simpson, 1979).

In addition to the school-age population, a growing number of adults in college and the work force are now being identified as suffering from learning disabilities that have never been treated or naturally compensated for. Thirty-two percent of incarcerated juveniles are estimated to be learning disabled, and in the prison population, estimates go as high as 80 to 90 percent.

The field of learning disabilities—even the term—is relatively new. "Word blindness" first appeared in the literature in 1911, followed by "dyslexia" in 1928, and "organic brain syndrome" in 1934. In 1963 Samuel Kirk first introduced the term "learning disabilities," followed by "the minimally brain-dysfunctioned child" in 1966 and "learning dysfunction" in 1967. Efforts by teachers and parents to minimize distressing effects of labeling have resulted in dropping references to brain "injury," "damage," or "dysfunction."

During the last decade of the nineteenth century the first observations appeared in the literature of bright children in England who were unable to read, write, or spell. In the 1920s Samuel Orton conducted detailed observations of school children in Iowa who had a variety of learning problems but were intelligent and neurologically intact. In the 1960s, the field began to grow at a fast rate and continues to grow each year. Since the 1970s theories concering etiology and treatment have multiplied, none enjoying universal acceptance.

The etiological theory, which most closely approaches gaining widespread acceptance, is that learning disabilities are based on a neurological condition. Because learning takes place in the brain, it is reasonable to assume that a problem in learning is a problem in brain function. The physiological basis of the disorder has been inferred since most learning disorders show no physiological change. This inference comes from studies of autopsies of adults with gross cerebral damage.

In the last few years, however, advances in the technology of brain research have made possible contributions supporting the neurological theory. In the late 1970s *Science* published information about one study indicating peculiarities in electrical brain activity and another indicating the presence of abnormal levels of toxic elements in the hair of learning disabled children. At an international meeting on epilepsy in Florence, Italy, in 1981, a method of using an electroencephalogram (EEG) to construct a "color-coded mapping system" to observe the working brain as it processes information was described.

Advances in brain research, however, do not ensure advances in serving the learning disabled population. The gap between the researchers and the practitioners—certainly not specific to this field alone—has been cited as an ongoing problem. Another example, among many, is the continuing acceptance of the perceptual deficit hypothesis by practitioners in schools and clinics despite strong evidence to the contrary (Cousins & Duhl, 1983).

As yet, no theory advanced seems to explain (a) the extent of learning disabilities, (b) the fact that some disabled are able to compensate and others are not, (c) the broad range of symptoms, (d) the lack of definitive treatment and (e) the power of this not obvious disorder to shape entire lives.

Some of the treatments studied, such as remedial education, perceptual training, gross motor exercise, and special diets indicate that only a portion of those identified are actually helped. It may be that each of the treatments addresses one form of disorder in a broad range of disorders. Or it may be that the treatments speak only to one aspect of a problem which involves a complex web of the person, technology, and the environment.

An important aspect of this social system has been recent legislation. Although there has been federal legislation dealing with the education of the handicapped since 1966, the Education for All Handicapped Children's Act of 1975 (EHC) was the first that directly addressed specific learning disabilities as a handicap of equal status along with other handicaps. On September 1, 1978, the EHC Act took full effect, requiring states to establish programs providing a free appropriate education to all handicapped children *if* they wanted to qualify for federal assistance. The law required the standardization of systems to identify those individuals requiring special help. On the federal, state, and local level this has resulted in a massive reorganization of services for the learning disabled. School districts all over the country are in various states of transition in order to be legally compliant. Private schools and agencies are being contracted by school districts to serve the needs of the learning disabled; medical and psychological professionals are being hired for purposes of diagnosis and programming; teacher licensing is being modified; new professional categories are being created to replace old ones; parent advocates and learning disabilities specialists in private practice are being hired as consultants by parents and schools alike; children are being mainstreamed, identified, tested, and remedial action taken.

Another part of the system is the development of technology and its social use. Technology for the learning handicapped can be thought of as ideas, social responses, and organizational structures, as well as objects or machines. The use of ideas, machines, and objects should be considered in light of the social context in which they are used. The social use of technology, of course, can make all the difference.

Because learning disabilities is a "soft" handicap, it can be addressed with a minimum of "hard" technology. Mainstreaming learning disabled children, for example, does not require ramps or modified plumbing. However, if mainstreaming is to appropriately address the needs of learning disabled children, teachers require training and support services to deal with the range of learning styles and learning needs. Mainstreaming, in and of itself, is not a cure for either learning problems or stigmatization. As yet, there is no scientific evidence that children with handicaps benefit from mainstreaming, to say nothing of research into what types of environments best address the development of individuals with various handicaps.

Is more "hard" technology what is needed for the learning disabled? Are social, organizational, or personal interventions more efficient, and effective, or are they parsimonious? How can technology help us to truly determine the needs of the learning disabled? What are the most effective ways of using technology and delivering services to the learning disabled?

Research and development needs in the field include: outcome studies for treatments and programs, particularly mainstreaming; factors that contribute to reading proficiency in the normal child; epidemiological studies with strict exclusion criteria; surveys of professionals and policymakers concerning definition, identification, and treatment. Research might do well to get around the problematic issue of definition. Then studies might be done of populations that have not been identified as learning disabled.

On this basis, we propose a study of the present field of learning disabilities that would include reviews and evaluations of:

- Surveys and epidemiological studies of various forms of learning deficiencies in order to map the types, the range, and the interrelatedness of the problem;

- Various methods of identification, current diagnostic categories, relationship of diagnosis to social and environmental context, the personal and organizational response to labeling;

- The range of available intervention techniques, personnel involved and institutions concerned with the problem, techniques which alleviate or exacerbate the problem;

- Research and development relating to technology and its social use; and

- Review of recent literature, state of the art, most pressing problems and questions.

The model used will be to look at learning disabilities as a system, including the history of its development as a field. Recommendations will be made in light of how this particular handicap is similar to other "soft" handicaps, particularly in respect to the utilization and development of "low" technology. Recommendations will also include addressing research and development, organizational change, and business, industry, and consumer needs.

Chapter 20

THE HEALTHY CITY

Its Function and Its Future

Talking to a group of international journalists, Prime Minister Nehru of India is reported to have said, "The climate of England is superb, but its weather is awful."

As with perceptions of England and its weather, describing the health of a city is complex and multifaceted. Cities break down. Parts of them ail and falter, and when this happens they need to be put into good working order. Persons trained in the health sciences may be particularly equipped to look at the city because not only are they trained to get people and systems to work—to be healthy—but, in the end, they may be able to judge the degree to which the healthy city contributes to the maximal well-being of the individuals in it.

But, what is the climate of the city? How can we look at the city to understand what is needed to make the city work at its highest level of competency? To enable us better to see the city, its complexities, and its weather and climate we will look at it here in health terms.

A city is a complex organism which, if one stretches this metaphor by comparing it to the human organism, has its many organs and connecting parts. What makes each of us humans work is a complex biological and psychological set of processes that are able to perform different kinds of functions. Each part has within it a set of functions that are unique, and within each part are materials and mechanisms that assist in connecting it to the surrounding organs in the human organism.

Think, then, of the city as having a heart and blood vessels, lungs with a respiratory system, a brain and central nervous system, a liver and metabolic system, and kidneys with an excretory system. These organs and systems with their functions could be compared to the energy, environmental, transportation, communications, nutritional, and disposal systems of the city—the infrastructure. There are also the connectors and a complex of interlinked organ systems of various kinds, the roads and communications networks that carry nourishment and waste as well as messages to the other parts so that either the other parts can act in concert or so that the total organism as a whole can work coherently. There is no action that takes place that doesn't affect the whole human. So is it with the city.

It is not difficult to see the contrasting and related functions of unique specialization and a system related to open learning that is needed for any part or for the whole of the organism that is the city to work well.

An example of this is the characteristic redundancy in the organism we are describing that permits messages to go through various pathways and the ability of one part to replace another if necessary. In an economy-conscious world, in the city organism, attempting savings, we tend to fight such redundancies when in fact their presence may permit a more cost-effective system. The human organism, as most of us have seen, is often saved because when one part doesn't work there is another part to take over.

The concept of "reciprocal maintenance," the need for each part of an organism to be assisted and nourished by another, is an important "rule" for healthy operation of the organism. Although this is the basis of current ecological belief, the idea is ancient. Old Sufi writings as well as Taoist concepts of thousands of years ago describe this idea.

REQUIREMENTS FOR A HEALTHY CITY

I am pushing the concept of the human metaphor, characterizing the city as an organism, because I believe the condition of urban health requires that we take a different kind of look at what makes a city healthy.

A healthy city must be a competent one for each of its members and for the community as a whole. Clearly we must see the city as a developing and changing organism which need not be like any other. However, the city must have, as must humans, other communities and cities with which it interacts for mutual gain. By using the words, "mutual gain," I am projecting a value which, along with reciprocal maintenance, takes us away from two existing theories: "In order to survive I must put the other [person] down" and "If I attain my goals, the excess will trickle down to others." Both of these theories can be shown to be destructive to the organism. For my liver to kill off the competitive kidney may be to destroy the human organism. Furthermore, at this time in our history, when we appear to be using up our resources, it is critical that we work out ways to use and revitalize what we have. We cannot ask the environment or others to maintain us unless we maintain ourselves and our environment.

What happens when chronic conditions, social problems, become exacerbated and "take over" the healthy body? What, then, are the requirements for a competent "healthy city organism?"

In my view, there are several overall requirements. First of these is that the city's responses to its developmental needs, its organizations, and its people be appropriate and effective. Second is that the city have the ability to cope with breakdowns of the system and its members. The third, then, is that the city have the ability to modify itself and change to meet the always emerging, changing requirements for life. This then leads, fourth, to the city's competence to enable its inhabitants to use it to their advantage. Finally, it must be understood that this cannot be accomplished unless the city is able to educate its inhabitants.

1. An Ability to Provide the Developmental Needs

What are the needs, the actions, and the infrastructure required at any stage in the development of a healthy city? What does the city need to develop into a healthy organism which, it-self, will allow others to grow and flourish?

Basic Needs.   Obviously the most basic needs must be met: food, clothing, shelter, safety, health care, as well as a human support system. Often, however, contrary to Gandhi's advice "to focus on needs, not wants," we have had a preoccupation with "wants." Indeed, we have created a society where *wants* are covering up real *needs* of the majority of the population. This ap-plies to both ends of the economic spectrum of the city's citizens. Sadly we see that the "wants industry" with its built-in obsoles-cence is central to our current values.

Often we believe that it is only the poor, the oppressed, and the so-called underclass whose needs are not met. However, in pursuing their wants the economically advantaged frequently lose sight of the fact that some of their basic needs must be met before they can go on to what Maslow calls "the higher needs." Although for the poor, too often some of the most basic needs are not met, for other poor they are met beyond anything that the "rich" can perceive. Many of the so-called minorities of our multiple communities have within them values, ways of being, relating, and of "knowing" that contain ideas for solutions to their problems and those of mainstream cultural and ethnic groups that are quite different and imaginative from those of the prevailing cultures.

A city, then, must have the ability to meet the bottom-line needs of its various citizens. It must be able to set the "climate" within which people can live their unique lives. To accomplish this it must "know" the needs of its diverse parts and people, to be deeply imbued in others' ways of being, putting aside preju-dices and preconceptions and firmly held points of view.

Functional and Aesthetic Needs.   There is more to life, how-ever, than the basic needs. *All* of the functions of life must be able to take place. Although there must be places to be born, to grow, learn, work, live, and die, there must also be places to play or to "just be," to waste time, to be with those we care about and who care for us—to nurture the spirit and grow. The city is made up of complex pleasures as well. People must be able to deal with the variety of activities that make up human life which include the aesthetic, artistic, cultural, and sports experiences where they can actively and passively participate.

The city must have room for "families" in all their forms, as well as for the entrepreneurship and creativity which allow people to express their unique skills and their cultural heritage and be rewarded. The importance of individual development and collective growth and the involvement of the family in the process of making the city a hospitable place cannot be underestimated.

Sometimes functional and aesthetic needs can be met by what seem to be small changes. Ideally the more groups involved, the better are the chances of successful outcome.

Communication and Networks.   Basic needs and places, cultural enrichment, and activities alone cannot make a city: connecting linkages are required which are different at different times. Linkages include not only paths, roads, highways, buses and airports, but they also include communication by mail and now, electronically, by radio, television, computer, and emerging variations.

The city needs ways to permit the flow of nourishment whether it be food, money, ideas, or touching between people. It needs communications within its boundaries and with the outside. It needs the nourishment of meaning, values, beliefs, and spirituality not only for the city but for its people. Only with communications can a city serve all of its parts allowing people of differing cultures and experiences to learn of other beliefs, value systems, and ways of doing.

A large number of studies in many disciplines have demonstrated that the ability of individuals to connect as part of a network of extended family and community decreases morbidity and mortality. People who are sick but are connected and linked to others become well faster and are less apt to continue in poor health or to die prematurely. The ability to link permits interconnections on levels not measured by standard means. Thus, to be part of a family or an immediate neighborhood or to have the ability to communicate, even by means of a telephone, becomes critical to an individual's ability to remain healthy (Duhl, 1968d; Duhl & Levinson, 1979).

Rebuilding the Infrastructure.   One of the ideas that seems to have a certain appeal these days is to "just go ahead" and rebuild the infrastructure of our cities. When people talk about infrastructure they usually refer to the hard structures—the water, sewage, transport, and communications systems—ignoring the interactional structure of how people govern, mediate, and cope with heterogeneous values and beliefs. The processes of governance and politics are, in reality, the battle of values between people who are able to separate their own views from their perceptions of reality. It is a battle of many "goods."

Governance and management of the infrastructure will be important in the next years. We must explore, study, innovate, and remember other styles. Such thinking and action can be seen in some of the fastest growing companies who are seeing that new participatory management patterns are critical to their survival and growth. A broad base for participatory input is most valuable, but it is also important not to throw out the baby with the bathwater.

Ecological Considerations.   The concepts of our own and reciprocal maintenance—humans needing each other, the basic needs, the aesthetic and recreational needs and the need for places, the necessity to modify and maintain the infrastructure—are all part of these concepts. But, as we struggle to deal with these aspects of our maintenance we must not lose sight of the most basic need of all, that increasingly, as we invade the spaces of the planet and elsewhere, we find that our need for Mother Earth to maintain us must be matched by our need to maintain her and her organisms. Each of us has a part and a role to play although at any given moment in time we may not be able to see it. In being unable to see it we may destroy what, in the long run, we may need the most, the earth's ability to regenerate herself.

2. Ability to Cope with Breakdown

In looking at the developmental needs, comparing people and cities, we must also be totally aware, capable, and ready to deal with a second need, self-maintenance following crisis and breakdown. Inherent or acquired weaknesses in a major, or even a minor system may cause it to wear out so that eventually a weak link can snap and break the chain of life. Responding to this requires an understanding of the problem and the means at any point to assist a person or organization that is in difficulty. In medicine we call this condition "dis-ease."

If and when "dis-ease" turns into illness or disease, the city must have all the complex, scientific, and other necessary skills to reverse the process and to assist the individual or organization to return to paths of competence and health. Often another problem is created because the means or institutions that were used which were successful for coping in the past do not meet the needs of the present. The city must know when that time, the breakdown, comes and be flexible enough to meet new, emerging conditions.

3. Ability to Change and Modify

When it recognizes that something is wrong, this city, this developing, changing organism, must have the ability to modify itself and change to meet the always changing requirements for life. Although such skills are necessary for coping once breakdown has occurred, breakdown may be avoided if the city is able to meet these changing requirements (Duhl & S. Blum, 1981).

As with humans, cities are different. Their location, their character, their genetic makeup are unique. We human organisms differ from each other in details of genetics, body design, and structure and we each have our unique strengths and weaknesses. History modifies and changes, requiring the city organism constantly to recreate itself and its parts. A city is a living, breathing, growing, changing, complex organism that has too often, of late, been looked at as only an economic entity. Focusing only upon economic cost criteria, or on "things," or the buildings and structures that make it up is to negate its living quality and hamper its ability to change and modify itself.

4. Competence Leading to Ability of Individuals or Groups to Use It

Here I return to Nehru's concern with the weather: no matter how fine the climate is, it is the weather that affects me. It is my mini-environment with which I am concerned. We may have a healthy city, but if I cannot use it or if, as a visitor, I am lost within its boundaries, the city is not healthy for me.

I want service for my kids. I need an overpass above the highway from my house to the playground so that my child doesn't get hurt. Although there may be wonderful food distribution through the supermarkets of my city, if I am poor, there is no food.

Thus, we raise what is, perhaps, the most important issue related to the requirements of the healthy city. If the city has the ability to respond to the specialized needs of all of its citizens, then the healthy city will allow the individual, family, or group to develop its own competence to use the city's resources. A healthy city not only listens, reacts, and responds to meet basic and changing needs, it responds in such a way that it aids the people or groups using it to learn.

5. Ability to Perform its Educational Role

To learn, to find within oneself the ability to cope, is of the highest importance. In the past, to educate has meant to replicate the society that exists, to teach those that follow how to preserve what it has and is. It now means teaching the learning of how to change or how to constantly recreate ourselves and our institutions, businesses, and our cities. But, to change requires taking a new look. We must learn how to "know" our city and its critical issues. We must see the "map" of the city to know how institutions and events and the parts relate and impinge on each other. New "maps" must be created that encompass the old, but they must start from where we are and lead to ways to reorganize our thinking about the old and the new, the emerging issues.

As my grandmother said when I asked her about her praying and the fact that I never heard God answer, "It is not the answer that is important, but the question that you ask."

Rethinking is learning to ask the right questions. *Knowing* is perceiving the question in its fullest form and in all its dimensions. *Education* is learning that permits asking the right question and leaving oneself open, free from prejudiced opinions, to the possibility that there are alternative ways to see the problem and to respond. A city must be able to educate its members to respond for themselves and to accommodate their private "weather" for the common good.

The more that the individual or small group, family, friends, or peers, have the ability to cope with issues, the healthier it is. The question of scale is such that unless one feels one's own power, one feels helpless. The more one learns to cope, the better is one able to cope. We must understand, then, that mistakes are not failure but a way to learn. As our complex life systems become even more complex and we have less control over them, we must expect mistakes as we learn how to respond and we must build experience upon experience. It is not difficult to see that many of the ways that the city responds to apparent need is to dehumanize and disenfranchise its citizens so that, in the long run, the citizens' ability to cope is diminished. It takes away that most precious "ability to command the events that affect one's life."

The city is also a crucible, and another way to educate oneself about the city is to define it by informational bits. Contributing to this is the surge of inmigration that has been occurring in our large cities in recent years which is not dissimilar to some of the migrations in the U.S. early in this century. Ghettos were and are places where people learn how to cope from earlier generations, from the streets, the businesses, and in other ways. This also is part of the process of the city educating its citizens. Something, however, is different. Now, as these immigrations are taking place the cities are changing. The middle class is moving to the suburbs leaving the poor, the migrants, the affluent singles. Now as the city becomes more fragmented, people are learning from their peers instead of at all levels from differing points of view and experiences. Many of these groups move away from being part of the whole. Some are oppressed and yet others form special interest groups.

When I was young, as I have described earlier, each weekend, until I was a rebellious thirteen-year-old, my father took my brother and me to different parts of the city, and we visited every culture, every business, park, hospital that we could. I saw and talked to the young and the old. My father had me meet people and walk the streets until I was unafraid and comfortable with whatever I saw or experienced. He helped to make the unfamiliar familiar and to show me that there are ways other than mine to solve problems. People looked different. Foods looked different. Healing was different. Even then, I was awed by the complexity and diversity of the city.

Throughout life the individual meets various crises with solutions or responses learned from his past. However, if the same old mechanisms are always used the individual with only one way of coping may become maladapted. We know that behavior can be influenced—that a new way to react can be taught. Presumably this is what education is all about (Duhl, 1964). The more we know and the more skills we have that enable us to do things for ourselves; the more able we are to ask others to teach us rather than going on alone, and the healthier we are.

ACTIONS THAT CREATE A HEALTHIER CITY

What, then, do we do if we, as citizens of the city, want to make our city healthier? There are two ways of answering. The first is an overt response, to choose a specific action to deal with a specific issue, and to accept or reject it as the concepts develop. This is the gut response, in fact the demanded response by most individuals and communities, the response to the symptom. The second, dealing with the underlying issues, is more complex.

1. Respond to the Symptoms

In responses there is usually a rising indication as to what needs to be done. The acting in response is important and clearly many programs would not have occurred without this kind of reaction. Consider the parent who organizes a helmet campaign after his or her child has been injured, or the single mother who creates a child-care school for her children and a job for herself, or the mental retardation programs, as responses to personal experience. A dramatic example of such a response in the U.S. has been the success of MADD (Mothers against Drunk Driving), the response of one woman, initially, to the death of her daughter.

In addition to these personal reactions are the responses to more complex issues: the changing taste and quality of drinking water, the need for security systems and planning regulations when streets get dark and unpopulated, traffic inconveniences and auto accidents and street and highway construction, nuclear waste, or eroding soil. Then there are the myriad of things that have created the advocacy programs that are responses to "victimization." We have become a society of victims, each hurting and trying to correct the imbalance to increase our equity in meeting our needs and pursuing our values.

2. Deal with the Underlying Issues

There is a time when "victimization" leads to polarization and fragmentation. It is here that the second, and to me the more important, response to needs is appropriate: to deal with the underlying issues of health. The issues are interconnected and they are complex and multidimensional. It is the interconnectedness and relationship between the parts and the sense of the whole community that is essential to making a city healthy. Toward that end there is a need to develop new approaches, to utilize a new kind of management of organizations and people and to recognize that "justice" involves meeting the essential needs of the community both by allocating resources and working to involve people in the responsibility to find answers to problems that affect their lives.

3. Specific Actions to Improve the City's Health

Now let us be explicit. What are some of the specific actions that we can take? Some that deal with ideas discussed here earlier immediately come to mind.

Create Community Round Tables.   The concept of round tables is an idea that has been with us for a long time. Although it is often used by business and in international meetings, it seems to have been all but forgotten in most of our U.S. cities. Leadership in America has always come from grassroots. Even more basic than the so-called big issues of the world are the responses people have to the issues that affect our daily lives. This isn't necessarily an easy or a peaceful process: the din may get overwhelming at times. The hope, of course, is that people from all walks of life will take a careful look at problems, assert their power, and find solutions together.

Meet Needs First, Then the "Wants". As people become more adept at handling the events in their community and lives by round tables or in other ways, they are going to see that it is possible for things to work for them. Then, through having to take some responsibility for what happens and in their being exposed to the views of others, they will be able to set priorities and to separate the varied individual and community needs from the wants.

Create Nonpolarizing Community-wide Responses. The KidsPlace program of Seattle is an excellent example of such action. A broad, diverse group of citizens came together, unified in the ultimate goal, that of reversing what they considered an alarming population trend in their city.

Seattle had enjoyed a reputation as a family town, a good place to raise kids. Then, residents became dismayed to discover that at the very time their city was being proclaimed for its livability for families, an outmigration of families with children was taking place. In the decade between 1970 and 1980, while the overall population of the city declined 7 percent, the number of residents age eighteen and under declined 36 percent.

To reverse the exodus of families, the mayor believed that not only must people's perceptions of Seattle as a place for young, affluent childless professionals be changed, but the city must assess itself and make appropriate changes. The project, KidsPlace, so named by the children of Seattle who wanted their city to be a place for children, was initiated to turn this population trend around. Through surveys, publicity, and public participation (in what began in small, nonthreatening, uncontroversial projects) families who already lived in the city were reminded of its advantages in the hope that those assuming that children belonged only in suburbia would be attracted. In addition, as citizens became involved in some of the small projects some complex ones surfaced. At least 20 groups examined issues such as child care, mental health, homeless youth, and television violence.

The broad spectrum of input into this project—in addition to that of the children themselves—was notable. Sponsors included the YMCA, the Junior League, and a private foundation which contributed about $20,000 to start the project up. Private enterprise and government worked side-by-side on this project: the regional office of the U.S. Department of Health and Human Services, the City of Seattle and a private advertising firm. The effects of KidsPlace could be far-reaching.

Recognize the New Management Styles.   Corporate management styles that are proving successful today may have applications in our cities and it is appropriate that we consider them. Among the more interesting trends is that of participatory management and of employee ownership. PEOPLExpress, a highly successful, no-frills airline company in the Northeast, is a particularly good model to describe this phenomenon which is enabling employees to release creative energies. A person cannot be hired at PEOPLExpress unless he or she buys a mandatory 100 shares of stock in the company. The resulting incentive and pride of employees with a sense of participation has been credited as having been largely responsible for the phenomenal success of this young airline (Frawley, 1984).

Another interesting management phenomenon is the "new populism." As U.S. business has looked for ways to resist external control by large government and institutions the concept, "to exert control over their own lives" is seen. In corporate decision making, it has created a demand for greater participation on the part of employees at all levels, including top executives and managers, as well as by public interest groups (Staff, *The Tarrytown Letter*, 1984).

Both of these trends—the trend toward participation in the process and interest by a broader spectrum of citizens—are in operation in our cities, and how we deal with them can be important.

Another thought-provoking concept for improving our American cities is the application of the pro-humanist ideas that are based on Japanese management styles. The connection of these ideas with our cities is being suggested by William G. Ouchi (1981, 1984), an authority on both Japanese and American business cultures, in his book, *The M-Form Model* (M for multidivisional). Professor Ouchi, in an earlier book, *Theory Z*, showed how Japan built its phenomenal economic rise on teamwork between government and industry and even competing companies.

In extending the techniques of Japanese business to American business, then to finding a model for American society, the themes that prevail continue to be teamwork, cooperation, and autonomy.

Dr. Ouchi points to Minneapolis-St. Paul as "an intermediate form—[of] an M-Form society (intermediate in comparison to the Soviet Union with its central planning and Los Angeles with its disconnectedness)." He characterizes the Minneapolis area as "a unique example of business cooperating with local communities to create a better living and working environment." He further describes it as a "region with strong social memory, strong cross-industry ties, and strong alliances between business and community groups."

Chief among the ideas in the best-selling book, *In Search of Excellence*, is the notion that companies have to encourage innovation, hire mavericks, and find people who are in close touch with the market. This is what the business community is calling "intrepreneurship"—encouraging people *within* the organization who know how to get things done to make things happen. It sees the value of people who *see*, then *do* (Peters & Waterman, 1984). In our cities there are people from all parts of the city who are "in touch." We need to find them and to create a context for success.

Educate to Produce "People Who Get Things Done".   Recent research by Pennsylvania State University behavioral scientist Dr. Siegfried Strufert reveals that most successful corporate leaders think in a way that he characterizes as "cognitively complex", his way of describing decision making that does not depend on IQ. This involves the capacity to acquire ample information for making decisions without being overwhelmed and the ability to grasp relationships between rapidly changing events (Goleman, 1984).

This view was substantiated earlier by Richard Boyatzis (1982) in his book, *The Competent Manager*, in which he identified 19 competencies in a study of more than 2,000 managers. Among these were ability to get different groups to collaborate, to spot hidden patterns in an array of facts, and managers' spontaneity in expressing themselves.

The ways in which these researchers describe thinking and decision making is particularly applicable to the skills we have been talking about in getting the parts of the city to work together, and we would be well advised to become aware of and responsive to alternative education goals that might produce "people who get things done." People trained in such thinking styles working in leadership roles in our cities could enhance the health of our cities.

THE GOAL: A CONTEXT FOR SUCCESS

If in our efforts to make our city healthier we have responded to the symptoms or dealt with the underlying issues, or both, we have set certain forces in motion. With sensitive, responsive, imaginative leadership that functions *both* from the "top down" and the "bottom up" we will have selected and implemented appropriate actions or programs that have created a context for success.

As in the healthy organism, the health of the parts as well as the vigor of the connections are essential to make the organism work at its highest level of competency.

The context for success can only be created when the people of the city realize that if the context works for them they can solve their problems. It is then that the people of the city, working together in a spirit of reciprocal maintenance, can address the complex and multidimensional underlying issues of health to create their healthy city.

Chapter 21

SUMMING UP

A Proposal

My lifelong concern with social change has been reflected in my own personal development, in my career, and in the diversity of my interdisciplinary interests. Underlying all of this has been a focus on healthy development rather than the physician's more conventional focus on illness. This includes a broad concern with the promotion of health as a way of preventing illness.

Since we are in the midst of all-encompassing social change where ways of living are being challenged, resisted, and modified, the question of growth and development becomes a central issue. Not only are business, social, and political institutions being challenged on their command of complex emerging issues; questions also arise on such competency in individuals evolved to the current developmental-learning context.

I do not question our potential for learning to cope; but rather whether this potential is optimized by the diverse experiences—biological, physiological, educational, and social—to which we are exposed.

Briefly, my belief is that the needs of past millennia have conditioned us biologically to control the environment: first the natural, then the social, and finally the human-made environments. This conditioning is manifested in our DNA.

At the time of the first major conceptual-paradigm revolution—the beginning of agriculture—humans were required to learn how to control a hostile environment, to attain food, clothing, and shelter, and then to protect themselves and what they had from others.

In learning how to do these things, they needed to acquire cognitive, precise language, to create new sets of skills, and slowly to adapt biologically to the new conditions. In order to control the environment, tools and skills were needed. To achieve this end, education, science, and other knowledge were required. To meet the consistent objective of controlling the environment and those enemies who would take away the power of those in control, they needed the full spectrum of social development, as experienced in the Western world. In doing so, we achieved the quality of life we now have in the Western world—a vast and awesome achievement, but one with a price.

What occurred was the unconscious repression and conscious oppression of other potentials of human development. These possibilities still exist as biological potentials. We find them developed and expressed in other cultures and in diverse individuals. Not being capable of expressing these other developmental abilities has not been considered as loss up to now since the skills we have attained have gained us much in a material sense, longevity, and human betterment.

It is only now, when we are faced by a transition as major as the agricultural revolution, that we have a need to explore alternative developmental models. These models have existed in so-called primitive peoples, in many non-Anglo-Saxon cultures, in Eastern philosophical-religious disciplines, and elsewhere. To meet our needs in our current crisis, there has been a "social search" for change. This search has occurred on multiple levels: "accidental," scientific, and experimental. It is as if in the sociology of knowledge the conditions of the time have created both the overt need and the potential solutions.

In the past few years many clues have emerged to indicate the different ways individuals could develop. Some may be blind paths. As a whole they point to important major conceptual paradigm shifts in the developmental processes. We can categorize these, in part, by a concern with evolving systems, "right-brain" development, synthesis, integration, and de-fragmentation. The ecological development of individuals has emerged as a major concern.

Communications, civil rights, the Third World, increased advocacy by apparent victims, new genetic modeling, virology, immunology, social biology and ecology, physics, holography, chemistry, astronomy, drug-induced states, psychology (Maslow, Jung), visualization techniques, biofeedback, Eastern philosophy, mysticism, alternative health and healing practices (including acupuncture), family and systems therapies, mutual aid and self-care, intermediate technology, steady-state economics, revisionist history, the social analyses of Illich, Friere, Schumacher, the works of Bateson and others—these are but illustrations of the emerging notions we cannot ignore, for they portend a major conceptual-paradigm shift that will affect all human development.

This adds up to a challenge. If we are indeed at the end of an epoch, then we are in the midst of a period where new developmental paradigms, with new languages, skills, and scientific disciplines are emerging. To use an historical, religious metaphor, when the Jews left Egypt where plagues were threatening, they needed to learn how to live in a different way. This learning process required 40 years of wandering in the desert preparatory to reaching and coping with the "promised land."

At such a time, demands are raised to meet merely the symptoms of crisis. Most economic, social, and educational programs respond reactively. Some people want to return to the "good old days." Some believe, by "letting it all be," it will take care of itself. Still others innovate cautiously. Others search for solutions requiring paradigm and conceptual shifts. The changes that need to occur will contain the best of what we have achieved to date, but they will integrate new models with the old. Some ways of living must of necessity die off—for example, central control. Others must be reborn or recreated. If alternative-conceptual paradigms emerge, a central question will be the choice of the appropriate solution from the paradigm that fits the particular problem.

Where the old epoch was one of control, the emerging one can be considered one of *non-control*. The word "non-control" should not be equivalent to anarchy but rather indicate an inter-dependent floating control. Depending on the issue of concern, different parts of a whole world would be in charge. Currently, presidents and chief executive officers of countries, corpora-tions, and universities, as well as parents and teachers, claim they are no longer in control using hierarchical power. Influence and floating, ad hoc control replaces hierarchical methods. These new forms of governance are already seen in families, in groups, in corporate models, informally structured work groups, and in some educational experiences.

What seems central is that data are increasingly available for a vast number of fields so that our biological organisms as well as our social institutions have the potential to cope with the emerg-ing needs. Since our biogenetic potential is socioenvironmentally determined, the change in needs creates new use of one poten-tial.

Change to new paradigms means letting go of a genetic so-cial history that we have assumed to be a permanent part of us. Letting go, loss, grieving, and moving on are different processes, both individually and socially.

Are we then in need of finding alternative human develop-mental models, or have these already emerged but not been per-ceived and utilized? We seem to be finding a pattern that has existed, submerged, and is now reemerging. We may not be dis-covering anything new. Rather, there is a pattern which has again found a time to be expressed, but this time in a form ap-propriate to our time and need. Our current crisis of control al-lows it to reemerge into consciousness and ultimately into per-sonal, social, and institutional behavior.

Optimal development, or what I would call health, is not a goal but a process. To me this process means the utilization of all our range of potential abilities. These include our senses, as well as our physical, social, psychological (cognitive, emotional), and spiritual potential exercised in an integrated manner through-out our lives. In this process we must use both "right" and "left" brain. It is the synthesis of the internal with the external envi-ronment (both immediate and universal in all its forms). It is learning how to problem solve and to cope, using the alternative conceptual paradigms and realities that exist. We must make choices consciously and unconsciously, fitting "solution" to problem in an appropriate way. Further, the process is the creation of living, evolving, and developing multi-interest and multigenerational organisms on a scale beyond the individual, where family, group, organization, community, governmental, and societal bodies deal with the issues of life on an appropriate level of response. Optimal developmental processes are both internal to the individual and part of an integrated, synthesized relationship to the physical, social, and universal environment.

Recognizing that ideal development does not exist, the concern is with a "normal" (optimal) development of all of us, including any so-called developmentally disabled, dis-eased, or ill individual. Sadly, too often those who are momentarily off the ideal developmental track follow a course of iatrogenic development, maximizing the disorder and oppressing the potential for health existing in even the most damaged or atypical person or group.

We must consider, therefore, development as including the ability to cope with disorder and breakdown. How we care for those who "can't make it" and our ability to return these people to healthy development is of prime importance. We must be concerned not only with the individual but with society as well. For example, "new organisms" of individuals, including those with apparent handicaps may turn out to be "more than human" because optimizing non-defect areas integrated with other areas may permit a new organism of higher and broader capacity to exist.

My proposal, therefore, is to focus on the changing paradigms of human development as they are emerging. It will be an attempt to synthesize a diverse set of knowledge and experience. Out of this should emerge a developmental strategy for human development, with focus both on the individuals and their social, institutional, human-created, natural environments which pattern the process and are its creations.

In doing so, I will call upon my own diverse, personal, scientific experience, changes in the current social, scientific, educational, and other available knowledge. For me this is a time for synthesis and integration.

REFERENCES

Alford, R. R. (1972). The political economy of health care. Dynamics without change. *Politics and Society*, (Winter), 127-164.

———— (1975). *Health care politics: Ideological and interest group barriers to reform.* Chicago: University of Chicago Press.

Anderson, O. W. (1968). *The uneasy equilibrium: Private and public financing of health services in the United States, 1875-1965.* New Haven, CT: College and University Press.

Archer, R. L., (Ed.) (1964). *Jean Jacques Rousseau, his educational theories selected from Emile, Julie and other writings.* Woodbury, NY: Barron's Educational Series.

Astrachan, B. M., Levinson, D. J., & Adler, D. A. (1976). The impact of national health insurance on the tasks and practices of psychiatry. *Archives General Psychiatry, 33*, 785-794.

Attneave, C. L. (1974). Medicine men and psychiatrists in the Indian health service. *Psychiatric Annals, 4*(11), 49-55.

Auden, W. H. (1976). *Collected poems.* In E. Mendelson (Ed.), *The poem, the art of healing.* New York: Random House, p. 627.

Barber, B. (1980). Regulation and the professions. *The Hastings Center Report*, (February), 34-36.

Barrett, W. (1979). *The illusion of technique: A search for meaning in technological civilization.* New York: Doubleday Anchor.

Bennis, W. G. & Slater, P. E. (1969). *The temporary society.* New York: Harper Colophon Books.

———— (1971). Searching for the "perfect university president," *Atlantic Monthly, 227,* (April), 39-41.

Berger, P. L. & Luckman, T. (1967). *The social construction of reality.* New York: Doubleday Anchor.

Berkman, L. F. & Syme, S. L. (1979). Social networks, host resistance, and mortality: A nine-year followup study of Alameda county residents. *American Journal of Epidemiology, 109*(2), 186-205.

Berlin, I. (1957). *The hedgehog and the fox.* New York: Mentor Books.

Beyond health care: Proceedings of a conference on healthy public policy. *Canadian Journal of Public Health, 76,* Supplement 1, May/June 1985.

Biller, R. (1973). Converting knowledge into action: Toward a postindustrial society. In J. S. Jun & W. B. Storm (Eds.), *Tomorrow's organization: Challenges and strategies.* Glenview, IL: Scott Foresman.

Birdwhistell, R. L. (1970). *Introduction to kinesics.* Louisville, KY: University of Louisville Press.

Blum, H. L. (1974). *Planning for health: Development and application of social change theory.* New York: Human Sciences Press.

———— (1976a). *Expanding health care horizons.* Oakland, CA: Third Party Press.

———— (1976b). Testimony at health insurance hearings, U.S. House of Representatives, Ways and Means Committee, San Francisco, March 19. (Available from Henrik Blum, School of Public Health, University of California, Berkeley.)

———— (1980). Social perspective on risk reduction. *Family and Community Health, 3*(1), 41-61.

———— (1981). *Planning for health* (2nd ed.). New York: Human Sciences Press.

Blum, S. R. (1973). *An unrequited war.* Unpublished doctoral dissertation, Berkeley, CA: University of California Press.

Blumer, H. (1969). *Symbolic interactionism—Perspective and method.* Englewood Cliffs, NJ: Prentice-Hall.

Bohm, D. (1978). The enfolding-unfolding universe. *Re-Vision Magazine, 1*(3-4), 24-51.

Boston Women's Health Book Collective (1973). *Our bodies, ourselves: A book by and for women.* New York: Simon & Schuster.

Bourne, P., Medrich, E. A., Steadwell, L., Barr, D. (1971). *Day care nightmare.* Berkeley, CA: University of California, Institute of Urban and Regional Development.

Boyatzis, R. E. (1982). *The competent manager: A model for effective performance.* New York: Wiley-Interscience.

Brody, H. (1973). The system view of man: Implications for medicine, science and ethics. *Perspectives in Biology and Medicine, 17*(1), 71-92.

Burn, M. (1956). *Mr. Lyward's answer.* London: H. Hamilton.

Calhoun, J. B. (1973). From mice to men. *Transactions and Studies of the College of Physicians of Philadelphia, 41*(2), (October), Serial No. 4, 92-118.

Califano, J. (1979). *Healthy people.* Washington, DC: Office of the Surgeon General, U.S. Government Printing Office.

Capra, F. (1975). *The Tao of physics.* Boulder, CO: Shambhala Publications.

——— (1982). *The turning point: Science, society, and the rising culture.* New York: Simon & Schuster.

Castenada, C. (1968). *The teachings of Don Juan. A Yaqui way of knowledge.* Berkeley, CA: University of California Press.

Churchman, C. W. (1971). *The design of inquiring systems: Basic concepts in systems analysis.* New York: Basic Books.

——— (1979a). *The systems approach* (2nd ed.). New York: Delacorte.

——— (1979b). *The systems approach and its enemies.* New York: Basic Books.

Committee on the costs of medical care (1932). *Medical care for the American people* (final report #531). Chicago: University of Chicago Press.

Conner, D. (Executive Producer) (1978). *Medicine in America: Life, death, and dollars* (Television special, January 3). National Broadcasting Company.

Cousins, C. & Duhl, L. J. (1983). *Technology and learning disabilities,* Health Technology Case Study 25, Technology and Handicapped People series, December. Washington, DC: Congress of the United States, Office of Technology Assessment.

Currie, E. (1971). Repressive violence. *Transaction, 8*(4), 12-14, 62.

Dewey, J. (1960). *The quest for certainty.* New York: Putnam.

Dubos, R. (1959). *Mirage of health.* New York: Harper.

——— (1968). *Man, medicine, and environment.* New York: Praeger.

Duhl, L. J. (Ed.), (1963). *The urban condition: People and policy in the metropolis.* New York: Basic Books.

———— (1964, July). *Social planning.* Paper presented at the meeting of the Center of Ekistics, Athens, Greece.

———— (1967). Planning and predicting: Or what to do when you don't know the names of the variables. *Daedalus, 96*(3), 779-788.

———— (1968a). *The poverty program: A national exercise in social change.* (A report. Available from author.)

———— (1968b). Introduction. In M. Dumont, *The absurd healer.* New York: Science House.

———— & Leopold, R. (Eds.), (1968c). *Mental health and urban social policy: A casebook of community action.* San Francisco: Jossey-Bass.

———— (1968d). The shame of our cities. *American Journal of Psychiatry, 124*(9), 1184-1189.

———— & Volkman, J. (1970). Participatory democracy: Networks as strategy for change. *Urban and Social Change Review, 3*(2), 11-14.

———— (1973). Education in a diverse society with emphasis on the mental health professions. In E. Garrison (Ed.), *Doctoral preparation for nurses.* San Francisco: University of California Press.

———— (1976a). Health, whole, holy, healing. *Gezar Magazine* (Spring), pp. 14-16.

———— (1976b). The process of re-creation: The health of the I and the us. *Ethics in Science & Medicine, 3*, 33-63.

———— (1976c). *The promotion and maintenance of health: Myth and reality.* Paper presented at a conference of the National Health and Welfare Department of the Government of Canada, "Health Promotion Through Design of Environment," held in Ottawa, October 1976. (Available from author.)

———— (1978). The future of mental health as a profession: Plugging psychiatry into the healing network. *Psychiatry Annals, 8*(5), 102-109.

———— & Levinson, S. (1979). The delivery of health care services. In G. Tobin (Ed.), *The changing structure of the city: What happened to urban crisis, Urban Affairs Annual Review, 16.* Beverly Hills, CA: Sage Publications.

———— (1980a). The social context of health. In Arthur C. Hastings, et al. (Eds.), *Health for a whole person.* Boulder, CO: Westview Press.

———— (1980b, August). *The dimensions of health, or health for a new epoch: Traditional healing and "modern" medicine.* Paper presented at the Conference on Traditional Medicine, Association of American Indian Physicians, Albuquerque, New Mexico.

———— & Den Boer, J. (1980c). *Making whole: Health for a new epoch.* Unpublished manuscript available from author.

———— & Blum, S. R. (1981). Health planning and social change: Critique and alternatives. In B. Checkoway (Ed.), *Citizens and health care.* New York: Pergamon Press.

Edelman, M. (1971). *Politics as symbolic action.* New York: Academic Press.

Ellison, R. (1953). *Invisible man.* New York: Signet.

Estes, C. L. (1979). *The aging enterprise.* San Francisco: Jossey-Bass.

Ferguson, M. (1980). *The aquarian conspiracy.* Los Angeles: J. P. Tarcher.

Foote, N. N. & Cottrell, L. S., Jr. (1956). *Identity and interpersonal competence: A new direction in family research.* Chicago: University of Chicago Press.

Forward, R. L. (1980). Spinning new realities. *Science 80, 1*(8), 40-49.

Frawley, M. G. (1984). PEOPLExpress: A new management formation flies "no frills" to success. *The Tarrytown Letter, 40,* 12-13.

Freedman, L. (1971, March). *The progress report of the President's task force on the extended university.* Los Angeles: University of California Press.

Fried, M. (1963). Grieving for a lost home. In L. J. Duhl (Ed.), *The urban condition.* New York: Basic Books.

Friedson, E. (1970a). *Medicine as a profession.* New York: Dodd Mead.

———— (1970b). *Professional dominance: The social structure of medical care.* Chicago: Aldine.

Future directions in health care: The dimensions of medicine. (1975). Report of a conference sponsored by the Blue Cross Association, the Rockefeller Foundation, and the Health Policy Program, University of California School of Medicine. Conference held in New York, December 1975.

Gaylin, W., Rothman, D., Marcus, S., & Glaser, I. (Eds.), (1978). *Doing good: The limits of benevolence.* New York: Pantheon.

Geddes, P. (1949). *Cities in evolution.* London: Williams and Northgate. (Original work published in 1915.)

Geiger, H. J. (1972). A health center in Mississippi: A case study in social medicine. In L. Corey et al. (Eds.), *Medicine in a changing society.* St. Louis: C. V. Mosby.

Goleman, D. (1984, July 31). Style of thinking, not I.Q., tied to success. *New York Times,* pp. 3, 15, 18.

Haggerty, R. J. (1972). The boundaries of health care. *The Pharos* (July), 106-111.

Hall, E. T. (1959). *The silent language.* New York: Doubleday.

———— (1966). *The hidden dimension.* New York: Doubleday.

Handler, P. (Ed.), (1970). *Biology and the future of man.* New York: Oxford University Press.

Harvey, P. (1974). *Art of creation* (a report). Berkeley, CA: The Wright Institute.

Hawken, P., Ogilvy, J., & Schwartz, P. (1982). *Seven tomorrows: Toward a voluntary history.* New York: Bantam Books.

Hillman, J. (1975). *Re-visioning psychology.* New York: Harper & Row.

Holmes, T. H. & Masuda, M. (1970). *Life changes and illness susceptibility in stressful life events: Their nature and effects.* New York: Wiley.

———— (1973). Life change and illness susceptibility. In J. P. Scott & E. C. Senay (Eds.), *Separation and depression.* Washington, DC: American Association for the Advancement of Science.

———— & R. H. Rahe (n.d.). *Schedule of recent experience SRE Questionnaire.* Seattle, WA: University of Washington, Department of Psychiatry.

Illich, I. (1976). *Medical nemesis: The expropriation of health.* New York: Pantheon.

James, D. (1972). *Poverty, politics and change.* Englewood Cliffs, NJ: Prentice-Hall.

Keatinge, M. W. (trans. and Ed.), (1967). *The great didactic of John Amos Comenius.* New York: Russell & Russell.

Keleman, S. (1975). *Living your dying.* New York: Random House.

Kesey, K. (1962). *One flew over the cuckoo's nest.* New York: Viking Press.

King, L. (1976). *Fanon Center restoration model for the education of all children with emphasis on the suppressed* (research report). Los Angeles: Fanon Research and Development Center.

Kitagawa, E. & Hauser, P. (1973). *Differential mortality in the United States: A study in socioeconomic epidemiology.* Cambridge, MA: Harvard University Press.

Knowles, J. (Ed.), (1977). *Doing better and feeling worse: Health in the United States.* New York: W. W. Norton.

Koestler, A. (1964). *The act of creation.* New York: Macmillan.

Kron, J. (1976, March). Designing a better place to die. *New York Magazine*, 43-49.

Kuhn, T. S. (1970). *The structure of scientific revolutions* (2nd ed.). Chicago: University of Chicago Press.

Laing, R. D. (1965). *The divided self.* Baltimore: Penguin Books.

Lalonde, M. (1974). *A new perspective on the health of Canadians.* Ottawa: Government of Canada, Ministry of National Health and Welfare.

Larson, M. (1977). *The rise of professionalism.* Berkeley, CA: University of California Press.

Leonard, G. B. (1975). *The ultimate athlete: Re-visioning sports, physical education, and the body.* New York: Viking.

Lifton, R. (1970). *Boundaries of psychological man in revolution.* New York: Vintage.

Lindemann, E. (1944). Symptomatology and management of acute grief. *American Journal of Psychiatry, 101,* 141-148.

Luce, G. G. (1979). *Your second life.* New York: Delacorte/Seymour Lawrence.

Marris, P. (1958). *Widows and their families.* London: Routledge and Kegan Paul.

———— (1962). *Family and social change in an African city.* African Studies Series No. 8. Evanston, IL: Northwestern University Press.

———— (1974). *Loss and change.* New York: Pantheon Books.

Maslow, A. H. (1968). *Toward a psychology of being* (2nd ed.). Cincinnati: Van Nostrand Reinhold.

———— (1970). *Motivation and personality.* New York: Harper & Row.

McKeown, T. (1976). *The role of medicine: Dream, mirage or nemesis.* London: The Nuffield Provincial Hospitals Trust.

Meiklejohn, A. (1932). *The experimental college.* New York & London: Harper & Brothers.

Meyerson, M., Rapkin, C., Collins, R., & Duhl, L. (1969). *The city and the university.* Toronto: Macmillan of Canada in association with York University.

Michael, D. L. (1973). *On learning to plan and planning to learn: The social psychology of changing toward future-responsive societal learning.* San Francisco: Jossey-Bass.

Milio, N. (1983). *Promoting health through public policy.* Philadelphia: F. A. Davis.

Moore, L. G., van Arsdale, P. W., Glittenberg, J. E., & Aldrich, R. A. (Eds.), (1980). *The biocultural basis of health: Expanding views of medical anthropology.* St. Louis: C. V. Mosby.

Morris, P. (1958). *Widows and their families*. London: Routledge and Kegan Paul.

Moynihan, D. P. (1969). *Maximum feasible understanding*. New York: Free Press.

Myers, N. (Ed.), (1984). *Gaia: An atlas of planet management*. Garden City, NY: Anchor/Doubleday.

Navarro, V. (1976). *Medicine under capitalism*. New York: Prodist.

Orleans, P. & Ellis, W. R., Jr. (1971). Race research: "Up against the wall" in more ways than one. In P. Orleans & W. R. Ellis, Jr. (Eds.), *Race, change, and urban society*. Beverly Hills, CA: Sage Publications.

Ornstein, R. (1971). *The psychology of consciousness*. New York: W. H. Freeman.

Ouchi, W. G. (1981). *Theory Z: How American business can meet the Japanese challenge*. Reading, MA: Addison-Wesley.

―――― (1984). *The M-form society: How American teamwork can recapture the competitive edge*. Reading, MA: Addison-Wesley.

Pearse, I. H. & Williamson, G. S. (1938). *The case for action. A survey of everyday life under modern industrial conditions with special reference to the question of health* (3rd ed.). London: Faber & Faber.

―――― & Crocker, L. H. (1947). *The Peckham experiment: A study of the living structure of society* (6th ed.). Rushden, England: Northamptonshire.

Pelletier, K. R. (1977). *Mind as healer, mind as slayer*. New York: Delacorte.

―――― (1979). *Holistic medicine: From pathology to optimum health*. New York: Delacorte.

Peters, T. J. & Waterman, R. H. (1982). *In search of excellence: Lessons from America's best-run companies*. New York: Harper & Row.

Pilusek, M. & Parks, S. H. (1986). *In search of a cure: Social support networks and loneliness in America*. Hanover, NH: University Press of New England.

Pioneer Health Centre. (1971). *Health of the individual, of the family, of society*. Rotherfield, Sussex, England: Author.

Preventive Medicine U.S.A. (1976). Task force reports sponsored by the John E. Fogarty International Center for Advanced Study in the Health Sciences, National Institutes of Health, and the American College of Preventive Medicine. New York: Prodist.

Pribram, K. (1971). *Languages of the brain*. New York: Penguin.

Proshansky, H. M. et al. (1976). *Environmental psychology: People and their physical settings.* New York: Holt, Rinehart & Winston.

Rahe, R. H. & Holmes, T. H. (n.d.). *Life crisis and disease onset: A prospective study of life crises and health changes* (mimeographed report). Seattle, WA: University of Washington, School of Medicine, Department of Psychiatry.

Rawls, J. (1971). *A theory of justice.* Cambridge, MA: Harvard University Press.

Relman, A. S. (1980). The new medical-industrial complex. *New England Journal of Medicine, 303*(17), 963-970.

Roemer, M. J. & Friedman, J. (1971). *Doctors in hospitals: Medical staff organizations and hospital performance.* Baltimore: Johns Hopkins Press.

Rogers, C. (1969). *Freedom to learn.* New York: Bobbs-Merrill.

Ryan, W. (1976). *Blaming the victim.* New York: Vintage.

Salk, J. (1973). *The survival of the wisest.* New York: Harper & Row.

Samuels, M. & Bennett, H. (1973). *The well body book.* New York: Random House.

Satin, M. (1978). *New age politics: Healing self and society.* West Vancouver, BC, Canada: Whitecap Books.

Satir, V. (1975). *Peoplemaking.* Palo Alto, CA: Science and Behavior Books.

Satprem (1970). *Sri Aurobindo: Or the adventure of consciousness.* Pondicherry, India: Sri Aurobindo Ashram Trust.

Schon, D. (1963). *Invention and the evolution of ideas.* New York: Barnes & Noble.

—— (1967). *Technology and change.* New York: Dell.

Schumacher, E. F. (1973). *Small is beautiful: A study in economics as if people mattered.* New York: Harper & Row.

Seeley, J. R. (1969). Personal science. In L. J. Duhl (Ed.), *The urban condition.* New York: Basic Books.

—— (1976). *Americanization of the unconscious.* New York: International Science Press.

Selye, H. (1974). *Stress without distress.* New York: Signet Books.

—— (1978). *The stress of life* (rev. ed.). New York: McGraw Hill.

Simpson, E. (1979). *Reversals.* Boston: Houghton Mifflin.

Skinner, B. F. (1948). *Walden two.* New York: Macmillan.

Slote, A. (1969). *Termination: The closure of Baker plant.* Indianapolis, IN: Bobbs-Merrill.

Somers, A. R. (1971). *Health care in transition: Directions for the future.* Chicago: Hospital Research and Education Trust.

Speck, R. V. & Attneave, C. L. (1973). *Family networks.* New York: Pantheon Books.

Staff (1984). Supermanaging in the 80s (an editorial). *The Tarrytown Letter, 40,* 3-6.

Stevens, R. (1971). *American medicine and the public interest.* New Haven, CT: Yale University Press.

Strauss, A. & Glaser, B. (1967). *The discovery of grounded theory.* Chicago: Aldine.

Thayer, F. C. (1980). *An end to hierarchy, an end to competition* (2nd ed.). New York: Watts, New Viewpoints.

Thomas, L. (1974). *The lives of a cell: Notes of a biology watcher.* New York: Viking Press.

Toffler, A. (1970). *Future shock.* New York: Random House.

Torrey, E. F. (1974). *The death of psychiatry.* Radnor, PA: Chilton.

van der Post, L. (1972). *A story like the wind.* Caldwell, NJ: Morrow.

———— (1974). *A far-off place.* Caldwell, NJ: Morrow.

Vargui, J. (1973). Creativity. *Synthesis, 3-4,* 60-120.

Veatch, R. M. & Bronson, R. (Eds.), (1976). *Ethics and health policy.* Cambridge, MA: Ballinger.

Vickers, G. (1965). *Art of judgment: A study of policy making.* New York: Basic Books.

Virchow, R. (1849). *Die einheits bestre bunger in der wissenschaftlichen medizin* (a pamphlet). Berlin: G. Reimer.

Vladeck, B. C. (1980). *Unloving care: The nursing home tragedy.* New York: Basic Books.

Webber, M. M. (1964). The urban place and the nonplace urban realm. In Webber & Dychman, et al. (Eds.), *Exploration into urban structure.* Philadelphia: University of Pennsylvania Press.

———— (1968). The post-city age. *Daedalus,* (Fall), *97*(4), 1091-1110.

———— & Rittel, H. (1973). Wicked problems: Dilemmas in a general theory of planning. *Policy Sciences, 4*(2), 156-169.

Webber, R. (1978). The enfolding-unfolding universe: A conversation with David Bohm. *Re-Vision, 1*(3-4), 24-51.

Williamson, G. S. & Pearse, I. H. (1947). *Biologists in search of material: An interim report on the work of the Pioneer Health Center, Peckham* (2nd ed.). London: Faber & Faber.

———— (1965). *Science, synthesis, and sanity.* London: Collins.

Winkelstein, W. W. (1972). Epidemiological considerations underlying the allocation of health and disease care resources. *International Journal of Epidemiology, 1*(1), 69-74.

Wiseman, J. (1970). *Stations of the lost: The treatment of skid-row alcoholics.* Englewood Cliffs, NJ: Prentice-Hall.

Zukov, G. (1979). *The dancing Wu Li masters: An overview of the new physics.* New York: Bantam.

INDEX